D1601643

Interpreting History in
Sino-Japanese Relations

The Nissan Institute/Routledge Japanese Studies Series

Editorial Board

J. A. A. Stockwin, *Nissan Professor of Modern Japanese Studies, University of Oxford and Director, Nissan Institute of Japanese Studies;* Teigo Yoshida, *formerly Professor, University of Tokyo, now Professor, Obirin University, Tokyo;* Frank Langdon, *Professor, Institute of International Relations, University of British Columbia, Canada;* Alan Rix, *Executive Dean, Faculty of Arts, The University of Queensland;* Junji Banno, *Chiba University;* Leonard Schoppa, *University of Virginia*

Other titles in the series:

Interpreting History in Sino-Japanese Relations

A case study in political decision-making

Caroline Rose

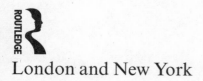

London and New York

First published 1998
by Routledge
11 New Fetter Lane, London EC4P 4EE

Simultaneously published in the USA and Canada
by Routledge
29 West 35th Street, New York, NY 10001

Typeset in Times by Routledge
Printed and bound in Great Britain by Biddles Ltd,
Guildford and King's Lynn

British Library Cataloguing in Publication Data
A catalogue record for this book is available from the British Library

Library of Congress Cataloging in Publication Data
A catalogue record for this book has been requested

ISBN 0–415–17296–9

For Louis Rose

Contents

List of illustrations

Figures

Tables

Acknowledgements

The idea for this book grew out of my undergraduate studies at Leeds under the guidance of Dr Penny Francks, and eventually developed into my Ph.D. thesis. Little did we imagine back in 1988 that ten years on this would be the result!

Thanks must go first and foremost to Penny – supervisor, mentor, role model, and now colleague and friend – whose enthusiasm never waned, and whose unstinting encouragement saw me through my frequent crises of confidence. A debt of gratitude also to Professor Don Rimmington whose moral support helped me through some tough years. Thanks also to Dr Delia Davin and Dr Wolf Mendl who examined my thesis, and to Professor Reinhard Drifte and Professor J.A.A. Stockwin for enabling its transformation into this final product. I am indebted to the British Academy for funding my Ph.D. and financing a much needed study trip to Japan, and to Monbusho for an extended period of study at Tsukuba University.

A debt of gratitude goes to my former colleagues at King Alfred's, especially Chris whose own determination and words of wisdom (honestly!) were an inspiration. Thanks also to all my colleagues at Leeds, many of whom have watched my research develop over the years and have provided invaluable support, advice and cups of tea.

My final words of thanks must go to my family: to my father whose unerring faith in me gave me the confidence to start this study, and to mum, Gabby, and Simon who gave me the strength and courage to finish it. This book is for you.

Series Editor's preface

Japan as the new century approaches is going through a turbulent period, in which some of her most entrenched political and economic institutions and practices are being increasingly questioned. The financial crisis which occurred in the latter half of 1997 affected most of the so-called 'tiger economies' of East and South-East Asia, and did not spare Japan. The collapse of several important Japanese financial institutions signalled both that the system was in crisis but also that the Government was no longer willing, or able, to rescue ailing institutions. The sense of crisis quickly dulled the lustre of the 'Asian model' in the eyes of the world's media, but also concentrated minds within Japan on the task of reforming the system. The extent to which the system needed reforming remained a matter of sharp dispute, but a consensus was emerging that many entrenched practices which derived from the immediate post-war period of the 'economic miracle' needed to be radically rethought. At the beginning of 1998, the extent and timescale of the desired revolution remained in doubt. Elements of the old regime seemed to be falling apart, but the shape of the new was still but dimly discernible.

Reading the world's press in the aftermath of the financial crisis one could well derive the impression that East Asia (including Japan) was heading for collapse and that the world could safely direct its attention elsewhere, notably to the dynamic and successful market economies of North America and Europe. Such an impression, however, was manifestly erroneous. Japan and its surrounding region remained a zone of intense economic production and interaction, resourceful and dynamic. Though there was a financial crisis, it was far less clear that there was an economic crisis. To use a hackneyed phrase, the fundamentals of the Japanese economy remained sound.

Radical reform was no doubt needed, but the occurrence of crisis made the road to that rather easier. If the world thought that the East Asian region could safely be ignored, it was likely to be in for a rude shock in a short span of years.

The Nissan Institute/Routledge Japanese Studies Series seeks to foster an informed and balanced, but not uncritical, understanding of Japan. One aim of the series is to show the depth and variety of Japanese institutions, practices and ideas. Another is, by using comparisons, to see what lessons, positive or negative, can be drawn for other countries. The tendency in commentary on Japan to resort to outdated, ill-informed or sensational stereotypes still remains, and needs to be combated.

This book concerns the international dispute that emerged in the early 1980s between Japan and China concerning alleged revision of Japanese school textbooks through the regular textbook screening process practised by the Ministry of Education. According to criticisms of Japan expressed at the time by the Chinese and South Korean Governments, the textbooks had been altered in such a way as to play down the barbarity of Japanese military actions in China during the late 1930s. A particular accusation was that the term 'invasion', referring to the actions of Japan from 1937, had been turned into 'advance'.

It turned out that the Chinese and Korean protests were based on inaccurate information, and that both 'invasion' and 'advance' had been used – and were still used – in textbooks over a considerable period. Nevertheless, the controversy focused international attention on the whole process of textbook screening, and the Japanese Government came under intense pressure to take Chinese (and Korean) views into account in the production of school textbooks, as well as to loosen Ministry control as such over the content of textbooks.

Caroline Rose dissects this dispute in a masterly fashion in the broader context of a balanced and perceptive study of Japanese–Chinese relations. Making extensive use of vernacular sources in both languages, she analyses the political dynamics of both China and Japan with expertise and insight. For Japan, no country apart from the United States is as important in the contemporary world as China. As a study illuminating the co-operation linked with mutual suspicion characterising the relationship between these two great powers, this book deserves the widest readership.

J.A.A. Stockwin

Conventions

Names and romanisation

Chinese and Japanese words have been romanised using the pinyin and Hepburn systems respectively. A macron has been used to denote long vowel sounds in Japanese words, e.g. *Chūō Kōron, Asahi Jānaru.*

Both Chinese and Japanese personal names are given in the conventional way with family name first followed by given name, e.g. Suzuki Zenkō; Mao Zedong. Chinese personal names are given in pinyin with the exception of names that would be unfamiliar in pinyin, e.g. Chiang Kai-shek as opposed to Jiang Jieshi. Similarly, Chinese place names are given in pinyin romanisation except for those which are more familiar in Wade Giles. With Japanese place names that are widely used in English, diacritical marks have been omitted (e.g. Tokyo, Osaka). Where place names have both Chinese and Japanese versions, both names are given (e.g. Senkaku islands (Japanese), Diaoyutai (Chinese)).

Since titles of Japanese newspapers are never translated into English, the same convention has been applied to Chinese newspapers for purposes of consistency. The names and positions of the key politicians and bureaucrats involved in the Textbook Issue are listed in Appendix 1.

Abbreviations and terms

ASEAN   Association of South East Asian Nations
CCP   Communist Party of China
COCOM   Co-ordinating Committee (on export control)
DPRK   Democratic People's Republic of Korea
FPA   Foreign Policy Analysis
IR   International Relations
JCP   Japan Communist Party
JSP   Japan Socialist Party (DSPJ after 1992)
JTU   Japan Teachers' Union (*Nikkyōso*)
LDP   Liberal Democratic Party
MFA   Japanese Ministry of Foreign Affairs
MOE   Japanese Ministry of Education
NPC   Chinese National People's Congress
PARC   Policy Affairs Research Council (LDP policy review body)
PLA   Chinese People's Liberation Army
PRC   People's Republic of China
ROC   Republic of China
ROK   Republic of Korea
TEC   Textbook Examination Committee
TARC   Textbook Authorisation Research Council

Japanese education-related terms

Chūō kyōiku shingikai   Central Education Council (permanent advisory body to the Japanese Ministry of Education).

Bunkyō bukai   Education Affairs Division (education committee in LDP's PARC).

Bunkyō seido chōsakai   Education System Research Council (education committee in LDP's PARC).

Kyōkasho mondai koiinkai	Subcommittee on the Textbook Problem (established by LDP in 1980 to address problem of textbook content. Chairman: Mitsuzuka Hiroshi).
Kyōkasho koiinkai	Textbook Subcommittee (established in 1981 by the Central Education Council to investigate textbook selection and authorisation methods. Chairman: Yoshimoto Jirō).
Gakushū shidō yōryō	Course of Study (curriculum guidelines for all textbooks set by Ministry of Education.)
Kyōkasho kentei kijun	Standards for Textbook Authorisation (guidelines for textbook content produced by MOE).
Kyōkayōtosho kentei chōsa shingikai	Textbook Authorisation Research Council (attached to MOE, responsible for passing or failing school textbooks in the authorisation process).
Kyōkasho chōsakan	Textbook Education Committee (attached to MOE, carries out initial evaluation of textbooks in the textbook authorisation process).
shinki kentei	'new authorisation' (screening process for newly-written textbooks).
kaitei kentei	'revision authorisation' (triennial process of revision/up-date of textbooks already in use).
seigo teisei	'correction of errors' (process by which publishers/authors can apply to MOE for errors in textbooks to be corrected during the three-year period between authorisation (*shinki kentei*) and revision (*kaitei kentei*)).
kaizen iken	'suggestion for improvement' (non-compulsory recommendation made by textbook examiners during textbook screening process).
shūsei iken	'suggestion for correction' (compulsory recommendation made by textbook examiners during textbook screening process).

1 Introduction

Qianshi buwang, houshi zhishi.

Past experience, if not forgotten, is a guide to the future.

Such was the title of the front page editorial of China's *Renmin Ribao* on 15 August 1982. This day marked the thirty-seventh anniversary of Japan's surrender in the Second World War and, as in other years, it was not unusual for the Chinese press to carry at least one article to commemorate the anniversary. In the summer of 1982, however, the anniversary coincided with a diplomatic furore between the Chinese and Japanese governments – the so-called 'Textbook Issue'[1] – which served to make the subject of the editorial particularly germane and its tone particularly cautionary.

The Textbook Issue concerned the alleged distortion and 'beautification' of Japan's wartime history in Japanese high school history textbooks, about which the Chinese and other Asian governments complained. According to the Japanese media, and later the Chinese, South Korean and Asian press in general, the Japanese Ministry of Education had instructed textbook authors and editors to delete, re-word or tone down certain passages or phrases relating, amongst other things, to Japan's actions during its colonialist period and the 1937–45 war in Asia. The result, according to Japanese and Asian press reports, was a 'prettification' of descriptions of the war and an ominous signal of a return to the prewar style of state-controlled textbooks. Some of the most frequently cited examples of the sorts of changes which were allegedly made to the manuscripts during the textbook authorisation process were those of the descriptions of Japan's 'invasion of China' (allegedly changed to 'advance into China') and the 'Nanjing Massacre'. The Chinese government argued that, by downplaying the nature of Japan's actions in China during the war, omitting, for example, details of the number of Chinese casualties and changing the wording relating to the cause of the Massacre, the Japanese government was 'not adopting a correct view of history', and this was detrimental to the development of Sino-Japanese relations. The editorial from the *Renmin Ribao* referred to above, for example, urged that it was important to 'once again reflect upon Japan's history of invasion of all countries in the Asian and Pacific region, especially China, in order to draw essential lessons for the development and consolidation of Sino-Japanese friendship'.[2]

The Chinese and South Korean governments took decisive action on the issue, both lodging official protests with the Japanese government demanding that the textbooks be corrected immediately and the original wording be reinstated. Throughout July and August the Chinese press carried comments by leaders of China's mass organisations, jurists and academics. Recollections of those who had witnessed or experienced Japanese conduct during the war appeared frequently; Chinese television programmes showed graphic pictures of the aftermath of some of the atrocities and interviewed eyewitnesses. Photographic exhibitions depicting the events of the war were held in a number of cities to coincide with the anniversary of the end of the war in August. In South Korea, too, the press followed the issue as it unfolded and was highly critical of Japan's slow response to the government's demands. Demonstrations were held in Seoul, and there were rallies in Taejon, Taegu and Inchon. Public feeling in South Korea was such that some shop owners boycotted Japanese goods, and some taxi drivers refused to take Japanese passengers.

The Japanese government came under fire from domestic circles also, with opposition parties criticising the LDP's response and signing a petition calling for speedy action. Public demonstrations were held in Tokyo, attended by members of China-friendly organisations, women's groups, teachers and textbook writers, again protesting at the government's actions and calling for a revision of the textbooks. News about the controversy spread further afield. Other Asian countries kept a close watch on developments and in the space of six weeks the issue escalated rapidly, threatening to develop into a region-wide anti-Japan movement. The major newspapers of North Korea, Hong Kong, Singapore, Taiwan and other countries contained considerable coverage of the controversy and warned against a revival of Japanese militarism. The issue even made it into the Western press with, amongst others, *The Times* and the *New York Times* charting the events throughout July, August and September.

Yet despite the intensity of the issue as suggested by the extent of reportage in the regional and international press, and the reactions of

Chinese and Korean governments, after several rounds of negotiations between the Chinese and Japanese governments, and the South Korean and Japanese governments, the issue was resolved – or at least temporarily defused – and disappeared from press reports as suddenly as it had appeared. At the end of August the Japanese government issued a vaguely-worded statement which agreed to (a) bring forward by one year the triennial procedure of updating textbooks, so that the 'problem' textbooks could be revised earlier, and (b) set up an inquiry into textbook authorisation criteria to ensure that in future years the spirit of the Joint Statements signed between Japan and China (1972) and Japan and South Korea (1965) would be fully reflected in textbook content. After some procrastination by both China and South Korea and further clarification by the Japanese government, the issue was brought to a close, although both China and Korea warned that they would be monitoring future developments.

By the end of September, when Prime Minister Suzuki arrived in Beijing to celebrate the tenth anniversary of diplomatic normalisation, the issue had been dropped by the Chinese press, which had regained an optimistic tone with regard to the past, present and future of Sino-Japanese relations. The issue was only mentioned in passing by Deng Xiaoping, Hu Yaobang and Zhao Ziyang, but all three acknowledged that the issue had been resolved and had not altered the course of China's policies *vis-à-vis* Japan. In contrast, throughout September the Japanese press continued to discuss the textbook issue and speculated upon Prime Minister Suzuki's forthcoming visit to China. Prime Minister Suzuki himself, though cautiously optimistic that the issue had not caused irreparable damage to Sino-Japanese relations, was nonetheless keen to reassure the Chinese government at every opportunity during his stay that Japan had no plans to become a military super-power. Suzuki's visit was hailed a success by both sides and by October the issue received no further mention in the daily press.[3]

It is significant that the Japanese government had not agreed fully to the demands of the Chinese and South Korean governments. The textbooks in question were not recalled and revised immediately. The reason for this is quite simple. The allegations about the wording of the textbooks, which had first appeared in the Japanese media in June 1982, were found to be incorrect. In fact, the changes to the textbooks as identified in such newspapers as the *Asahi Shimbun*, the *Yomiuri Shimbun* and the *Mainichi Shimbun*, though perhaps 'recommended' for change by the Ministry of Education during the textbook authorisation process, had not been implemented. Indeed, some of the alleged changes had never even been 'recommended' in the first place. Therefore, the

Japanese government was unable to 'revise' the textbooks or reinstate the 'original wording' as it was being asked to do by the foreign governments, precisely because the textbooks had not been 'rewritten' in the first place.

In a sense then, the textbook issue turned out to be a 'virtual crisis', albeit one which seriously jeopardised Sino-Japanese relations on the eve of the tenth anniversary of normalisation. Japanese foreign ministry officials were quoted at the time as saying that the issue set back Sino-Japanese relations by ten years, and all this because of what the *Japan Echo* later described as a 'historic blooper by the Japanese media.' [4]

However, the issue cannot be dismissed as insignificant on the grounds that it was all 'a big mistake,' since it raises important questions about the use of history in Sino-Japanese relations, the nature of that relationship in the 1980s and, given that similar events are still happening in Sino-Japanese relations, in the 1990s as well. Throughout the 1980s, beginning with the Textbook Issue, there was a string of issues relating in some way to the legacy of Sino-Japanese history, (for which one must read Japan's aggression during the war), and what the Chinese government perceived to be evidence of residual pro-militarist elements in Japan. The Textbook Issue can perhaps be seen as the event which brought into the international arena for the first time the issue of Japan's responsibility for the war in Asia. The main aim of this book, therefore, is to examine how and why the Textbook Issue became such a critical issue in Sino-Japanese relations, and what it reveals about the dynamics of contemporary Sino-Japanese relations.

History in Sino-Japanese relations

The Textbook Issue was concerned with the writing and interpretation of history. History, we are frequently told, plays a particularly important role in Sino-Japanese relations. China and Japan share a history that goes back beyond the fifty years of conflict, to a two thousand-year period of friendship and cultural exchange. This combination of a 'good' period of history and a 'bad' period of history appears to figure large in their contemporary perceptions of each other.

In 1987, Deng Xiaoping said that 'Japan is indebted to China more than any other nation in the world.' [5] Japan is generally considered to owe two types of debt to China. Deng could have been referring to Japan's cultural debt accrued over two thousand or more years of friendly, or at least cordial, relations involving trade and cultural exchange. With the 1894–5 Sino-Japanese War however, the friendship turned to enmity and the ensuing fifty years of Sino-Japanese relations entered a period of what is euphemistically termed 'unfortunate history'.[6] This period gave rise to the second debt, incurred by Japan through the damage and suffering inflicted on China and the Chinese people during the Sino-Japanese war, and it was in fact to this debt, and not the 'cultural debt', that Deng was referring in 1987. Though never explicit, 'repayment' of this debt has been, and continues to be, made in the form of Japanese aid and investment in China's modernisation programme. Deng made it clear in his speech that China considers Japan's assistance obligatory not only because of the suffering of the Chinese during the war, but also because China did not claim war reparations when China and Japan normalised diplomatic relations in 1972. Ijiri comments that Deng raised the 'debt' issue in 1987 as a reminder of this obligation, and as a way to embarrass the Japanese government into making 'much greater contributions in order to assist China's development'.[7]

Before considering how Sino-Japanese history has influenced more recent events in Sino-Japanese relations, it is worth considering how the two types of debt referred to above came about, and how the two different periods of history have been perceived and manipulated over time by both Chinese and Japanese leaders and governments.

Sino-Japanese relations to 1894: creating a cultural debt?

In his speech to the Committee of Non-Governmental Organisations in 1992, General Secretary Jiang Zemin, talking of the 'International Situation and Sino-Japanese Relations', made the following comments:

> China and Japan are friendly neighbours separated only by a strip of water, and the people of the two countries have forged a profound friendship through their exchanges for more than two thousand years. . . . Culturally our two countries have a lot in common that makes it easy for us to communicate with each other and helps increase our mutual understanding and trust.[8]

This is the standard fare of speeches on Sino-Japanese relations, but what are the origins of this 'profound friendship', and what is it that enables such 'mutual understanding and trust'?

It is generally agreed that the cultural affinity and lengthy friendship to which Jiang Zemin was referring had their origins in the third century BCE.[9] The nature of these very early contacts is not clear, but by the Qin (221–207 BCE) and Han (206 BCE–CE 220) dynasties it seems that Chinese immigrants reached Japan and introduced such techniques as weaving and rice cultivation. Even if there was little direct contact between China and Japan, Chinese cultural influence entered Japan via Korea.[10]

Formal relations, although sporadic, began in the early Christian era, with a mission from the country of 'Wa' (the Chinese term for Japan until the seventh century) to China in CE 57, and another in CE 107. There seems to be no record of further missions until the middle of the third century, and then none again until the fifth. Yet despite there being fewer official missions, Chinese immigrant artisans and craftsmen brought new knowledge and skills, and were even put into service for the imperial family.[11]

The period from the fifth to the tenth centuries was the apogee of China's influence on the development of Japanese cultural, social, political and economic spheres, and it is this period which created what the Japanese and Chinese see as Japan's cultural debt to China. The social stability and economic prosperity of the Sui (581–618) and Tang (618–907) dynasties spurred development in all aspects: military, political, economic, social and cultural. This provided a model for Japan, itself developing from a slave to a feudal society. As a result Sino-Japanese contact began to take place on a much larger scale than previously and this period is commonly referred to as a 'high tide' in Sino-Japanese relations. The most significant and lasting influences were the introduction of the Chinese writing system, Confucian and Buddhist thought, and Chinese arts and crafts. These influences, along with some of the economic and political borrowings, helped to transform Japan into a 'civilised' nation.[12]

After this first 'China boom', Japan moved away from its fascination with all things Chinese and concentrated instead on domestic matters.[13] Although there were no official relations between the Chinese and Japanese courts from the tenth to the fourteenth century, cultural and economic exchanges were maintained. Trade played an increasingly important role in the relationship, with as many as forty or fifty ships sailing between China and Japan annually during the Song dynasty.[14] Formal relations remained strained during the Yuan dynasty (1271–1368) due to the Yuan's attempted attacks on Japan and because of the activities of the Japanese pirates (*wakō*) on the China coast.

During the Ming dynasty (1368–1644) Japan reluctantly entered into a somewhat faltering tribute relationship with China.[15] Ming China's Sinocentric view of the world determined its relations with all its East Asian neighbours. Countries were ranked hierarchically, and graded according to geographic proximity and/or cultural similarity. Fairbank suggests three zones: the first containing Korea, Vietnam, the Ryukyu

(Liu Qiu) islands and, at times, Japan; the second zone included the non-Chinese Inner Asian nomadic people; and the third zone consisted of those at a greater distance, the 'outer barbarians' (*wai yi*) including Southeast and South Asia and Europe and, by the late Ming period, Japan.[16]

Japan paid tribute between the beginning of the fifteenth century and the middle of the sixteenth century, but with only nineteen missions to China during this time, Japan's ranking in China's hierarchical world view was clearly very low (compared with Korea, which paid tribute annually). Relations were severed intermittently either by Chinese emperors or Japanese shōguns, and by the middle of the sixteenth century Japan withdrew from the 'Chinese world order'. The lack of tribute relations can be attributed not only to China's disdain for Japan as an 'Eastern Barbarian', but also to Japan's reluctance to acknowledge China as a superior state.[17] For example, when shōgun Ashikaga Yoshimitsu decided to enter into tribute with the Ming court in the fifteenth century, he was criticised for going against the 'traditional foreign policy concepts of Japan's ruling class, which had considered Japan to be China's equal'.[18]

In the late sixteenth century, Sino-Japanese relations deteriorated. Authorised 'tally' trade diminished and *wakō* raids on China increased. The Ming court severed relations with Japan in 1557, and in the 1590s Japanese and Ming troops came into conflict when Japan made an early attempt at expansionism into Korea. In the seventeenth century, Japan's formal relations with the Qing dynasty were minimal. Toby points out that in the Japanese 'world order' of the time the 'bakufu had demoted China to the lowest rung of its hierarchy of partners'.[19] The so-called *sakoku* or 'isolationist' policy of the Tokugawa shogunate, aimed initially at the Portuguese, eventually had the effect of restrictions on the number of Chinese trading ships allowed to the ports of Nagasaki and Hirado after 1616. Nevertheless, trade with China did increase up to the late seventeenth century,[20] but thereafter declined due to the imposition of stricter regulations on Japan's China trade that remained in place throughout the eighteenth century.[21] Toby suggests that the restriction of trade with China in the eighteenth century was a means of forcing China's acceptance, or at least recognition, of Japan's centrality in Asia and of reinforcing China's low status in Japan's 'hierarchy of partners'.[22]

While trade with China was curtailed in the seventeenth and eighteenth centuries, *sakoku* certainly did not extend to curtailment of cultural and intellectual exchange with China. Toby argues that contrary to popular belief the *sakoku* policy did not cut Japan off from the rest of the world: 'Japan was not closed to Asia, nor even entirely closed to Europe.'[23] On the contrary, cultural exchange between China and Japan experienced a renaissance during this period. Scholars, doctors, veterinarians and Zen monks entered Japan via Nagasaki, many at the invitation of the shōgun Yoshimune. There was a revival of interest in Confucianism and Chinese literature on all subjects was studied, especially books on law and administration, some of which were used in schools to teach about respect for elders and village harmony. Chinese artists were highly regarded and contributed to Japanese art by introducing the genre of nature scenes, and Chinese music and songs also became popular.[24]

Thus, during this period the Japanese elite came to hold what Jansen describes as an idealistic view of China as a 'land of sages and tranquillity'. But just as Japan's reverence of Tang China had faded with time, by the nineteenth century when China's military weakness and internal disorder were becoming apparent, there was a change of attitude in Japan. The change was also prompted by Japan's growing self-sufficiency and cultural confidence[25] as 'the Japanese first became fully aware of themselves as a national entity'.[26]

The myth of the cultural debt

As described above, Japanese society developed firmly within the Chinese 'culture area', influenced at various times and to varying degrees by Chinese cultural, political, religious and ideological systems. Jansen suggests that when one considers the incomparably high level of development of Chinese society during for example the Han, Tang and late Song, Japan's reverence for Chinese superiority is understandable. For Japan, 'China was . . . a Greece and Rome that remained powerful, a Renaissance Italy and a classical France, all rolled into one; a single, unitary and unique cultural colossus.'[27]

Through cultural borrowing, Japan's early development clearly owed much to continental influence, particularly in the Sui and Tang periods when Japan's enthusiasm to learn from China was at a peak. However, Chinese culture and civilisation were not transferred completely in their original form, but underwent careful selection and adaptation. Many aspects of Chinese civilisation were not incorporated into Japanese society, some failed to work, and some were completely redefined to suit Japanese circumstances (for example, government by merit, equal land distribution). In Varley's words, 'Japan's cultural borrowing was sufficiently selective to bring about the evolution of a society which, although it owed much to China, became unique in its own right.'[28]

Furthermore, as Japan developed, attitudes towards China began to change. Hints of a Japanese sense of superiority, or at least aspirations to equality with China, began to emerge at the beginning of the seventh century. A Japanese envoy to the Chinese court in 607 delivered a message which read: 'The Son of Heaven in the land where the sun rises addresses a letter to the Son of Heaven in the land where the sun sets.' This was regarded as an affront by the Chinese emperor who 'told the official in charge of foreign affairs that this letter from the barbarians was discourteous, and that such a letter should not again be brought to his attention'.[29]

Hane talks of the 'growing ethnocentrism' in Japan in the seventh century, illustrated by the style of the *Kojiki* and *Nihongi*:[30]

> Japan is viewed in these accounts as a unique land. In fact, it was depicted as being at the center of the universe, and the ancestral god of Japan, the Sun Goddess, was seen as the ruler of the entire world. From around the middle of the seventh century the term Nihon, the place where the sun rises, came to be used to identify Japan. Much of the cultural activity of this era sprang from the Japanese desire to rise to the level of China.[31]

Japan was never as closely incorporated into the Chinese world order as were, say, Korea and Vietnam. Japan was never under direct Chinese control, and never became a 'full' tributary state. Indeed, for many centuries, 'the Japanese islands held little interest for China . . . They were off world trade routes.'[32] The Japanese, for the most part, were not willing to be subordinated to China's hierarchy of states.

Japanese attitudes towards China were not consistent, but varied according to changes in Japan's domestic politics and at times of domestic disorder and cultural stagnation in China. By the end of the Tokugawa period, China's economic and intellectual importance to Japan was in decline and China's response to Western imperialism had highlighted China's weakness. Jansen suggests, for example, that 'Tokugawa participation in the Chinese world . . . left no consciousness of benevolence on the one side and even less sense of obligation on the other.'[33]

In the mid-nineteenth century both China and Japan faced the threat of Western imperialist incursion, and were subjected to a series of unequal treaties which forced open their markets to the foreign powers. By the end of the nineteenth century, China, unable to withstand foreign pressure, had not only become victim of the Western powers in their 'scramble for concessions' but was also suffering at the hands of a newly-transformed, expansionist Japan. In the words of Iriye, 'Japan's cultural indebtedness to China did not prevent its military assertiveness on the continent'[34] and, ironically, the concept of Japan's cultural debt to China was even used by some Japanese as a means of justifying and rationalising their actions on the continent. Here, then, we see that the concept of the cultural debt owed to China by Japan was being used or manipulated by some in order to serve their own political agenda. This is not very different from the way in which history was used in the Textbook and other issues as a symbol or tool to gain leverage for other, unrelated reasons.

1894–1945: 'Fifty years that overshadow two thousand.'

The 'unfortunate' period of Sino-Japanese history began with the first Sino-Japanese war in 1894 and ended in 1945. Japan's imperialist ambitions in Asia grew rapidly in the twentieth century. From 1895 on, Japan acquired more and more territory and rights through a series of wars, rebellions and 'incidents'. By 1931, the Japanese Empire encompassed the Ryukyu islands, Taiwan, Korea, the Kwantung Leased Territory (Liaodong) and South Manchuria, Sakhalin (Karafuto) and the Micronesian islands. In China, it enjoyed the same rights and privileges in treaty ports and concessions as did the Western powers and had established itself as China's major trading partner. At its 'peak' in China, Japan controlled nearly all the major cities, was manipulating the puppet government of Manchukuo, and was reaping the benefits of a vast industrial and commercial base.

This section will provide an overview of the 'unfortunate' period of history so that the context of the Chinese protests during the Textbook Issue can be understood, and also to highlight some of the events and themes which have since influenced Sino-Japanese relations.

1894–1931: Japanese expansionism

In 1894, after more than two decades of growing friction, China and Japan came into military and naval conflict over Korea, an event which was a turning point in the history of Sino-Japanese relations. Prior to the outbreak of war, some Chinese, particularly those who were advocating 'self-strengthening' reform in China such as Li Hongzhang and Zeng Guofan, had been charting Japan's rapid rate of change brought about after the Meiji Restoration. For this minority of people, Japan was clearly seen as a potential rival, and among them there was a 'grudging admiration' of Japan's development.[35] For the majority, however, ignorance and preconceptions of Japan had blinded them to the possibility that Japan would even dare to attack the mainland, let alone stand any chance of defeating the 'Middle Kingdom'. On the eve of the 1894 war, most Chinese felt not only condescension but also contempt for the Japanese.[36]

When war broke out, the Chinese army and navy, although superior in numbers, were overwhelmed by 'Japan's swift and decisive action,'[37] and highly-trained Japanese troops armed with modern ships and equipment.[38] For China, defeat at the hands of the 'Eastern barbarians' was a huge shock, and signalled the demise of the Qing dynasty. Despite thirty years of 'self-strengthening', China had been humiliated by a small, insignificant country that had nevertheless overtaken China in the race towards modernisation.

After the war, Chinese resentment of Japan was mixed with admiration and a feeling that China could perhaps learn something about modernisation from Japan.[39] Chinese foreign students were first sent to Japan in 1896, and numbers rose dramatically in the following years.[40] Suddenly the relationship had been reversed; no longer was China Japan's cultural mentor. Instead Japan had become a role model for China to emulate. The decade from 1898 has been called a 'golden age' of Sino-Japanese relations, with the flow of Japanese ideas into China and Chinese students into Japan.[41] Japan's impact on Chinese education, militarisation, constitutionalism and nationalism is considered to have been 'more direct, profound, and far reaching' than that of Britain in the nineteenth century or even the Soviet Union in the 1950s.[42] Chinese reformers were optimistic that what Japan had achieved in the thirty years since the Meiji Restoration, China could achieve more quickly, particularly because, in the course of their own modernisation, the Japanese had already selected the most appropriate elements of Western science, technology and political thought.[43]

For Japan, the Sino-Japanese war brought Japan her first colonies: Taiwan, the Pescadores and the Liaodong peninsula (although the Triple Intervention later forced retrocession of the latter). Japan also gained 'most favoured nation' status, thus putting her on an equal footing with the Western powers in China.[44] Victory and the subsequent growth in prestige and status also affected Japanese attitudes towards the Chinese: 'Japanese respect for China changed with extraordinary speed to condescension and even contempt.'[45] This reversal of attitudes was partly brought about by the accounts of the armies of the Sino-Japanese and later Russo-Japanese wars who had witnessed China's poverty and backwardness; a far cry from the traditional image of China as the 'land of sages and tranquillity'. Negative views of China

12   *Introduction*

were introduced in government-written school textbooks of the early 1900s which imparted to Japanese schoolchildren images of a rude, arrogant and weak China that failed to 'recognize Japan's true desire to promote peace and enlightenment in East Asia'.[46]

On the other hand, there was also a certain amount of sympathy for China's plight, a sense that Japan could now try to help China modernise, and that this could be some sort of repayment of the cultural debt. The late nineteenth century saw the emergence of Pan-Asianism, the concept that 'Japan, as the first successful non-European modernizer, was obligated to assist the uplift of less fortunate neighboring peoples.'[47] Fears of a collapse of the Qing dynasty and subsequent partition of China by the Western powers bent on a racial war in Asia were widespread, and produced a sense of commitment to an 'Asian cause' based on ideas of kinship, that is, 'same script, same race' (*dōbun dōshu*).

While some pan-Asianists may have genuinely felt a sense of duty to Asia, there were, however, far less altruistic dimensions of Pan-Asianist ideas. China's modernisation was considered not only of vital importance to China's own survival but to Japanese national interests also. At the turn of the century, political leaders such as Prince Konoe Atsumaro talked of the need for Japanese 'to study China, travel to China and meet Chinese' in order to 'adopt policies appropriate to the danger both countries face'.[48] China was believed to be of great economic significance to Japan also. After the Sino-Japanese war, Japanese governments concentrated on developing Japan's commercial interests in the new colonies and in the treaty ports in China in order to achieve the goal of transforming Japan into an industrial and commercial power. Not only could China supply raw materials such as cotton, coal and iron ore, but it also possessed a potentially huge market for Japan's exports of manufactured goods.[49]

Both government-backed and privately-owned companies began to prosper in China, especially in the two decades after the Russo-Japanese war when Japan's domestic economy was undergoing rapid growth and produced surplus capital that could be invested in China. In addition to employees of large companies (NYK, OSK, Nisshin Kisen, Mitsui, Ōkura and so on), from the 1890s increasing numbers of Japanese traders and shopkeepers began to move to China. They settled not just in the concession areas of treaty ports, but also in China's hinterland. By the 1930s, Japanese expatriates outnumbered Western expatriates in China.[50] Bilateral trade between China and Japan developed to the extent that by the 1920s Japan had become China's most important trading partner,[51] and direct investment, particularly in Manchuria,[52] meant that the South Manchurian Railway, gas and electricity companies, mines and iron foundries all received massive injections of capital in the early 1900s as a result of the policy of economic modernisation and resource development.[53]

After the Chinese revolution of 1911 there was an upsurge in nationalist, anti-imperialist feeling in China. Chinese suspicions of Japan's ambitions in Asia were confirmed by Japan's aggressive foreign policy and growing economic presence. Much of the anti-imperialist feeling was directed at Japan, and fears were expressed that Japan's 'economic invasion' would soon lead to military invasion.[54] It is interesting to note the historical precedent of sentiments expressed in present-day China, most notably during the student demonstrations in 1985 when students accused Japan of launching a 'second economic invasion'.

Chinese fears were soon realised. By 1914, taking advantage of Germany's preoccupation with affairs in Europe, Japan had added Qingdao and other German-held territories in the South Pacific to her formal empire. The Twenty-One Demands imposed on China in 1915 revealed the 'true nature' of Japan's long-term objectives in Asia,[55] and were regarded by the Chinese as a plan to take advantage of a 'helpless neighbour' while the powers were engaged in a war in Europe.[56] Furthermore, the superficially friendly policies of Prime Minister Terauchi Masatake only served to strengthen Chinese suspicion and opposition to Japanese imperialism.[57] Chinese nationalism manifested itself in boycotts of Japanese goods in response to the Twenty-One Demands, student demonstrations against the Nishihara loans, and the May 4 demonstrations against decisions taken in Japan's favour at the Versailles Peace Conference in 1919.

Japan's China policy in the 1920s alternated between caution and aggression, intervention and non-intervention, reflecting the debate in Japan as to the solution of the 'China problem'. Shidehara's 'weak-kneed diplomacy' (1924–7) was followed briefly by Tanaka's stronger approach, which manifested itself in a series of military manoeuvres in Shandong and Manchuria. The murder of Chinese warlord Zhang Zuolin by 'rebel' officers of the Kwantung army led to Tanaka's downfall, but was an ominous sign of what was to come. Shidehara returned to 'power', replacing Tanaka in 1929, and tried to re-establish a policy of non-intervention in China's affairs, but Shidehara was faced with growing opposition from the military and those in favour of an autonomous Japan. Furthermore, the worldwide economic depression of the late 1920s created a sense of vulnerability and national danger. Japan needed to retain markets for its manufactured goods, ensure continued access to raw materials and find space for its surplus population.[58] For the military especially, Manchuria was seen as Japan's lifeline.

1931–45: the Fifteen Year War

The 1931 'Manchurian Incident,' or 'September 18 Incident,'[59] though not sanctioned by central government, presented Tokyo with a *fait accompli* and led to the subsequent establishment of the puppet state Manchukuo in 1932. This signalled the end of Japan's 'peaceful' economic exploitation of China and the beginning of nearly fifteen years of continual violence and aggression. 'Pan-Asianist' sentiments were revived as rationalisations for Japan's actions. In the textbooks of the 1930s, schoolchildren were told that although China was weak and underdeveloped, by combining the efforts of the Chinese, Japanese and Manchukuo people, peace would be preserved in East Asia. Indeed, the textbooks taught, it was the duty of the Japanese people to help China, because Japan had borrowed so much from China in the past. However, the textbooks also made it clear that Japan's national interests took priority, stressing that 'those students who went to the continent would strengthen those nations' economies, overcome shortages for Japan, and help to build a brilliant future for Japan.'[60]

After 1931 there were 'daily occurrences' involving gunfire or guerrilla action in areas occupied by Japanese forces,[61] and in 1937 the Marco Polo Bridge Incident[62] brought all-out war between China and Japan. The Japanese military and government had expected that the 'China Incident' could be dealt with quickly, but they had underestimated the strength and tenacity of Chinese resistance. Furthermore, as Hata notes, the Japanese military created for itself a vicious circle; the larger the area it seized, the more troops it needed, and the deeper it became bogged down in the China 'quagmire'.[63] As the fighting went on, rationalisations for Japanese actions broadened from the idea of the Japan-China-Manchukuo bloc of the early 1930s to the 'Greater East Asia Co-Prosperity Sphere' that would incorporate Southeast Asia and the Pacific.

The Nanjing Massacre of 1937 stands out (in Chinese and Western sources) as one of the most horrendous atrocities committed by the Japanese in China, and deserves some attention here as it became one of the focal points of the 1982 Textbook Issue. Chinese, Western (and some Japanese) versions of the massacre relate that for six weeks after the capture of Nanjing on 12 December, Japanese troops engaged in execution, rape and random murder of Chinese soldiers and civilians, men and women, young and old both in Nanjing itself and in surrounding villages.[64] This mass slaughter of Chinese citizens and the plundering and burning of homes, shops and government buildings was witnessed by foreign observers, whose accounts, along with those of survivors, provided the outside world with a picture of an army intent on systematic annihilation of all Chinese resistance. The exact death toll will never be known, and the subject has been and continues to be a matter of great controversy. As with the overall number of Chinese casualties of the war, different sources give different estimates of those who died during the Nanjing Massacre, with estimates ranging from 40,000 to 300,000.[65]

The Nanjing Massacre is notorious for its scale and intensity, but it was not an isolated incident. Huge numbers of Chinese were killed during the capture of smaller cities – Hankou and Guangzhou, for example – and the peasantry and villages of northern China were terrorised during the 'rural pacification' campaigns. In Kwantung (Liaodong) and Manchukuo, discrimination against Chinese was total and policies of assimilation, similar to those imposed in Taiwan and Korea were introduced. Chinese employees of the South Manchurian Railway coal mines were exploited financially and physically, with lower wages and poorer working conditions than their Japanese counterparts.[66]

In China proper, labourers were either mobilised to work at the front or were shipped to Japan. Chinese labourers were amongst those mobilised to build the Burma railroad; Chinese girls and women were forced into prostitution as 'comfort girls' for the Japanese troops; Chinese prisoners of war were used in Japanese training exercises, and unknown numbers of Chinese were secretly taken to Manchuria (Unit 731) and died as a result of the bacteriological experiments inflicted upon them.[67] Experiments carried out on human guinea pigs at Unit 731 were put into practice in China after 1940 in the form of germ warfare. [68]

It is difficult to quantify the atrocities committed by Japanese troops against Chinese soldiers and civilians alike, and Chinese, Japanese and Western sources differ tremendously. Chinese and Western sources agree that violence, killing, rape, and torture were committed arbitrarily by the Japanese army. Prisoners of war were maltreated, tortured or murdered, civilians were massacred, women and children were raped.[69] Japanese textbooks generally estimate that 10 million Chinese soldiers and civilians died in the Sino-Japanese war, and Dower suggests this is a 'reasonable' figure. Many other estimates have been suggested, however, ranging from several million to 15–20 million deaths. [70]

This account is the standard 'accepted' version of the events of the Sino-Japanese war on which Chinese, Western and *many* Japanese scholars agree, [71] but an 'alternative' view has been expressed on many occasions by Liberal Democratic Party (LDP) politicians, right-wing scholars and journalists in Japan. Apart from disagreeing on the number of Chinese soldiers and civilians sacrificed during the war, the 'alternative' view rests on the premise that for Japan the war was not one of aggression but a war of liberation, and that Japan was carrying out its duty in freeing Asia from the grip of Western colonialists and Chinese communists. In this respect, Japan's actions in Asia have even been likened to the US war in Vietnam in that the war was not a war with China, nor was it about seizing territory; rather, it was 'a defence action against communists and their allies in China.'[72] The testimony of Generals Matsui and Tōjō at the Tokyo War Crimes Trials attests to the belief among Japanese at the time that the hostilities could be likened to 'a fight between brothers', or ' a family quarrel, in which the younger brother, China, was being made to reconsider its various illegal acts'.[73]

This interpretation has changed little among the LDP and right wing since 1945, and while Japanese governments admit that Japan caused much suffering in Asia and have begun to acknowledge this suffering in recent years, the underlying view of the war with China appears to have remained the same. This explains the reluctance of successive Japanese governments, until 1993, to apologise to its Asian neighbours, and the continuing occurrence of controversies over remarks made by Japanese LDP politicians about, for example, Japan not intending to launch a war of invasion against China, which have enraged Chinese and other Asian governments throughout the 1980s and 1990s. As this study will illustrate, it is not simply the legacy of the atrocities carried out during the war, but also the *different interpretations of these events* that have had such a significant impact on the development of Sino-Japanese relations in the postwar period.

The legacy of history

The juxtaposition of a two thousand-year, predominantly peaceful relationship on the one hand, and a fifty-year relationship of acrimony on the other, appears to have set the tone of postwar Sino-Japanese relations. As described below, any discussion of Sino-Japanese relations invariably contains some reference to the long and illustrious history of Sino-Japanese friendship, and there is no reason to dismiss this as total rhetoric. But as the Textbook Issue exemplifies, memories of Japanese atrocities are, understandably, still very much alive in China, or perhaps more accurately, are kept alive in China. In Japan, on the other hand, it seems that they would much rather be forgotten,[74] and the Japanese are frequently accused of suffering from amnesia on the subject of the war.[75]

The title of the *Renmin Ribao*'s August 1982 editorial, 'The past, if not forgotten, is a guide to the future', has become, suitably perhaps, a standard maxim in Sino-Japanese relations and points to the central role of 'history' in this relationship, not only in the sense of the events of the past but as a powerful symbol. Most of the descriptive accounts of Sino-Japanese relations, be they in English, Japanese or Chinese, invariably include some reference to the 'long and illustrious history' that the two countries share (*lishiyoujiu*), and their 'two thousand years of well-established friendly contacts' (*youhaojiaowang yuanyuanliuchang*). There is of course reference also to the period of 'unfortunate history' (in Chinese, *buxin de guocheng*, in Japanese, *fukō na keika*) which, for China, 'brooks no distortion' (*buneng waiqu*), and for which Japan has expressed 'deep self-reproach' (*fukai hansei*); but for which until 1993 she had not apologised, a fact in itself a bone of contention for the Chinese. In addition to historical factors, Sino-Japanese relations are also said to benefit from geographical proximity, 'separated by only a narrow strip of water' (*yiyidaishui de linbang*) and cultural and racial affinity (*dōbun dōshu*, 'same script, same race',[76] *ibōkyōdai*, 'brothers by a different mother'). Such characteristics, these accounts say, provide Sino-Japanese relations with a solid foundation on which to build a 'special relationship', one which benefits from mutual understanding, trust, communication and co-operation.

Such descriptions of Sino-Japanese relations are not merely restricted to textbooks or history books, but are to be found in preambles to the various agreements and treaties that the two countries have signed, and are also frequently heard in the speeches, statements and essays of Chinese and Japanese politicians, bureaucrats and academics, who frequently reaffirm their commitment to the principles of peace and friendship, mutual benefit and long-term stability on which Sino-Japanese relations are based. Furthermore, governments in both countries have long talked of the need for peace and stability in Asia in order to achieve not only their own respective economic goals, but also regional economic prosperity. Both governments are aware of the central role of the Sino-Japanese relationship in East Asia, and believe that maintaining peace between them will contribute to the region's stability.

Yet despite these frequent proclamations of friendship and solidarity, Sino-Japanese political relations have been characterised by sporadic controversies and conflicts ever since the end of the Second World War. While this may have been understandable before normalisation, it does not explain why problems between the two governments were not significantly reduced even after diplomatic relations were normalised in 1972. Disputes have centred on various problems, ranging from territorial issues (Senkaku islands/Diaoyutai) and economic issues (plant cancellations) to diplomatic issues (Japan's recognition of Taiwan) and issues related directly to the 'bad' history (textbooks, apologies, Manchurian orphans issue). The latter appeared with regularity during the 1980s, beginning with the Textbook Issue of 1982 (which recurred in 1984 and 1986), which can be seen as a 'prototype'; but all types of issue tended to include some degree of reference to the past, specifically some reference by the Chinese government to a revival of militarism in Japan or renewed attempts at economic domination of China in the region.

After the textbook controversy, the next major political issue occurred in August 1985, when Prime Minister Nakasone, in his official capacity, chose to visit the Yasukuni Shrine where the spirits of the Japanese war dead, including war criminals, are enshrined. In the same year, student demonstrations in China protested against what they saw as Japan's 'second (economic) invasion'. In 1986 there was a renewal of the Textbook Issue, when a history textbook produced by an ultra-nationalist Japanese group became the object of renewed Chinese and Korean criticism. A number of events in 1987, including an increase in Japan's defence expenditure and a legal wrangle over ownership rights of a student dormitory in Kyoto, added to tension already caused by the continuing trade imbalance and brought Sino-Japanese political relations to another low ebb. Comments by leading LDP politicians about the war became the focus of Sino-Japanese tension in 1988 and 1989.

In the 1990s there have been similar patterns of events with frequent resignations of Japanese government ministers over insensitive remarks about the events of the war, disagreements between the Chinese and Japanese governments over Japanese apologies (or lack of them) for the war, and the wording of the Japanese government's 1995 'no-war resolution'.[77] Prime Minister Hashimoto's 1996 visit to the Yasukuni shrine and the latest instalment of the Senkaku Islands dispute in the summer of 1996 have provided further evidence to the Chinese that Japan is planning to reassert itself militarily, and analysts have commented that 1996 saw Sino-Japanese relations at their lowest ebb since normalisation.[78]

Interpreting history: the Textbook Issue

Clearly the legacy of the events of the Second World War plays a significant role in contemporary Sino-Japanese relations. The Textbook Issue was the first 'full-scale' controversy which appeared to be about history and its interpretation. Specifically, it was about the difference between the Chinese interpretation of the 'unfortunate' history between the two countries, and the Japanese interpretation of the same period.

The Chinese interpretation is one which sees China (and the Chinese people) as the victor in the war but the victim of Japanese aggression. In turn, the War of Resistance against Japan is seen as one part of the 'century of humiliation' which the Chinese suffered at the hands of the imperialists. Chinese history textbooks contain full details of the War of Resistance, and the fight against colonialism in general. A description of the Nanjing Massacre in a middle-school textbook in use in the 1980s contains photographs and graphic details of the events of December 1937, commenting that 'the fierce brutality of the Japanese troops roused unparalleled anger in the Chinese people.'[79] In Chinese lore, the Nanjing Massacre has become one of the most powerful symbols of the atrocities committed by Japanese troops in China. Attempts of Japanese journalists or politicians[80] to deny or reinterpret the events of the Nanjing Massacre are akin to denials of the Holocaust, and are certainly not taken seriously in academic circles in Japan. But in Chinese eyes, they are proof that Japanese militarism still has a stronghold in Japan. Seen in this context, it is therefore understandable that the Chinese and other Asian governments protested at what they saw to be an attempt by the Japanese government to cover up the facts of history.

The Japanese interpretation of the war is more complex. While the Chinese see themselves as victims and the Japanese as victimisers, the Japanese have been slow to acknowledge their role as victimisers. On the contrary, in the early postwar period, the view of history became dominated by a 'victims' consciousness' where the Japanese people themselves were seen as victims, that is, of the actions of Japanese leaders (who were responsible for leading the country to war), and of the atom bombs.

While journalists and academics did address the issue of Japanese history from the point of view as Japan as the victimiser, this was not an officially accepted, or acceptable, point of view. The 'official', conservative (right-wing) view of the events of the Second World War related mostly to the events of 1941 onwards, i.e. the Pacific and not the Asian 'part' of the war. This was very much the result of the Tokyo War Crimes Trial and the Occupation-inspired 'reinterpretation of history.' What has become known as the 'Tokyo War Crimes Trial view of history', i.e. that Japanese expansionism and aggression were carefully planned and executed but the villains were identified and punished as a result of the Trials, meant that by 1945 the war issue had been 'dealt with' and enabled the country to 'break with its past.'[81] By then focusing heavily on Japan and the Japanese as the victims of the war, it meant that a huge chunk of history was omitted, specifically the part that explained what the Japanese did in Asia before war broke out with the USA. This history came to be ignored not just in history books but in the 'collective memory' as well. Dower explains how the horror and devastation of Hiroshima and Nagasaki:

> became icons of Japanese suffering – perverse national treasures, of a sort, capable of fixating Japanese memory of the war on what had happened to Japan and simultaneously blotting out recollection of the Japanese victimization of others. Remembering Hiroshima and Nagasaki, that is, easily became a way of forgetting Nanjing, Bataan, the Burma–Siam railway, Manila, and the countless Japanese atrocities these and other place names signified to non-Japanese.[82]

If and when the Asian part of the war was addressed, it tended to be by 'progressives' or 'revisionists'. Progressives, though by no means united on their views of Japanese history, fought a long battle with the establishment against the reintroduction of any prewar 'symbols' (imperial ideology, nationalism) into education, but found their position weakening as the years of LDP rule turned into decades.[83] Revisionists, on the other hand, sought to explain the rationale for Japanese actions during the war, which was described in terms of the role Japan played in the struggle against colonialism and the liberation of Asia from Western imperialists; a point of view which can be found amongst LDP Diet members to this day.[84]

The implication of the neglect of the Asian war (or the 'Fifteen Year War') was that prior to the 1980s there had been relatively little questioning of the issue of Japanese responsibility for the events of 1931 to the early 1940s. The Textbook Issue helped to bring this issue out into the open (though by no means resolved it), and revealed the huge perception gap between Chinese and Japanese views of their shared history.

However, if the Textbook Issue revealed nothing more about Sino-Japanese relations than how Sino-Japanese history is interpreted by both parties, then this study need go no further than an outline of the events and an assessment of the way it influenced the subsequent debate on Japan's war responsibility. As the book will show, however, the Textbook Issue in fact raises many questions which cannot be explained merely in terms of a gap in historical interpretation. Why, for example, did the Chinese government take up the issue at such a crucial juncture (on the eve of the tenth anniversary of normalisation), when it was not the first time that textbook content and interpretation of the past had been on the Japanese political agenda? Why did the Japanese government fail to make the press retract the erroneous reports immediately, and why did they not explain the error to the Chinese immediately so as to contain the damage? Why was the Chinese government pacified so easily by the non-committal pledge of the Japanese government?

The answers to these questions can provide an insight into the way the Chinese and Japanese governments go about dealing with one another in a 'crisis', how they perceive their relationship – past and present – and to what extent (if at all) these perceptions determine the way they deal with one another. They encourage us to explore the decision-making processes in both countries and to examine the key factors which are most likely to influence decision makers under certain conditions. This book attempts to provide answers to these questions with the aim of reaching a better understanding of the factors which influence Sino-Japanese political relations, and the way in which Chinese and Japanese decision makers formulate domestic and foreign policies. To find the answers to these questions, it is necessary to look beyond the narrow confines of the events of July and August 1982 and the idea that the issue was bound up only with the writing and interpretation of history. To understand how and why the Chinese and Japanese governments acted and reacted in the way they did requires an understanding of the interconnection of, for example, the patterns of Sino-Japanese relations before and since 1945, of domestic political and economic developments in China and Japan since the 1970s and their influence on decision makers at the time, and of changes in the international system in the late 1970s and early 1980s and the effect these had on domestic and foreign policies of both governments.

By considering these factors the study will show that the Textbook Issue had less to do with history and its interpretation than it did with responses to changes in domestic and international politics, and the use and manipulation of collective memory and history as a means of serving the interests of both the Chinese and Japanese governments. In so doing, the study rejects some of the standard explanations of Sino-Japanese relations, favouring instead an approach which combines findings from the fields of area studies and international relations. Chapter 2 will assess the applicability to the Textbook Issue of the standard explanations of Sino-Japanese relations, before outlining a framework for an interdisciplinary approach which, it is suggested, can better explain Chinese and Japanese decision-making in the Textbook Issue.

2 The Textbook Issue
Methodology and approaches

As described in Chapter 1, 'history' appears to play a significant role in Sino-Japanese relations. Indeed, history is one of the key themes in the literature which seeks to explain the nature of postwar Sino-Japanese relations. In addition, there are two other arguments which are regularly put forward to explain Sino-Japanese political relations: firstly, the linking of politics and economics, and secondly, the *use* of history as a means of gaining political or economic concessions. This chapter discusses these three standard explanations, but questions their applicability to the Textbook Issue suggesting instead an alternative framework which combines findings from the fields of international relations and area studies.

Standard explanations of Sino-Japanese relations

History and attitudes

The history argument suggests that Sino-Japanese relations cannot be understood without due consideration of the history the two countries have shared and the attitudes and perceptions that have evolved as a result. There has been a considerable amount of work on the role of attitudes, perceptions and mutual images in the Sino-Japanese relationship.[1] This sort of literature attributes the way Chinese and Japanese governments interact to the attitudes and images that have developed over time. Thus, the argument goes, the 'special affinity' between China and Japan, Japan's 'cultural debt' and 'guilt complex', are the key to understanding the way the two governments interact. The literature produced in the 1950s and 1960s tended to focus mainly on Japanese attitudes to China, attributing Japan's friendly attitude towards China to such factors as kinship, nostalgia for China and desire for trade. On the other hand these studies also pointed to such factors as fear, disdain and a guilt complex which have tempered excessively friendly feelings of Japan towards China.[2] The origins of these attitudes are cultural and historical, stemming from centuries of cultural exchange and nearly half a century of warfare.

The idea that the Japanese people had (or should have) a 'guilt complex' about Japan's wartime actions in China first became popular in Japan in the 1950s and 1960s amongst those whom Ogata describes as 'progressive intellectuals' who considered 'Japan's rise to the status of great power as having been attained through the sacrifice of China'.[3] Leng Shao Chuan is a proponent of this point of view, pointing out that:

> To the Japanese people's sentimental feeling toward CHINA [*sic*] must be added a certain guilty conscience, which is a combination of sincere gratitude toward Chinese contributions to Japan's cultural development and deep regrets for what Japanese militarists have done to China in recent wars. This gives rise to a compelling feeling, especially among Japanese intellectuals, that something must be done to remove the unhappy memory of the recent past and to restore traditional friendship with the Chinese people.[4]

While studies of foreign policy have shown that perceptions and attitudes born of historical dealings and experience *do* play a role in the foreign policy making process, the studies of Sino-Japanese attitudes usually fail to address how, and to what extent, such attitudes affect both governments' decision-making processes *vis-à-vis* bilateral problems. This has been addressed recently in Allen Whiting's study of the influence of Chinese images of Japan on the bilateral relationship.[5] Whiting notes the ambivalence of Chinese attitudes towards Japan, the simultaneous admiration and fear of Japan for its rapid economic development and the threat (of economic dominance) that Japan's rapid development has brought with it. Furthermore, Chinese memories of Japan's aggression during the war still have, according to Whiting, a tremendous effect on Chinese decision makers. Any perceived sign of a revival of militarist tendencies is greeted in China with alarm, and an 'automatic' reaction. Whiting uses this history/attitudes argument to explain the Textbook Issue, suggesting that Chinese decision making was a 'conditioned reflex'-type response to Japan's actions, and arguing that the Textbook Issue was an example of the way that 'provocative events in Japan associated with the war trigger an automatic response in China that combines anger over the past with apprehension about the future.'[6]

While Whiting provides us with a much-needed insight into the possible influence on decision makers of images and perceptions, as with the earlier works on attitudes and images, the case is perhaps over-stated and results in an over-emphasis on the role of perceptions which are in fact just one determinant in the decision-making process. Nonetheless, it is still commonly argued in this sort of literature that the perceptions about guilt and debt have a strong influence on decision makers and are manifested in the ambivalence both sides feel towards each other. Specifically:

> the Chinese have a superiority complex deriving from their cultural influence in pre-modern history and hatred stemming from Japanese military aggression against China in the modern period, while having an inferiority complex based upon Japan's co-operation in their modernization, and admiration for Japan's advanced economy. On the other hand, the Japanese have an inferiority complex due to their cultural debt to China and the sense of original sin stemming from their past agression against China, while having a superiority compex based on their assistance to China's modernization and contempt for China's backwardness.[7]

Politics and economics

A second argument commonly used to explain Sino-Japanese interaction stems from studies of the way politics and economics have become closely linked. This argument does not accept the dominant role of history, but argues that the Sino-Japanese relationship is dominated more by the practicalities of politics and/or economics. A common theme in this literature is that China and Japan have used politics for economic ends and/or trade for political ends. For example, when China and Japan resumed trade relations in the 1950s and 1960s, Japan adopted the slogan of 'separating politics from economics' (*seikei bunri*) as a way of circumventing the fact that the two countries lacked diplomatic relations. The government of the PRC however refused to acknowledge the separation of politics and economics (*shengji bukefen*), and in fact manipulated trade with Japan for political reasons.[8] Lee rejects the idea that culture and geography were key determinants of Sino-Japanese behaviour before normalisation. Rather, he argues, mutual misunderstanding of each other's domestic and international situations meant that 'neither common cultural background nor geographic proximity had any appreciable beneficial effect upon their conceptual differences, political estrangement, or diplomatic confronta-tion.'[9] Furthermore, because the Japanese 'sense of guilt toward China diminished as a determinant of Sino-Japanese relations', until 1972 'China used, or sometimes abused, trade as a primary, material instrument of its political operations in Japan',[10] China was useful to Japan as well, with political parties, notably the LDP and Japan Socialist Party (JSP), 'using Chinese issues as a central instrument for their partisan political interests'.[11]

After 1972 politics and economics became even more 'inextricably intertwined.' The literature describes how China began to use political issues for economic purposes, and Japan used the development of economic relations for political purposes.[12] Zhao, for example, comments upon the way Japanese have used 'extensive *tsukiai*[13] activities including ODA programs, thereby expanding their political access in China'. Japan's ODA programme in China is seen as a means of promoting a 'friendly social environment' which in turn can help Japan to cultivate better political ties with China.[14] Economics has also been viewed as a means of reducing friction between China and Japan. Zhao notes that during the Textbook Issue and the 1985 student demonstrations, Japan's leaders 'pledged large-scale soft loans to China, and 'although there were no direct connections between the controversies and the loans, the Japanese used government loans as goodwill gestures to smooth over the friction and to promote better ties with the Chinese'.[15] Another example of the use of economics to improve political relations is Japan's reaction to the Tiananmen Square incident of 1989. Reluctant to see China isolated from the international community – and therefore dangerous – the Japanese goverment was the first to restore frozen aid projects, provided new grant aid in December 1989 (for a Beijing TV station and a Shanghai hospital), and Prime Minister Kaifu was the first leader to visit China after the incident, negotiating a new loan package while he was there. This again is seen as a goodwill gesture, but one which makes little distinction between politics and economics.[16]

History used for political/economic gains

The third type of argument commonly used to explain Sino-Japanese relations combines the history/attitudes approach and the politics/economics approach. This argument states that when history-related issues arise there is a pattern of behaviour between the two governments whereby the Chinese government reacts to perceived trends within Japan by protesting or making certain demands, to which the Japanese government meekly responds (out of guilt) on an *ad hoc* basis with appropriate measures.

This argument is very much based on the assumption that the Japanese guilt complex is still extant. However, some analysts do not share the opinion that the Japanese feel guilty about the war, or are seeking 'absolution' through their dealings with China. Ogata, for example, concedes that while some individuals did feel a sense of guilt 'derived from the memory of their personal war-time experiences', many others experienced no 'guilt complex'.[17] This is no doubt true but, as Johnson argues, the themes of 'guilt complex', 'cultural debt' and 'special affinity' created by intellectuals in the 1950s and 1960s had the detrimental effect of making 'China diplomacy much harder for the Japanese to control and much easier for the Chinese to manipulate.'[18]

Thus, the Chinese government is seen to be manipulating the Japanese government, taking advantage of the 'unfortunate history' and Japan's supposed guilt complex, as a way to get political and/or economic gains. For example, Arnold argues that 'many Japanese feel that China resurrects the spectre of Imperial Japan for political purposes when in need of concessions, funds or aid',[19] and suggests that the loans given to China by the Japanese government in 1984 and 1988 helped to alleviate the discontent over the textbook and other political issues. This view is echoed by Ijiri who also comments on the convenience of the 'revival of militarism' slogan which is 'bandied about by Beijing as it suits its purpose at any given time'.[20] Similarly, Kojima talks of Japan's diplomacy of appeasement *vis-à-vis* China, and explains how 'Beijing uses the issues of Taiwan and past aggression as levers to extract increased economic co-operation, and Tokyo docilely complies'.[21]

As described above, all three of these standard arguments have been applied to the Textbook Issue. Whiting explains the issue in terms of the history/attitudes argument, where the Chinese react 'automatically' to perceived revival of militarism. Zhao suggests a political/economic argument arguing that Japanese governments agreed loan packages in the 1980s as a means of easing the tension in the relationship and as a 'goodwill gesture'. Arnold uses the 'history for economic gain' argument, suggesting that the Chinese government launched an anti-Japan campaign not with the aim of getting Japanese history textbooks rewritten, but as a way of making the Japanese government feel guilty and therefore increase its economic assistance to China.

On closer examination, however, and as this book will show, none of these arguments fully explain the actions and reactions of the Chinese and Japanese governments in the Textbook Issue. The so-called 'automatic' response of the Chinese government must be questioned, since it took nearly a month before the Chinese press launched its anti-Japan campaign and before the Chinese government lodged its official protest.

The analysis of the Chinese government's decision-making yields little proof that the Chinese were seeking any economic gain from the Textbook Issue, even indirectly. They may have been seeking a political gain but, as the study will show, the gain was related more to domestic politics than to bilateral politics. Thus the Textbook Issue cannot be understood in terms of political or economic 'points' that the Chinese government hoped to score over the Japanese government. Finally, the Japanese government's response cannot be seen as another example of Tokyo's so-called 'policy of atonement', since there is little evidence of the Japanese government reacting out of guilt and making large concessions.[22]

Alternative explanation of Sino-Japanese relations

If the 'standard arguments' fail to explain the Textbook Issue, then a different approach is needed, one which takes into consideration factors other than history, attitudes and the narrow confines of the Sino-Japanese bilateral relationship. The case studies of key events in Sino-Japanese political relations, such as the signing of the Joint Statement, and the conclusion of the Peace and Friendship Treaty provide a good starting point,[23] since these studies use a framework which allows consideration of the internal and external influences on Chinese and Japanese foreign policy decision-making. In addition, Japanese academics have examined Japan's foreign policy-making *vis-à-vis* China, and vice versa, using methods drawn from the field of international relations (IR)[24] which again consider external and internal factors.

The main problem with these studies, however, is that they have proceeded in a fairly non-systematic and 'non-cumulative' manner. They have tended to be one-sided, in that they deal either with China's Japan policy or Japan's China policy, and they have not resulted in many comparative studies or the development of any 'grand' theory of Sino-Japanese relations. Nevertheless, they do provide a firm foundation on which to build a more 'integrated' study of Sino-Japanese political relations. Tanaka, for example, looks at the influence of the Prime Minister, the Cabinet, the LDP and interest groups on Japan's policy-making on China in general,[25] while Fukui considers the influence of these groups in his case study of diplomatic normalisation, and Ogata focuses solely on the influence of the business community on the negotiations.[26] Tanaka's study, in particular, is useful in that he acknowledges that it is not enough to consider Sino-Japanese relations simply in terms of their mutual actions (bilateral interactions); rather, Sino-Japanese relations must be considered within the context of both the international environment and the domestic political situation of each country.[27]

This is clearly the sort of approach necessary for a deeper understanding of the Textbook Issue, given that the standard explanations are inadequate. Thus, rather than focusing solely on the historical/cultural and narrow bilateral aspects of Sino-Japanese relations to explain the way the Textbook Issue was resolved, this study considers the influence of factors such as changes in the international sysem, or in domestic and foreign policies. In so doing, this book attempts to bridge the gap between the general, universally-applicable ideas and specific ideas about Chinese and Japanese decision-making. The study therefore adopts an interdisciplinary approach, drawing upon frameworks and hypotheses from IR, in addition to findings of country-specific studies from the field of area studies. This sort of approach inevitably brings with it the problem, discussed below, of how to combine two fields of study which tend to be regarded as mutually exclusive. If, for example, one adheres to the argument that a nation's foreign policy behaviour is patterned behaviour which shares certain characteristics with that of other states in the international system, then one favours generally-applicable theories to test their validity against a case study. On the other hand, if one agrees with the view that a nation's foreign policy can only be fully understood by taking into account that nation's peculiar characteristics, then one adopts a country-specific approach. That this choice presents itself reflects the long-standing and on-going battle between advocates of general theories produced in international relations and those of country-specific theories from the field of area studies. IR theorists seek to establish universally-applicable theories, whereas area studies specialists focus on the characteristics/particularities of individual countries. Each field has yielded useful research but at the same time both fields of study have been widely criticised: the general approach because it 'denigrates factual detail', the single-country approach because it amasses 'empirical data but [is] usually devoid of theoretical value'.[28]

The matter becomes complicated, however, when one considers that within the discipline of international relations there has been, and remains, constant 'competition among theories'. IR comprises many different areas of study, and there has never been a consensus on a single paradigm.[29] The debates in IR have moved on from the so-called 'inter-paradigm' debate of the 1970s and 1980s where 'realists', 'liberalists' (and later Marxists) offered contending views of the world system, to the 1990s where there is a profusion of contending theories including neo-realism, neo-liberalism, IPE, feminist theory, critical theory and so on.[30] Even within one area of IR, such as foreign policy analysis, there are a number of discrete approaches (for example, domestic politics, comparative foreign policy, or middle-range theories).[31]

There is a similar range of choice of hypotheses and models in the country-specific approach. Thus, although proponents of this approach agree to the extent that the domestic attributes of a nation are considered to be the main determinants of a nation's foreign policy, there is little agreement beyond that point. As with IR, there are divisions of opinion. To take China as an example, while some argue that ideology plays a greater role in decision-making than national interests, others argue that the top leadership (such as Mao Zedong or Deng Xiaoping) has a greater impact than does factional politics on Chinese decision making. Similarly, students of Japanese decision-making have long been divided as to whether elitism, pluralism or patterned pluralism best characterises the Japanese decision-making process.

Thus the task of finding a framework of analysis for a case study of Sino-Japanese relations is complex, given not only the choice between general and specific, but also the choice of contending theories within the separate disciplines. The biggest bone of contention in IR appears to be the split between those who argue that the international system determines nations' actions (macro level), and those who argue that the nations that make up the international system determine the nature of that system (micro level). In a sense the same division can be seen between IR as a whole (the macro approach) and area studies (micro approach).

In an attempt to resolve this conflict, there have long been calls for some sort of synthesis of the macro and micro levels (both within IR and between area studies and IR) which could broaden the narrow confines of each approach and result in a better understanding of the way international politics works. What is required is an intradisciplinary *and* an interdisciplinary approach, one which combines the findings of, on the one hand, the macro and micro levels within IR, and on the other, area studies and IR. In IR, many scholars have argued for an approach that allows international and national system approaches to be combined in order to determine how they influence each other and how they are linked.[32] As for combining area studies and IR approaches, Samuel S. Kim, writing on the study of Chinese foreign policy, urges that 'we must study Chinese foreign policy as if international relations matters, or conversely ... we must study international relations as if China mattered'.[33] The same argument could be put forward for Japanese foreign policy, and by extension for studies of Sino-Japanese relations also.

In fact, recent research on single-country studies in IR and on Chinese and Japanese foreign policy in area studies, discussed below, has gradually begun to adopt this sort of intra/interdisciplinary approach, although it is clearly still in its infancy. As Rosenau remarks, with the world becoming ever more interdependent, the 'continuing erosion of the distinction between domestic and foreign issues' requires foreign policy analysts to 'expand their horizons, enlarge their kit of analytical tools, and probe for meaning in heretofore unexplored areas of social, economic, and political life'.[34] By the same token, specialists are urged to shed their preferred modes of analysis (e.g. historical narrative) and their aversion to scientifically testable theories about their region or country.[35]

Before considering how these new approaches can be applied to the Textbook Issue, it is worth outlining the main arguments (and counter-arguments) of the international systemic and nation-state approaches in IR and the single-country studies in area studies.

International relations approaches

As described above, the field of international relations has been marked by conflicting debates and the constant emergence of new subjects of study. The conflict within the field is probably best understood in terms of the level-of-analysis problem which was identified originally by Kenneth Waltz,[36] but elaborated upon by John D. Singer in 1961. Singer suggested that there were a number of levels from which one could approach a study of international relations.[37] The highest level is that of the international system, followed by the nation-state, then the bureaucracy and finally the individual decision maker. Singer debated whether it was better to explain the actions of nation-states in terms of the international system, or the international system in terms of the nation-states that comprise the system. Moving down the levels of analysis, Singer identified the potential problems of selecting one level over another: whether, for example, at the nation-state level, foreign policy behaviour is determined more by external (international) factors or internal (domestic) factors; and at the bureaucracy level, whether bureaucratic systems determine the behaviour of the bureaucrats or bureaucrats determine the nature of the bureaucracy.

Singer concluded that one's research results would depend largely on which approach one took. Adopting a systemic approach will not shed any light on how a state's internal organisations function, but will provide an explanation of how the system determined a state's actions in a given circumstance. By contrast, a nation-state approach will have the effect of opening up the 'black box' to reveal the way a state's government and bureaucracy go about reaching a decision, but in so doing will de-emphasise the role of the international system (though not necessarily the effects of external influences). The problem with favouring one approach over another, Singer held, is that there is a tendency to overemphasise the influence of the level one is studying:

> The unit or state level exaggerates the differences among states, and underestimates the impact of the system on the actions of states; the systems level assumes that states are more homogeneous than they are and overestimates the impact of the system on the behaviour of the units.[38]

Furthermore, because of this inherent bias, Singer concluded that the levels cannot be combined to produce one overall explanation of international relations. In other words, the separate approaches are to be kept separate. This point of view has been challenged, however, by those who advocate that models and theories produced at various levels of analysis and in different fields of study *must* be integrated in order to gain a better understanding of foreign policy.

The international system approach states that the nature of the international system (for example, bipolarity or multipolarity) has a greater influence on a state's foreign policy orientations and actions than do domestic factors. This is a 'top-down' view of the world, which sees the international system as greater than the sum of its parts (that is, the nation-states) and which takes the view that global politics is dominated by the pursuit of power, with each nation state acting in its national interest to attain international political power.[39] According to this approach, international relations can be explained without detailed reference to the internal workings of a nation-state, such as the ideologies, political processes and values of individual decision makers.

This approach has been criticised precisely for ignoring the influence of domestic factors. Even those studies that do acknowledge the presence of domestic influences nevertheless conclude that systemic influences play a greater role in determining a state's behaviour. Thus, in his study of consistency in Chinese foreign policy, Ng-Quinn concludes that analysis at the level of decision makers and domestic politics fails to provide a 'coherent explanation' because 'Chinese foreign policy . . . cannot be seen in isolation, but as part of the greater international environment.'[40] This international environment, whether it is considered to be bipolar or tripolar in structure, imposes a set of constraints on Chinese foreign policy behaviour, and other variables such as domestic politics are only relevant 'to the extent that they cause changes in Chinese capabilities, leading to changes in the distribution of power, thus structural transformation'. Thus in a bipolar structure, Ng-Quinn argues, China will always lean towards one or the other superpower (neutrality or independence is ruled out), and its policies, for example towards East Asia, will be constrained by bipolar competition.[41]

The nation-state approach helps to 'explain the whole by analysing the attributes and interactions of the parts'[42] and examines the various factors that may influence decision makers during the policy-making process. In contrast to the international systemic approach, this is a 'bottom-up' approach which opens up the 'black box' and looks at the operational environment (domestic and foreign influences), and psychological environment (personality, perceptions of decision makers) which together influence foreign policy decision makers. As Rosenau points out, analysis of even the simplest foreign policy action requires close scrutiny of any number of 'causal layers'. For example, one action:

> reflects the decision of an individual, the deliberations of a committee, the outcome of a policy making process, the sum of clashing interest groups, the values of a dominant elite, the product of a society's aspirations, the reinforcement of a historical tradition, the response to an opportunity or challenge elsewhere in the world . . . [43]

The nation-state level, then, takes into account such factors as the way decision makers perceive a situation, the way bureaucratic organisations function and the influence they have on foreign policy making, the type of government structure and level of economic development, and so on. The vast number of potentially relevant 'causal layers' has meant that a number of subfields have emerged which have examined each individual potential variable of the foreign policy-making process to determine its relative influence on policy outcome.

The nation-state approach is still very much concerned with universally-applicable theories and does not attempt to argue that each nation is unique by virtue of political, ideological, cultural and historical factors. Rather, it has tried to categorise nations (for example, by type of political system, level of development), issues (strategic, economic, diplomatic), and decision-making structures (bureaucratic politics, organisation process) in order to create general theories as to how nations of a certain type will act or react in a given situation.

As the international systemic approach was criticised for ignoring details, so the nation-state approach has been criticised for its overemphasis on the internal processes of a nation's foreign policy-making, and for de-emphasising the 'reality' of the international system (since foreign policy analysis is concerned with how decision makers *perceive* the international system and with their reactions based on their 'definition of the situation'). Indeed, foreign policy analysts have been their own stiffest critics, disillusioned by the failure 'to produce the all-encompassing IR theory its early proponents assumed would ensue if the "black box" was opened and investigated'. [44]

Area studies approaches

In contrast to the universally-applicable approaches described above, area studies is concerned with specific countries and by its very nature is pitched at the level of the nation-state, but the aim of area studies is to examine the influence of a country's ideology, historical legacy, political culture, geopolitical aspects and so on its domestic and foreign policy outputs. The study of Chinese and Japanese foreign policy has 'grown up' within this tradition, and until recently has tended to overlook IR theories. This inevitably has resulted in a vast body of literature that tends to overemphasise the influence on the foreign policy process of characteristics (e.g. politico-cultural, historical, ideological and so on) that are specific or 'unique' to China and Japan.

The study of China's foreign policy

Writing in 1989, Samuel S. Kim commented that 'the study of Chinese foreign policy has been advancing in divergent directions in an atheoretical, noncomparative, and noncumulative manner' and lamented that 'we are still some distance from capturing its increasingly complex, involved, and multifaceted nature'. [45] The literature is indeed replete with many different explanatory approaches, including historical legacy, ideology, political culture, bureaucratic structure, and national capability and attributes (i.e. level of economic development, military capacity and so on). [46]

The chief proponent of the historical legacy approach, John K. Fairbank, asserts that it is essential to refer to the history of imperial China in order to understand its present-day international behaviour. [47] According to this type of study, then, China's historical 'tradition' of superiority in a hierarchical international structure (e.g. within the 'tribute system') persists in the minds of Chinese leaders, influencing their foreign policy-making behaviour. This approach has been rejected by other Sinologists who argue that the Sinocentric world view was destroyed by China's century of 'humiliations' and by the rise of nationalism. Instead, the counterargument goes, 'China seems to conform more closely to the realities of world politics than anything derived out of the past'.[48] Still others argue that even if the Sinocentric view is no longer dominant, the historical legacy of one hundred years of suffering at the hands of Western and Japanese imperialism has superseded it.[49]

Other studies stress the role of ideology in China's foreign affairs, that is, of Marxism–Leninism and Mao Zedong thought. Proponents of this view argue that Chinese foreign policy cannot be fully understood without reference to 'the Marxist perspective of international relations, the Leninist theory of imperialism, the Maoist principles of contradiction, the Communist united front strategy, the Chinese revolutionary model'.[50]

Advocates of political culture argue that Chinese foreign policy is best explained in terms of China's 'traditional' political culture and the domestic political situation. Factional politics, for example, is thought to be so culturally rooted that foreign policy is the product of conflict between two or more groupings. In addition, cultural traditions are said to explain concepts and styles of Chinese foreign policy behaviour.[51] The political culture approach, which fell out of favour in the 1970s, is currently enjoying a renaissance, not only in area studies but also in IR.[52] An opposing argument comes from those who consider that China's national attributes, that is, the resource and population levels, degree of economic and technological development and military capabilities, are the key to understanding China's role in the world since these capabilities act as constraints on the nation's foreign policy behaviour.[53]

Wu has criticised the separate approaches described above for their 'unrealistic attempt to explain a complex phenomenon like Chinese foreign policy by a single causal variable'.[54] As discussed above, one foreign policy decision involves a number of 'causal layers'. Multi-causal approaches attempted to rectify this problem by combining a number of explanations. Yet multi-causal analysis[55] still had its problems because it failed to explain how each causal factor related to and affected the others, and which factors were more influential. Thus, it is not enough to set out a list of all the possible causal factors without exploring the linkages between them. This then makes it all the more necessary to make use of 'concepts, hypotheses and research techniques' from the field of comparative foreign policy, a point which will be discussed in more detail below.

The study of Japan's foreign policy

In area studies, much of the literature on Japanese foreign policy has been devoted to Japan's economic policies, security policy and, more recently, its international role. This is not remarkable given the main foreign policy goals adopted by successive Japanese governments in the postwar period, namely prosperity, security and international recognition.[56] Consequently, however, there are comparatively few studies which discuss the diplomatic and political aspects of Japanese foreign policy, and those which do tend to adopt either a purely diplomatic history approach or a multi-causal one. Multi-causal explanations tend to emphasise similar characteristics to those noted above in the review of literature on Chinese foreign policy, for example historical legacy, political culture, bureaucratic structures, national capability and so on. Similar to the multi-causal analyses of Chinese foreign policy, multi-causal studies of Japanese foreign policy fail to identify the links between the various determining factors.

As is the case with the literature on Chinese foreign policy, Japan's historical legacy is said to play an important role in her contemporary foreign policy. The most frequently cited factors are Japan's history of isolation, militarisation and defeat in the Second World War, and a guilt complex about her actions during the war. Reischauer argues, for example, that contemporary Japan's aloofness from the international stage is a 'natural continuation' of her history of isolationism. Moreover, isolationism has resulted, for the Japanese, in 'their strong self-identity, their extraordinary homogeneity, and their close-knit society' which in turn prevent them from dealing effectively with the outside world.[57]

Advocates of the political culture approach to Japan's foreign policy argue that 'traditional' Japanese behavioural patterns, such as social hierarchies, collectivity and sense of uniqueness, affect the style and substance of Japan's foreign policy, acting as constraints on Japanese interaction with foreign countries. Satō for example talks of Japan's 'deep ethnic and cultural dissimilarities' from other nations, which, along with Japan's history of isolation from and peripheral position with regard to the other powers prior to the Second World War, helps to explain the inactive stance taken by Japan on the international stage.[58] Reischauer takes a similar position, arguing that international relations is the area in which the Japanese feel self-conscious and lacking in confidence because of their 'traditional consciousness of cultural borrowings from China and of catching up with the West in modern times'.[59] Japanese social organisation is used to explain Japan's approach to international relations which is said to be fashioned along hierarchical lines mimicking the domestic hierarchy of superiors, inferiors and peers.[60] The structure of Japan's bureaucratic and political system (for example, bureaucratic dominance, factional politics) has also been considered an important factor in the country's foreign policy process, as have national capabilities, such as Japan's lack of natural resources and reliance on foreign trade.[61]

As Wu concluded in his appraisal of the literature on Chinese foreign policy, clearly no one aspect can explain everything about Japanese foreign policy behaviour, and even if all the factors are combined to produce a multi-causal approach, there is still the danger that one fails to identify which factors are more influential. Recent studies of Chinese and Japanese foreign policy, however, have begun to address this problem, and will be discussed below.

Towards an integrated approach

As described above, the result of the single-country studies has been an over-emphasis on the unique, or peculiar, distinctive aspects of a specific country's decision-making process, which immediately brings this discipline into conflict with the international systems and the foreign policy anguish approach, given area studies' 'theoretical deficiency' and 'unsystematic nature'.[62] Yet attempts at theory-building in both systemic and foreign policy analysis approaches have themselves not been as rigorous as originally hoped, nor have they been able to produce a 'metatheory' (understandable given the huge nature of the task) against which to test case studies or events data.

However, despite the atheoretical development of studies of Chinese and Japanese foreign policy, and the lack of a single paradigm in IR/foreign policy analysis, each approach has considerable value if integrated with the other. The single-country studies, for example, are based on specialist knowledge that can only enhance understanding of a country's foreign policy when combined with IR organisational frameworks and analytical devices. Talking of Chinese foreign policy, Rosenau advocates that:

> IR theorists need to tool up in the details of Chinese culture and politics, just as China specialists need to enlarge their horizons to incorporate the processes that sustain world politics. . . . *Our ultimate theoretical task is to trace how the external and internal are interactive*, how international dynamics impact upon and shape Chinese conduct at home and abroad and, conversely, how these domestic dynamics impact upon and shape international structures and the actions that other countries direct toward China [italics added].[63]

It must be noted that application of 'general' IR theories to the study of Chinese and Japanese foreign policy has indeed been carried out by an increasing number of scholars in recent years. Ng-Quinn's application of the international system approach to Chinese foreign policy was discussed above. The volume edited by Segal advocates an interdisciplinary approach in order to determine which factors played the more influential role in China's foreign policy reforms of the 1980s.[64] Robinson and Shambaugh have provided another contribution to the interdisciplinary approach to Chinese foreign policy,[65] and Zhao has applied the macro–micro linkage approach to his appraisal of postwar Chinese foreign policy.

The study of Japan's foreign policy is also beginning to benefit from an interdisciplinary approach. Some of the contributors to Curtis's book have treated Japan's foreign policy within a broader, inter-disciplinary framework.[66] More recently, Drifte has analysed Japanese foreign policy at a regional and international level using the concepts of hard and soft power. However, most of the research that has tested the applicability of IR theories against the case of Japan has been carried out by Japanese scholars, notably Aruga *et al.*[67] and Satō,[68] who have relied heavily on US theoretical approaches to the study of foreign policy. Inoguchi notes that there is now a growing trend towards developing a 'Japanese approach' to international relations,[69] a move which resembles the trend among Chinese scholars who feel that US-developed theories fail to explain Chinese foreign policy sufficiently.[70]

It would seem, therefore, that the response to Kim's call for China (and Japan) specialists to view China/Japan 'as though international relations matters' is being made, and that an integrated approach to the study of Sino-Japanese relations is becoming as viable as it is desirable. The next section will consider how an 'integrated' approach can be applied to a case study of the Textbook Issue.

The Textbook Issue as a case study

In order to 'trace the interaction' between the external and internal factors in the Textbook Issue, it is useful to turn to some of the organising frameworks developed by IR scholars. These frameworks, or system models, though of varying degrees of complexity, help to identify the potentially relevant variables, locating each one in a certain part of the foreign policy-making process.[71] All the frameworks are similar inasmuch as they depict the foreign policy process as an input–output model where inputs (international system, domestic structures, individual decision makers and so on) act as constraints on or opportunities in the decision-making process. The output of the system (foreign policy decision or foreign policy behaviour) feeds back into the environment, affecting the international system, other nation-states and so on. The whole process is seen as dynamic, constantly changing in response to stimuli from foreign policy output, systemic changes etc (see Figure 2.1). This sort of framework enables systematic analysis and comparison of the foreign policies of different nation-states in different issue types and areas, and over a period of time. In addition, it allows for an inter-disciplinary approach. McGowan and Shapiro, for example, recognised the necessity of contributions of historians, economists, psychologists, political scientists and others.[72]

Some explanation of the variables depicted in Figure 2.1 is necessary before discussing how the framework is to be applied to the Textbook Issue. In the international environment, 'systemic changes' refer to changes to the characteristics of the international system, such as shifts in the balance of power between two superpowers, or a change from bipolarity to multipolarity.[73] Regional, bilateral or international organi-sational influences are actions taken by one or more nations/organisations which would prompt a reaction from the nation under study.

The internal influences or domestic environment encompass a nation's attributes and capabilities (i.e. geographical factors such as resources and size, economic factors and military-strategic factors such as the level of development, stability, dependence, influence of the mili-tary establishment and so on). Cultural factors describe a nation's 'cultural system', that is, the degree of cultural pluralism, degree of nationalism, the role of the media and ideology, and cultural attributes such as race and religion. The historical factor of 'traditions of past foreign economic and political involvement' which influence current and future behaviour must also be included into this category.[74] Political

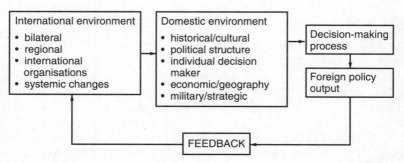

Figure 2.1 Organising framework

structure refers to the characteristics of a nation's political system such as the type of government (presidential, parliamentary), the competitiveness of the party system, the level of political conflict and the influence of pressure groups on the foreign policy process.[75] 'Individual decision maker' refers to the personality, beliefs and perceptions of key foreign policy decision makers such as prime ministers and presidents.[76]

As the organising framework suggests, the decision-making process is influenced, to varying degrees, by each of the independent variables described above and produces a foreign policy output: an action upon which other nations then act. The element of feedback is therefore essential to complete the framework in order to convey the dynamism of the foreign policy system which is always changing in response to the foreign policy outputs of different nations.

This sort of framework is a useful organising tool with which to analyse a foreign policy issue such as the Textbook Issue. It enables one to 'deconstruct' the event, identify all the variables, then 'reconstruct' them to achieve a clearer picture of the process through which foreign policy decisions were reached, how the variables interacted and which factors were the most influential. By focusing not just on the actions within the nation-state but on events or changes in the international system and the way all the variables affect each other, the framework allows us to see the linkages between the macro (international) and micro (domestic) levels.

While it would be unwise to draw sweeping generalisations from the results of one case study, it is hoped that it at least contributes to the process of 'theory building' in the study of Sino-Japanese relations.[77] By comparing the Textbook Issue with, for example, some of the later similar controversies using a similar framework, it might be possible to discern a pattern of behaviour in Sino-Japanese relations comparable to other bilateral relationships. One of the main aims of this book, therefore, is to challenge the assumption that the Sino-Japanese relationship is special, unique, dominated by the influences of a long history of interaction in times of war and peace, and explicable only within an East Asian or more specifically Chinese and Japanese cultural and historical context. By looking more closely at the events of the Textbook Issue, at the workings of Chinese and Japanese domestic and foreign politics and the various influences upon them, the book will show that the standard explanations of conflict in Sino-Japanese relations have considerable shortcomings and certainly fail to explain fully the actions and reactions of the Chinese and Japanese governments during the Textbook Issue.

Chapter 1 provided the contemporary context for the Textbook Issue and suggested that the basis for the so-called 'debts' that Japan has accrued in its relations with China over 2,000 years needs to be re-examined. Chapter 3 provides an overview of Sino-Japanese relations from 1945 to 1982 within an international context, and examines the changes that were taking place in the international system in the early 1980s which could have affected Chinese and Japanese foreign policies. Chapter 4 then considers in detail the domestic political issues facing China and Japan in the early 1980s which could also have influenced the decision-making process in the Textbook Issue.

Chapter 5 describes the day-to-day events of the Textbook Issue, identifying the key decision makers and their actions and reactions, in addition to the responses of Chinese public opinion, Japanese opposition groups and the reaction of other East and Southeast Asian countries. This account relies heavily on Chinese and Japanese newspapers, in particular China's *Renmin Ribao* and Japan's *Asahi Shimbun*, since these two newspapers are generally regarded as having taken the lead in the press campaigns in both countries. The *Renmin Ribao* is considered to be the mouthpiece of the Chinese Communist Party (CCP), and hence the *Renmin Ribao* anti-Japan campaign reveals the 'official line'. The *Asahi Shimbun* is renowned for its frequently anti-establishment stance and pro-China attitude, and, according to Yayama,[78] it played a leading role in coverage of the Textbook Issue. Other newspapers, current affairs and 'special interest' journals which carried articles on the controversy as it developed helped to fill the gaps left by the *Renmin Ribao* and *Asahi Shimbun*. These included Chinese-language newspapers and journals such as *Jiefangjunbao*, *Hongqi*, *Shijie Zhishi*, *Zhongguo Qingnianbao* and *Banyuetan*, the important articles of which are reproduced in *Fuyin Baokan Ziliao*, published by Zhongguo Renmin Daxue. The additional Japanese language material was found in newspapers and journals such as *Mainichi Shimbun*, *Sekai*, *Seiron*, *Chūō Kōron*, *Asahi Jānaru* and *Shokun*. Finally, English translations of other national and regional Chinese and Japanese newspapers found in the BBC's Summary of World Broadcasts (SWB), the FBIS Daily Report: China, and the Daily Summary of Japanese Press provided further information.

The analysis of the behaviour of the Chinese and Japanese governments in Chapters 6 and 7 once again draws upon the two key newspapers, but also on the profusion of articles filling the October and November issues of the Japanese current affairs journals, in addition to English, Chinese and Japanese language retrospective analyses of the Textbook Issue published in the mid-to-late 1980s. These chapters address the question of *why* key decisions were reached by considering the linkage between the systemic, external, and internal factors described in the previous chapters. They make use of some of the findings of country-specific studies, in particular, models of Japanese decision making, and studies of linkages between Chinese domestic and foreign policies.

The final chapter draws the findings of the analytical chapters together, suggesting that an integrated approach provides a more convincing explanation of the way China and Japan interacted in the Textbook Issue than does a purely historical explanation. It also considers the development of patterns and cycles in Sino-Japanese relations, and discusses whether these are comparable to similar patterns of behaviour observed in other bilateral relationships, and suggests how the Textbook Issue can help us to gain a better understanding of how Chinese and Japanese governments interacted during the 1990s.

3   Postwar Sino-Japanese relations
An overview

The 1987 edition of the Chinese foreign ministry's yearbook of foreign affairs, *Zhongguo waijiao gailan*, says of Sino-Japanese relations that:

> Since the founding of the People's Republic of China, Chairman Mao Zedong, Premier Zhou Enlai and other leaders have frequently made it clear that Japanese militarists' invasion of China was merely a counter-current in the long river of history. China has consistently adopted a forward-looking attitude on this period of history, and has made enormous efforts to strengthen friendship between the two peoples and improve relations between the two countries.[1]

The problems that occurred in Sino-Japanese relations both before and since normalisation seem to suggest that, far from taking a forward-looking approach, the Chinese government has retained a firmly 'backward-looking' stance in its dealings with Japan. Studies of Chinese political culture have described how Chinese governments frequently refer to the past as a way of justifying current sentiment,[2] and the diplomatic and political problems that have arisen between Chinese and Japanese governments since the war appear to provide many examples of this phenomenon. In addition, many of the issues in Sino-Japanese relations point to an increasingly complex relationship between politics and economics, one which has allowed both sides to manipulate events at certain times. This chapter will consider some of the major issues in Sino-Japanese political and, where relevant, economic relations, which occurred between 1945 and 1982 to see how history influenced, or perhaps more accurately, was used to influence the development of relations, and to consider the interplay of politics and economics. The aim of this chapter is not to provide a complete history of postwar relations, but to highlight patterns of behaviour in the relationship which will in turn help to place the Textbook Issue into context.

The first section considers the development of relations prior to normalisation in 1972, while the second part of the chapter examines some of the issues that arose between the signing of the Joint Statement and the conclusion of the Treaty of Peace and Friendship in 1978. The final section focuses on international and bilateral developments from 1978 up to the summer of 1982, just prior to the Textbook Issue.

1945–72: politics in command?

The period between 1945 and 1972 was marked by a lack of diplomatic relations between China and Japan which inevitably had an effect on their political, economic and cultural interaction. The PRC, intent on achieving diplomatic normalisation, used many devices to try and attain that objective, while Japan, restrained by US policy dictates, could respond only in a limited fashion. Furthermore, the international system of the Cold War period had an enormous influence on the relationship, bringing China and Japan into the 'subsystems' of the two superpowers and placing them as Cold War 'enemies'.

As the following account will show, before normalisation Sino-Japanese relations were marked by a number of recurring issues, many of which related directly or indirectly to the legacy of both the 'good' and 'bad' periods of Sino-Japanese history described in the Introduction. Some issues centred around PRC criticisms of Japan for attempting to revive militarism, or for pursuing a 'two Chinas' policy by recognising Taiwan. Others involved the PRC's manipulation of Japan's 'guilt complex' for trade and/or cultural exchange. However, the underlying theme during this period was the 'overt injection of politics' into the, albeit limited, cultural and economic aspects of the relationship.

Suspicious of Japan's relations with the US 'imperialists', the PRC was initially hostile to Japanese governments in the late 1940s and early 1950s, especially when Japan began to negotiate treaties with the US and Taiwan and became subsumed into the Western camp in the Cold War. The PRC considered these actions a sign of Japan's preparing for a war of invasion, which prompted the earliest accusations by the PRC of a revival of Japanese militarism.[3] Between 1953 and 1957, however, the PRC adopted a softer line in its dealings with Japan. During this period, the PRC initiated 'people's diplomacy', a policy designed to promote friendly relations between the Japanese and Chinese people through the exchange of cultural delegations. The chief objective of 'people's diplomacy' was to create a large body of public opinion in Japan favourable to the PRC that would put pressure on the government to normalise relations with China. Increasing numbers of delegations from Japanese organisations such as 'friendship' groups, women's and youth groups, labour unions and groups of Diet members visited China after 1954, and by 1957 a number of non-governmental agreements and joint statements were concluded on trade, fishery, cultural and scientific arrangements.[4]

For their part, many Japanese shared China's enthusiasm for improved bilateral relations, and welcomed what has been termed 'cumulative diplomacy' (*tsumiage hōshiki* or *tsumikasane hōshiki*), albeit for different reasons.[5] Many were keen to resume the 'traditional' friendship with the PRC.[6] Some expressed feelings of guilt for the actions of the Japanese during the war, and a sense that Japan had a duty to make amends for the suffering inflicted.[7] Showing a commitment to China's revitalisation was considered one way of repaying the debt, but businessmen also sought a resumption of commercial relations for their own interests, seeing the potential of the huge China market.[8] Japanese governments, though restricted in their actions, also considered trade with China an important means of avoiding economic dependence on the USA and facilitating Japan's own economic development.[9]

Trade resumed in August 1950, but was immediately restricted by the imposition of COCOM export quotas during the Korean War.[10] Private trade agreements, of which four were signed between 1952 and 1958, led to a gradual increase in bilateral trade (see Table 3.1) but were also used as a political weapon in China's quest for normalisation with Japan. For example, Lee notes that whereas the first trade agreement carried no political message, the subsequent trade agreements of 1953 and 1955 included 'politically inspired demands and obtained various promises and concessions from Japanese negotiators, some of whom were influential leaders of the ruling political parties'.[11]

Thus, as early as 1953, the Chinese government set a trend that would continue until normalisation. That is, rather than complying with the Japanese policy which sought to 'separate politics from economics' (*seikei bunri*), and which allowed both the Chinese and Japanese governments to circumvent the absence of diplomatic relations, the Chinese government insisted that 'politics and economics could not be separated' (*shengji bukefen*). Thus, for the next twenty years 'trade was viewed and used as an instrument to persuade and pressurize Japan to recognize Beijing and modify its China policy'.[12]

A major instance of the use of trade as a political tool occurred in 1957 and 1958 and related to the negotiations for the fourth private trade agreement and an apparently unrelated issue, the so-called Nagasaki Flag Incident of 1958. The Nagasaki Flag incident culminated in the suspension of trade between China and Japan as a result of the

Japanese government failing to take any legal action against a Japanese youth who had pulled down a Chinese flag at an exhibition in Nagasaki in May. In fact, as Johnson points out, China's 'real' motive for the suspension of trade must be seen in terms of the deterioration in relations since 1957 when Kishi Nobusuke became Prime Minister.[13] Well-known for his pro-Taiwan leanings, Kishi visited Taiwan soon after gaining office, thereby offending the PRC government. Difficult negotiations for the fourth private trade agreement reflected the worsening of Sino-Japanese relations. In 1958, the agreement was finally signed, the Japanese side having agreed to a resident PRC trade mission in Tokyo and attendant privileges of semi-diplomatic status for its personnel and the right to fly its national flag over the trade mission. However, Taiwan saw this as tantamount to Japan's recognition of mainland China and forced the Kishi government to rescind the PRC's privileges. In retaliation, the PRC then threatened to cancel the trade agreement unless the Japanese government rectified the situation. Using the Nagasaki flag incident as a pretext, the PRC carried out its threat by cancelling the trade agreement and suspending all business and cultural dealings with Japan.[14] Consequently, bilateral trade declined drastically during 1959 – approximately a 79 per cent decrease on the previous year – and remained at a low level until the early 1960s[15] (see Table 3.1). Other reasons have been cited for the deterioration of Sino-Japanese relations in the late 1950s, and the similarity of some of the domestic and external factors with the situation prevailing in 1982 is noteworthy. Tanaka considers three factors in particular: a shift in China's perception of the international situation, the Chinese domestic political situation, and the Japanese political situation. In China's international relations, tensions had increased with both the Soviet Union and the US and prompted China to take a more assertive stance in its foreign policy.[16] Under these circumstances, it was unthinkable for China to take a conciliatory stance with Japan, associated as it was with the USA. China's domestic situation further prevented a soft stance in China's economic relations, with the introduction of the policies associated with the Great Leap Forward and a new emphasis on self-reliance. Similarly Japanese domestic policies were less conducive to Sino-Japanese friendship with the emergence of the pro-US/Taiwan Kishi government intent on strengthening relations with the USA in the run-up to the revision of the Security Treaty.[17]

All these factors can be seen behind the continuing hard line in China's Japan policy in the late 1950s and early 1960s. For example, the three 'principles' necessary for normalisation of Sino-Japanese relations announced by Zhou Enlai in August 1958 stipulated that the Japanese

Table 3.1 Japan's trade with China, 1950–72 (in $US millions)

Year	Exports to China	Imports from China	Total	Balance
1950	19.6	39.3	58.9	−19.7
1951	5.8	21.6	27.4	−15.8
1952	0.6	14.9	15.5	−14.3
1953	4.5	29.7	34.2	−25.2
1954	19.1	40.8	59.9	−21.7
1955	28.5	80.8	109.3	−52.3
1956	67.3	83.6	150.9	−16.3
1957	60.5	80.5	141.0	−20.0
1958	50.6	54.4	105.0	−3.8
1959	3.6	18.9	22.5	−15.3
1960	2.7	20.7	23.4	−18.0
1961	16.6	30.9	47.5	−14.3
1962	38.5	46.0	84.5	−7.5
1963	62.4	74.6	137.0	−12.2
1964	152.7	157.8	310.5	−5.1
1965	245.0	224.7	469.7	20.3
1966	315.2	306.2	621.4	9.0
1967	288.3	269.4	557.7	18.9
1968	325.4	224.2	549.6	101.2
1969	390.8	234.5	625.3	156.3
1970	568.9	253.8	822.7	315.1
1971	578.2	323.2	901.4	255.0
1972	608.9	491.1	1,100.0	117.8

Source: Morino, 1991, 88; Nihon Bōekishinkōkai (JETRO), 1990, 273.

government should stop treating China as an enemy, stop attempting to create 'two Chinas', and not obstruct normalisation of relations between Japan and the PRC. Kishi's cabinet was perceived by the PRC government as the main obstacle to normalisation of Sino-Japanese relations, and accusations about Japan's supposed attempts to revive militarism appeared regularly in the PRC's media after 1958 and continued into the early 1960s.[18]

In 1960, Zhou Enlai put forward three conditions for the resumption of trade between the two countries signalling a temporary relaxation in China's Japan policy. Three types of trade were to be allowed: trade guaranteed by the two governments, trade by contract between Japanese and Chinese companies, and trade with those Japanese businesses that relied on supplies of Chinese raw materials. These conditions became the basis of a dual system of trade in the 1960s, namely 'Friendly Trade' and 'L-T Trade',[19] both of which were once again used by the PRC for political means. Japanese companies wishing to trade under the terms of 'Friendly Trade' were obliged to join a Sino-Japanese 'friendship' organisation and were then 'vetted' by the Chinese government. If they were considered 'friendly', that is, if they were willing to accept China's conditions and policies, then they were permitted to trade with China. L-T Trade was initiated in 1962. It differed from 'Friendly Trade' in that it was a semi-official, long-term (five-year) agreement under which the annual volume of two-way trade was fixed, and details were negotiated collectively by representatives of Japanese companies and Liao's liaison office. 'Friendly Trade' grew rapidly after 1960, but proved to be of limited benefit to the Chinese government in terms of its political influence on Japanese policy making. On the other hand, the volume of L-T trade, though much lower than that of 'Friendly Trade', was initially of greater value politically to the Chinese government, and it was considered 'a barometer of political relations . . . and a useful instrument through which the Chinese could exercise pressure on the pro-PRC elements within the LDP and in business circles.'[20] Commercial relations between China and Japan began to suffer during the Cultural Revolution when the 'overt injection of politics into economic matters' reached a peak. Lee describes how Japanese companies in favour of an improvement in relations between China and Japan were rewarded with contracts or increased volumes of trade. However, in return for the privilege of trade with China, Japanese trade negotiators and companies had to show active support for Chinese positions by participating in mass demonstrations or by issuing joint communiqués.[21]

In the 1960s, political relations became increasingly fraught. Despite Prime Minister Ikeda's supposedly 'tolerant and patient' (*kanyō to nintai*) policy towards the PRC, his stance on China's representation in the United Nations angered the PRC, which denounced him, as they had his predecessor, for obstructing Sino-Japanese normalisation.[22] A number of other, Taiwan-related incidents prompted further criticism from the PRC, which accused Ikeda of attempting to create 'two Chinas'.[23] By the mid-1960s, China's overall hard-line foreign policy during the Cultural Revolution, and Prime Minister Satō's 'anti-PRC' policies, led to a further deterioration of Sino-Japanese political relations. For example, Satō's pro-Taiwan stance and the signing of a treaty between Tokyo and Seoul in 1965 was seen by the PRC as evidence of an attempt to create a military alliance in Northeast Asia aimed against China, and a step towards a revival of militarism. The PRC government accused Satō of allowing Japan to become a military base and of attempting to resurrect the concept of the Greater East Asia Co-prosperity Sphere.[24]

But the PRC's most bitter attacks against Prime Minister Satō were reserved for his visits to Taiwan in 1967, and Washington in 1969. In Taiwan, Satō agreed with Chiang Kai-shek that Japan and Taiwan should forge closer political, economic and cultural links, a move which was perceived by the PRC as Japan's attempt to 'spread its tentacles of aggression into China's territory of Taiwan'.[25] In the Nixon–Satō joint communiqué of 1969, Satō reiterated his pro-Taiwan position by stressing that the security of both Taiwan and South Korea was essential to that of Japan. Furthermore, Satō declared that Tokyo would assist the USA to 'fulfil its obligation in regard to "the peace and security of the Far East"'.[26] These events, plus the renewal of the US–Japan Security Treaty in 1970 reinforced the PRC view that Japan and America had formed a military alliance with the aim of committing further aggression in Asia. The campaign against a revival of Japanese militarism that ran from 1969 through to the early 1970s in the PRC media shares many similarities with the campaign against Japanese history textbooks in 1982, and will be examined in more detail in Chapter 6.

While levels of trade increased at the end of the 1960s, Satō's pro-Taiwan, Korean and US stance led to the enunciation in 1970 of Zhou Enlai's stringent trade policy *vis-à-vis* Japan – the 'Four Conditions for Sino-Japanese Trade' – which 'caused turmoil in the Japanese business community'.[27] It is interesting to note, however, that in spite of the vehemence of the attacks on Satō's policies, the PRC never threatened to suspend trade as it had done after the Nagasaki Flag Incident. This attested to the growing importance to the PRC of trade with Japan. Similarly, the willingness of Japanese companies to accept the 'four conditions' was an indication that Japan was equally keen to continue its trade with China.[28]

By the early 1970s changes in the international and domestic situations ushered in a climate conducive to an improvement in Sino-Japanese relations. In international politics, the two superpowers had achieved parity in strategic nuclear arms, had concluded the Nuclear Non-Proliferation Treaty, and had begun the strategic arms limitation talks (SALT). The USA was no longer 'Number One' in economic terms because of the disastrous effects of the Vietnam War on the US economy, and the rise of Japanese and European economies which began to rival that of the USA.[29] In China, the emergence of a more pragmatic leadership meant that the 'militant and xenophobic foreign policy' of the early years of the Cultural Revolution gave way to a more relaxed stance. By the early 1970s, fifty-seven countries had normalised relations with the PRC and the US announced that it was also seeking rapprochement with the PRC.[30]

Refusing to deal with Prime Minister Satō, the Chinese government signed a Joint Statement in 1972 with Japan under the leadership of Tanaka Kakuei. The preamble to the statement declared that both countries wished to terminate the 'abnormal state of affairs' that had existed between them. In reference to Japan's wartime actions, it also read 'the Japanese side is keenly aware of Japan's responsibility for causing enormous damages in the past to the Chinese people through war and deeply reproaches itself'.[31]

The main body of the statement contained a number of paragraphs, the most important of which declared that Japan recognised the PRC as the sole legal government of China and that Taiwan was an inalienable part of PRC territory; that the PRC renounced its demand for war reparations; and that Japan and the PRC agreed to 'establish durable relations of peace and friendship . . . on the basis of the principles of mutual respect for sovereignty and territorial integrity, mutual non-aggression, non-interference in each other's internal affairs, equality and mutual benefit and peaceful coexistence'.[32]

The new relationship between China and Japan helped to defuse Chinese fears of a revival of Japanese militarism and displeasure over the renewal of the US–Japan Security Treaty.[33] Expectations for much improved economic relations between China and Japan were high after the signing of the Joint Statement. Lee talks of the 'new sense of shared accomplishments and commitments' and the way both governments 'tended to bend backward in their efforts not hurt each other's feelings and interests'.[34] It was hoped that the Joint Statement would lay to rest the various diplomatic and political problems that had hitherto plagued Sino-Japanese relations. Lee comments, for example, that with the signing of the Joint Statement 'the immediate political saliency of diplomatic conflict between Japan and China was reduced, if not eliminated'.[35] Similarly, Jain argues that with the Chinese government's willingness after 1972 to 'tolerate the US presence in Japan and the rearmament of Japan' the concern about Japanese militarism seemed to have disappeared.[36]

As we have seen, Sino-Japanese relations between 1945 and 1972 were dominated by the Chinese insistence on placing political considerations (ultimately diplomatic normalisation) above commercial ones. The emphasis on 'politics in command', reflecting Mao's preference for ideology over economics in domestic politics, was extended to China's dealings with Japan but jeopardised the economic relationship on more than one occasion. With the goal of normalisation achieved, however, it was hoped that a 'new stage in Sino-Japanese relations' could commence, accompanied by the 'new era in Asian international relations' which saw amicable relations between the USA, China and Japan for the first time in the twentieth century.[37]

1972–8: a new stage in Sino-Japanese relations?

Between 1972 and the conclusion of the Treaty of Peace and Friendship in August 1978, the Chinese and Japanese governments concluded twelve agreements ranging from aviation and maritime transport agreements to meteorological communications agreements.[38] The volume of trade increased steadily throughout the 1970s (see Table 3.2), and by 1975 Japan became China's principal trade partner.[39]

As described above, the prime goal of China's Japan policy up to 1972 had been diplomatic normalisation. This achieved, China's policies on Japan began to focus on the development of economic relations. This was partly due to the emergence of a new leadership in China after Mao's death in 1976, which sought to implement new economic policies aimed at modernisation. For this, Japan's assistance was actively sought, and even (albeit tacitly) expected given Japan's wartime record in China and China's renunciation in 1972 of its claim to war reparations. However, a number of problems between 1972 and 1978 meant that progress in economic relations was slower than anticipated. The problems related to the negotiations for the various economic agreements described above (most notably the aviation and fisheries negotiations), and the wording of the Treaty of Peace and Friendship.

Talks to negotiate the aviation agreement began in 1973 but soon stalled over the Taiwan issue. The PRC objected to the continuation of Taiwanese airline CAL's flights between Tokyo and Taipei, viewing it as proof that Japan was carrying out a 'two Chinas' policy. The Chinese government demanded that CAL flights be re-routed or cancelled, and that CAL be renamed and not carry Taiwan's flag. Resistance to these demands came from the pro-Taiwan lobby in Japan which did not want to see a disruption in either Japan's 'traditional ties' with Taiwan or the lucrative Japan–Taiwan route. The actions of some of the pro-Taiwan group (demonstrations, brawls in Diet meetings) caused some concern in the Chinese government, which accused the group of attempting to resurrect the 'Greater East Asia Co-Prosperity Sphere'.[40] The aviation agreement was finally concluded in April 1974, after many rounds of negotiations between Japan's Foreign Ministry and the pro-Taiwan lobby on the one hand and the Chinese government on the other. The aviation 'issue' was seen as a 'diplomatic coup' for China. The agreement was not sought primarily for economic reasons but rather for political reasons, and for Beijing 'it meant a step . . . towards the achievement of a one-China situation and towards the improvement of Sino-Japanese relations, one of the indispensable elements in the ultimate solution of the Taiwan issue'.[41] According to Hsiao, the conclusion of the agreement can be interpreted 'as a demonstration of the Japanese government's readiness to recognize Taiwan as part of China's territory', and this augured well for the negotiations of the Treaty of Peace and Friendship.[42]

However, negotiations for the treaty did not go as smoothly as hoped. Talks began in 1974 but were suspended in May 1975. The problem this time was not Taiwan, but a deadlock over the inclusion of an 'anti-hegemony' clause. The Japanese government was reluctant to agree to the inclusion of the anti-hegemony clause because of fears that the USSR would interpret it as directed against them. China's insistence on the inclusion of the clause was precisely to persuade Japan to take a less equidistant stance and 'tilt towards China', although Chinese leaders maintained that the clause was not directed against any third power.[43]

Domestic political crises in both countries in 1976 meant that negotiations on the treaty were not resumed until the end of 1977, but even then Prime Minister Fukuda remained reluctant to conclude the treaty promptly. The Chinese are said to have instigated the Senkaku island incident which is thought to have been a 'shock tactic' designed to pressurise Prime Minister Fukuda into positive action on the treaty talks. The incident was a dispute over the appearance of Chinese fishing boats in the territorial waters of the Senkaku islands (Diaoyutai) in April 1978.[44] When the Japanese government asked the Chinese government to instruct the boats to leave the area, the Chinese insisted they were entitled to be there since they were in Chinese territory. Since neither side wanted the problem to escalate and disrupt the treaty negotiations, the problem was settled within weeks, with the Japanese government accepting China's explanation that the intrusion was not intentional. The issue was once again 'shelved', but as events in recent years have shown, it remains a useful political device.

The peace treaty negotiations resumed in July, and by August the Japanese finally agreed to the anti-hegemony clause while stressing that the treaty was not an anti-Soviet alliance.[45] The Chinese government, on the other hand, regarded the treaty as a 'political and psychological victory against the Soviet Union since it was the first international legal document in which the principle of anti-hegemonism was prominently asserted'.[46]

With the treaty concluded, the Chinese and Japanese governments anticipated greater 'political consultation' and regular ministerial meetings which would 'promote mutual understanding and co-operation on matters of common interest'. In a broader context, the treaty was considered to usher in (again) 'a new era of co-operation among Japan, China, and the United States' and promote East Asian 'stability and security'.[47] The problems that occurred between 1972 and 1978 were perhaps outweighed by the remarkable 'record of cooperative efforts made in the field of Sino-Japanese economic diplomacy',[48] and Lee commends the two governments for their success in 'containing actual and potential controversies over Taiwan's status, the Diaoyu Islands . . . '.[49] However, as described above, political and strategic considerations played a large part in Chinese (and Japanese) decision making on the issues, though to a lesser extent than the previous period of Sino-Japanese relations. After 1978, economic considerations appeared to take on a much more important role as the next section will show.

1978–82: economics in command?

The conclusion of the Long-Term Trade Agreement in February 1978 had instilled Japanese government and business leaders with optimism that trade with China would increase still further. Under the terms of the non-governmental agreement, there was to be a two-way trade of $20 billion between 1978 and 1985 whereby Japan would export industrial plant and equipment to China, and China would export crude oil and coal to Japan.[50] The factors of mutual complementarity of the Chinese and Japanese economies, the geographical proximity of the two countries and their cultural affinity were cited by both sides as providing the potential for a rapid and vast expansion of bilateral trade. China perceived Japan as 'a convenient and near source of plant imports, advanced technology, and credits on favourable terms, which would facilitate the speedier realization of China's Four Modernizations'. Japan, for its part, was keen to develop economic ties with China 'in order to diversify its export markets and its sources of raw materials as well as reduce the degree of economic dependence upon the United States'.[51]

For Japanese business and government circles, the lure of a China finally open to trade was very attractive, but the 'new stage' of Sino-Japanese relations once again proved to be of limited duration and by the early 1980s optimism had turned to realism after a number of setbacks and disappointments. The first of these setbacks began in February 1979 with China's unilateral cancellation of a number of plant

Table 3.2 Japan's trade with China, 1972–92 (in $US millions)

Year	Exports to China	Imports from China	Total	Balance
1972	608.9	491.1	1,100.0	117.8
1973	1,039.5	974.0	2,013.5	65.5
1974	1,984.5	1,304.8	3,289.3	679.7
1975	2,258.6	1,531.1	3,789.7	727.5
1976	1,662.6	1,370.9	3,033.5	291.7
1977	1,938.6	1,546.9	3,485.5	391.7
1978	3,048.7	2,030.3	5,079.0	1,018.4
1979	3,698.7	2,954.8	6,653.5	743.9
1980	5,078.3	4,323.4	9,401.7	754.9
1981	5,097.2	5,291.8	10,389.0	−194.6
1982	3,510.8	5,352.4	8,863.2	−1,841.6
1983	4,912.3	5,087.4	9,999.7	−175.1
1984	7,216.7	5,957.6	13,174.3	1,259.1
1985	12,477.4	6,482.7	18,960.1	5,994.7
1986	9,856.2	5,652.4	15,508.6	4,203.8
1987	8,249.8	7,401.4	15,651.2	848.4
1988	9,476.0	9,858.8	19,334.8	−382.8
1989	8,515.9	11,145.8	19,661.7	−2,629.9
1990	6,129.6	12,053.5	18,183.1	−5,923.9
1991	8,593.1	14,215.8	22,808.9	−5,622.7
1992	11,949.0	16,952.8	28,902.0	−5,003.8

Source: Morino, 1991, 88; JETRO, *China Newsletter*, 1993, no. 106, 21.

contracts. The 'Baoshan shock', so named after the Baoshan steel complex near Shanghai, the 'symbol' of Sino-Japanese friendship and China's modernisation programme, was to be just the first of a number of cancellations and postponements lasting for two years which resulted in disillusionment and bitterness, not to mention financial loss, amongst the Japanese business community. In 1980 China postponed or cancelled 295 projects, and announced in early 1981 that work on the major projects at Baoshan, Nanjing, Shengli and Dongfang was to be cancelled. Discussions took place to try to salvage the situation, and the PRC intimated that the plant projects could be restarted on the condition that the Japanese government agreed to provide low-interest loans. A $1.3 billion loan agreement was therefore signed at the end of 1981, and construction work on the Baoshan, Daqing and Nanjing plants gradually resumed.[52]

The Baoshan shock was the result of China's unrealistic planning, but nevertheless had serious consequences for Sino-Japanese relations. China initially blamed Japanese companies for the failure of plant transfer, accusing them of bungling the arrangements and of deceiving the Chinese into making unnecessary purchases.[53] The real reason for the cancellations stemmed from decisions made during the Eleventh Party Congress of December 1978, when a reappraisal of the PRC's economic policy judged earlier forecasts of the modernisation programme to be unrealistic. The decision was taken, therefore, to shift the focus from heavy to light industry.[54] According to Newby, the PRC's handling of the matter and the high demands it made on Japan to help rectify the problem clearly indicated 'that China perceives technology transfer as part of the historical debt it is owed by Japan.'[55] By the same token, some Japanese (most notably Okazaki Kaheita, adviser to the Japan–China Economic Association), expressed the view that it was Japan's duty to provide governmental aid to China since China had renounced the demand for compensation for the war.[56]

Economic relations suffered badly from the Baoshan shock and left Japan's business and government circles disenchanted with China and dubious about China's commitment to stable economic relations with Japan.[57] While the problem of plant cancellations appeared to be resolved by late December 1981, the Chinese government frequently reconfirmed its commitment to economic co-operation with Japan in 1981 and 1982 to try and reassure Japanese government and business circles. Nonetheless, two-way trade between China and Japan in 1982 fell by 14.7 per cent on the previous year – the first drop since 1976 – as a result of the retrenchment measures and import restriction policies adopted by China in 1981.[58] This caused alarm in Japanese business circles, which feared that Sino-Japanese trade would continue to suffer under China's new policies of development of 'technical transformation of existing Chinese enterprises'.[59] Furthermore, in negotiations for the 1982FY yen loan which had started in June 1982, the Chinese government asked for ¥90 billion in low interest loans, but the Japanese government agreed only to provide ¥65 billion because of the delay in construction work on other projects.[60]

Other aspects of relations were less fraught, and by 1982 it could be argued that China and Japan were beginning to enjoy the fruits of normalisation. In June, Japan agreed to ¥64.8 billion investment in the construction of the China–Japan Friendship Hospital and technical co-operation in all fields continued, with exchange of researchers and specialists, and co-operation on development surveys.[61] Cultural relations had gone from strength to strength in the ten years since normalisation.

Exchange of 'personnel' numbered 150,000 in 1982, against 9,000 in 1972. The scale of cultural exchange had broadened considerably to encompass exchange of scholars, students, young people, artists, sports people, exhibitions, performances, lectures and so on. Furthermore, to commemorate the tenth anniversary of Sino-Japanese normalisation, twin cities and private organisations arranged various cultural events.[62] Japanese political and government circles also set up a fund for the construction of a Sino-Japanese Friendship Hall, which both governments welcomed and agreed to support actively.

At the political level, there were no signs of tension between the two governments in the main diplomatic 'events' of late 1981, early 1982. In early March, State Councillor Gu Mu gave a report to a meeting of the Standing Committee of the Fifth National People's Congress on the results of the second meeting of the 'Sino-Japanese parliamentary consultation' held in December 1981. According to Gu Mu's report, both governments stressed the need for greater co-operation in economic relations, and the conference helped to further Sino-Japanese understanding, strengthen friendship and promote close co-operation. This general line was reiterated during the Sino-Japanese foreign minister's conference held in Tokyo at the end of March which addressed international and bilateral issues, including discussion of the exchange of visits of government leaders to celebrate the tenth anniversary of normalisation.[63]

The first of these visits took place from 31 May to 6 June when Premier Zhao Ziyang travelled to Japan. According to both governments, there were no serious bilateral problems and no major unsettled problems.[64] Zhao remarked on the favourable conditions enjoyed by China and Japan in their relationship, namely, diplomatic relations, traditional friendship and the 'topographical advantages' of geographical proximity and complementary of China's resources and Japan's technology. Discussions between Premier Zhao and Prime Minister Suzuki centred on economic relations and international issues. Zhao spoke of 'establishing long-standing and stable ties of economic co-operation in the spirit of peace and friendship, equality, and mutual benefit'. He put forward three principles for the promotion of economic relations: that economic relations should be developed energetically on the basis of the Joint Statement and Treaty of Peace and Friendship; they should grow in depth and scope according to each other's 'needs and possibilities'; and that they should be 'lasting and stable and impervious to international storms'.[65]

Tanaka suggests that Zhao Ziyang indicated his eagerness to maintain friendly relations by stressing the importance of the third principle, rather than the first and second. For example, Zhao referred to the first two of the three 'principles' in the past tense acknowledging that much had already been achieved. In reference to the third principle, however, he stated at a press conference that 'Sino-Japanese relations will not be influenced by the current "excitement" in the international situation, and we must make every effort to maintain and develop long-term, stable friendly co-operation'.[66] Tanaka argues that Zhao was not merely trying to reassure the Japanese government of China's commitment to long-term economic relations in the wake of the Baoshan shock, but that he was in fact trying to 'signal' to the Japanese government that it should not alter its China policy in response to 'current international trends'. The trends to which Zhao was referring were probably the deterioration of Sino-US relations and the improvement of Sino-Soviet relations (discussed below).[67] Whether this much can be read into Zhao's comments is debatable, but the fact remains that in May 1982, there was nothing to suggest that the friendly relationship between China and Japan was in any danger. Both Zhao and Suzuki expressed satisfaction with the development of economic, political and cultural relations since 1972,[68] and looked forward to Suzuki's return visit to China in September to celebrate the tenth anniversary of normalisation.[69] While the Baoshan shock had been an economic problem between the two countries and revealed economic incompatibilities, political relations had developed amicably, and the issues that had plagued the earlier period seemed to have disappeared. It is surprising, therefore, that serious problems in the political arena began to emerge so soon after Zhao's visit, bringing into question the so-called 'special affinity' of the relationship.[70] The roots of the problem can be found, perhaps, in the changes in the international environment to which Zhao was referring in his press conference.

The international environment in 1982

While Sino-Japanese bilateral relations appeared to be relatively problem-free before the Textbook Issue broke out, changes had been taking place on the international environment since the 1970s which inevitably affected Chinese and Japanese domestic and foreign policies. The most significant trend in the international system of the 1970s had been a shift in the balance of power between the two superpowers, and a move away from bipolarity towards multipolarity with five centres of power (USA, USSR, PRC, Japan and Europe).[71] The USA's previously unrivalled economic might was being threatened by the high levels of growth in Japan, Germany and France, despite Reagan's attempts to turn the economy around.[72]

After a brief period of East–West détente in the early 1970s, by the end of the decade there was a heightening of the rivalry between America and the Soviet Union. A reassessment of Soviet military spending carried out by the CIA revealed that the USSR had been spending significantly more than the USA had previously thought.[73] President Reagan's pledge to 'restore US military might' and his policies of all round confrontation with the USSR led to a new arms race, with the USA rapidly rearming and modernising its navy and nuclear arsenal in an attempt to 'catch up' with the USSR.[74]

As Paul Kennedy argues, the USSR had undoubtedly enhanced its military strength during the 1970s and was much more powerful in both economic and military terms than it had been under Stalin.[75] Moreover, the USSR's insistence on its right to conduct its foreign and domestic policies without interference from the West further heightened US (and Chinese and Japanese) fears about burgeoning Soviet influence. The Soviet Union's economic and military backing of the Vietnamese invasion of Cambodia, its invasion of Afghanistan and its role in the suppression of the Polish trade union Solidarity seemed to confirm those fears.[76]

Thus by the late 1970s, amidst an atmosphere of increasing mistrust, the shift in the global balance of power inevitably affected the way the Chinese and Japanese governments perceived their own position in the international system and how they were perceived by other nations. For example, US policy on China began to change in the early 1980s, in line with President Reagan's hard-line against the USSR and the removal of pro-PRC top personnel in the US administration. In response, the PRC's foreign policy began to change away from its previous pro-US stance towards a more neutral posture. While US and Japanese policy makers still identified the Soviet Union as the biggest threat to regional and global security, by late 1981/early 1982 the PRC began to show a softer attitude. This was prompted partly by a change in China's perceptions of the Soviet situation. By the early 1980s, the USSR was suffering from domestic economic failure and political problems in the form of a succession of leaders and a political elite resistant to change. The Afghanistan invasion had become a 'quagmire' and the USSR was losing its appeal as a model to other eastern European states.[77] Relations with the PRC had improved little after the signing of the Treaty of Peace and Friendship between Japan and China, and the PRC's rapprochement with the USA fuelled the USSR's fears of encirclement by the three 'allies'.[78] To prevent this scenario from developing further, the USSR began to make conciliatory gestures towards the PRC, which by 1982 was formulating its 'new' independent foreign policy, and began to respond more favourably than in previous years to Soviet suggestions about a rapprochement.[79]

The USA's Japan policy also underwent a change in the late 1970s, and whereas China had been in favour throughout the 1970s, by the 1980s Japan was judged 'to be pre-eminent as a regional power because of its industrial prowess'. Facing what it perceived to be a serious military threat from the USSR, the Reagan administration sought a closer relationship with Japan, and encouraged Japan to 'fill out its economic capability with commensurate (or at least modestly appropriate) military power'.[80] To a certain extent this was welcomed by the Japanese governments, which also identified the USSR as a greater threat than in previous years and felt the need to alter Japanese defence policy accordingly (see Chapter 4). Reagan's new 'pro-Japan' policy therefore encouraged Japan to adopt a more assertive, or at least a (pro-)active, foreign policy position in the Asian region. It could be argued that Japanese foreign policy was beginning to change anyway by the 1980s, and not necessarily just because of external pressure (*gaiatsu*) from the USA. As the next chapter will describe, Japan's economic success had brought with it a change of attitude among many Japanese people and politicians, who saw Japan's previously passive role in world affairs as no longer suitable to its international status. Though barely palpable, Japan's foreign policy could be seen to be moving towards a more active stance in the early 1980s. Prime Minister Suzuki's tour of ASEAN countries in 1981, for example, was aimed at developing co-operation and harmony in the region, and Japan's support of ASEAN countries on the Cambodian issue also helped to improve Japan's diplomatic relations in the region. These moves were seen, and to some extent welcomed, by Southeast Asian countries as evidence of Japan's growing independence of Washington.[81]

As Chapters 6 and 7 will elucidate, these general changes in the international system, and Chinese and Japanese responses to them, contribute to some extent to a better understanding of Chinese and Japanese actions and reactions during the Textbook Issue. However, they are by no means the only contributing factors, and as the next chapter will highlight, it is necessary to consider also the changes taking place in the domestic political situations in both countries.

4 Background to the Textbook Issue

Domestic issues in the 1970s and 1980s

As suggested in Chapter 2, there are many factors at work in the process of foreign policy decision-making which remain 'in the background, affecting the decision makers on almost every foreign policy choice'.[1] The particular mix and relative influence of the main determinants of a foreign policy output depends on the particular situation and the actors involved.[2] Broadly speaking, the determinants are external and internal factors, but these categories subsume a number of variables as the organising framework illustrated. In addition the external and internal cannot be considered as separate, discrete clusters, since international events exercise pressure on domestic events and vice versa. In studying a particular foreign policy event, therefore, it is necessary to identify the most relevant external and internal factors and examine how they interact to produce a foreign policy output. This chapter considers some of the internal factors, and explores some of the linkages between these and the external factors discussed in the previous chapter. The first section examines changes in Japanese domestic politics in the 1970s and early 1980s, the second section looks at developments in China, and the final section examines some of the similarities in Chinese and Japanese domestic and foreign policies which may also help to explain the actions and reactions of the Chinese and Japanese governments in the Textbook Issue.

Japanese domestic dynamics

Japan's rapid economic development from the 1950s led to her becoming the world's 'Number One'[3] economic power by the 1980s, surpassing the USA to become the world's largest creditor nation. Japan's success was lauded by both Western and Japanese analysts, who began to examine the causes of Japan's remarkable rapid economic growth and political stability. Yet despite Japan's economic prowess, her role in world politics remained peripheral. The so-called 'Yoshida doctrine' had committed

Japan to the pursuit of economic growth in the postwar period, provided the protection of the US security umbrella, and allowed successive Japanese governments to steer clear of international politics through a low-key foreign policy. By the late 1970s, Japan's mercantilism and passive foreign policy became the focus of much criticism and tension between Japan and the USA. By the 1980s, the incongruity of Japan's international economic strength but political weakness prompted much debate about whether or not Japan should create for herself a new, more active world role commensurate with her economic power. Before considering the debates about Japan's new international role, it is necessary to chart the political changes which took place at the end of the 1970s.

LDP resurgence and the 'new mood'

One of the most frequently cited reasons for Japan's postwar success is the political stability brought about by the Liberal Democratic Party's protracted stay in government. From 1955 until the early 1970s, the LDP had maintained a stable majority in both houses of the Diet and had brought the Japanese people peace and prosperity. During the 1970s, however, the LDP suffered a series of setbacks, faced with the oil crises, the Lockheed and other scandals, weak leadership, factional struggles, and the breaking away of 'young dissidents' to form the New Liberal Club.[4]

As the decade progressed the LDP's majority in the Lower and Upper Houses dwindled as a result of election losses in 1972, 1974, 1976 and 1979. There was a period of nearly equal power in the Diet between the opposition parties and the LDP (*hakuchū kokkai*) which meant that opposition parties finally had a greater say in policymaking due to their increased power in the Diet committees. The revision of the budget in 1979 was one of the major successes of the opposition parties, and was seen as a strong indication that the fall of the LDP was imminent.[5] The general election of 1979 had left the LDP with only 48.6 per cent of the seats (44.6 per cent of the vote), although with the support of a number of 'independent' candidates the LDP was able to gain a narrow majority in the Lower House. However, when the opposition parties brought a vote of no confidence against Prime Minister Ohira in May 1980, the abstention of 69 LDP 'rebels' meant that Ohira was defeated by 243 votes to 187. Ohira was forced to dissolve the Diet, and called for a June election to coincide with the Upper House election.[6] Forecasters predicted a victory for a coalition government between the Japan Socialist Party and the other opposition parties, but to the surprise of many the LDP managed to retain its place in government, winning a stable majority in both houses of the Diet in June 1980.

Various reasons have been cited for this double victory. Perhaps the most significant was Ohira's sudden death at the end of May, an event which produced a large-scale sympathy vote for the LDP, left the opposition parties without their 'primary target – Ohira and his "power supported by money" ', and which also allowed wavering LDP, voters (amongst who Ohira had not been popular) to return to the fold.[7] Murakami suggests two other factors for the LDP's resurgence, a revival of 'tradition-oriented conservatism' and the LDP's success in widening its support base and transforming itself into an 'interest-oriented catchall party'. Murakami concludes that the 'interest-oriented' hypothesis best explains the surprise victory of 1980, but the 'tradition-oriented' hypothesis cannot be rejected out of hand since it does seem to tally with the 'general mood' of the time, and with the changes that were to take place after 1980. The 'tradition-oriented' hypothesis refers to the way in which the crises of the 1970s (oil, trade and so on) and 'the increasing Russian military threat in East Asia stirred the Japanese out of their complacency resulting from material affluence, leading to a tradition-oriented conservatism among Japanese voters'.[8] Opinion polls certainly seemed to indicate that the Japanese were growing in confidence as a result of the country's success. Pyle, for example, points to the results of the five-yearly government surveys on 'Japanese national character' as evidence of the growth in national self-esteem. Compared to just 20 per cent in 1953, by 1983 over 53 per cent of Japanese thought they were superior to Westerners.[9] In addition, the (re-)appearance of *nihonjinron* literature in the late 1970s attributing Japan's phenomenal success to its traditional and unique cultural values helped to reinforce this 'new mood'. [10]

The resurgence of power gave the LDP the opportunity to put forward proposals for many new policies. Former Prime Minister Tanaka Kakuei apparently commented that with the 'landslide victory', the LDP could do anything it wanted.[11] While Prime Minister Suzuki's priorities were concerned with state finances, social welfare, administrative reform and political ethics,[12] other proposals from within the LDP were perceived to be 'a tilt to the right' or a return to 'tradition-oriented conservatism'. These included 'preferential treatment of the defence budget', and a debate about an 'independent' constitution.[13] The new mood also gave rise to calls for return of the Northern Territories, for 'nationalisation' of the Yasukuni Shrine and calls for more education about national defence and patriotism.[14]

The mood in the LDP was paralleled by the popular mood described above and was accompanied by the debates in the press about Japan's new role in international affairs, but there was little consensus on how to resolve the incongruity of Japan as 'economic giant, political dwarf'. The debates that filled the pages of the current affairs journals and magazines reflected the confusion as to precisely what Japan could and should do with its newfound wealth and prestige. Pyle describes the four main arguments put forward in the early 1980s as the progressive view, the liberal-realist view, the neo-mercantilist view, and the new-nationalist view.[15] The most 'radical' of the arguments was put forward by proponents of the 'new nationalism', who rejected the 'traditional' values of the postwar period in favour of a military build-up and an independent foreign policy.[16] Alarmed by this view, opponents in the progressive and liberal-realist schools saw these ideas as a call for a return to prewar militarism. With requests from the USA for Japan to increase its military power in line with its economic power, China's accusations during the Textbook Issue that Japan was once again trying to revive militarism may seem quite justified.

But, as Pyle explains, the 'new nationalists' were seeking to increase Japan's military might not with the aim of conducting another war, but to become a 'normal nation' that would no longer be vulnerable to other countries. Nor were the 'new nationalists' the only group who argued for some degree of rearmament. Furthermore, Pyle concludes, nationalism of the type that led to Japan's expansionism in the 1930s would be unlikely to recur given the transformation of social structure and politics in postwar Japan.[17] Buzan also states that despite the new feelings of national confidence a renewal of Japanese military aggression was unlikely. He posits four main reasons: the commitment of postwar Japanese society to democracy and pacifism, Japan's dependence on trade, the deterrent of Chinese, Soviet and US military power, in addition to the greater power of other regional states, and the absence both of European colonies in East Asia and of a weak, 'decaying' Chinese empire.[18] Thus the arguments in favour of Japanese rearmament should be seen not as evidence of a growing pro-militarist tendency, but within the context of the debate about Japan's role in international affairs in the 1980s which was in turn a response to changes in the international environment.

The LDP's debates on such matters as defence, revision of the constitution, and changes to the education system represented most clearly the new sense of confidence in the LDP, given that in previous years these issues had been considered taboo. In terms of defence, Farnsworth notes a shift in Japan's defence strategy from the late 1970s away from an omni-directional diplomacy which sought to develop relations with 'all other nations regardless of their political structure, size and geographical location'.[19] Instead, by 1980 the policy was responding to changes in the international environment such as the Soviet threat and shifting balance of power, and to US criticisms of Japan's low defence contributions. Both the Defence White Paper and Diplomatic Blue Book in 1980 called for awareness of the Soviet threat and for expansion of armaments. Dahlby suggests that although the Defence White Paper showed a 'new assertiveness' it did not represent any radical changes in policy. Rather, it was 'the first effort to concentrate on Japan's own shortcomings and also to pinpoint the build-up of Soviet naval, land and air forces in the Pacific and the Soviet invasion of Afghanistan as "posing an increased potential threat to Japan's security"'.[20] The White Paper intimated that in the interests of national security Japan should procure more sophisticated military equipment, and make greater efforts to fulfil its obligations to the USA and the 'West'.[21] These greater efforts were to be in the form of LDP hawks pushing for an increase in defence expenditure right up to the 1 per cent ceiling.[22]

The issue of Japan's defence and increased armament had increasingly gained the support of the more hawkish LDP politicians who, emboldened by the LDP's stable majority, raised the subject of revision, even deletion, of the war-renouncing Article Nine of the Constitution.[23] In particular, Justice Minister Okuno Seisuke called for the 'enactment of an independently written constitution'. Debate about revision of the foreign-imposed Constitution has been ongoing behind LDP closed doors ever since the Occupation, but the provocative nature of the issue has meant that the debate has rarely been aired in public for fear of alienating the electorate. Indeed, two-thirds of the LDP were said to be in favour of constitutional revision in 1980,[24] but Prime Minister Suzuki's harsh condemnation of Okuno's remarks made it clear that the 'official' government position was not in favour of Constitutional revision and Cabinet members expressing views to the contrary would be forced to step down.[25]

One topic on which debate was not stifled and where 'tradition-oriented' conservatism was enjoying a true renaissaince was education, in particular textbook content and revision of the Fundamental Law of Education. LDP members who called for a more patriotic tone to be incorporated into textbooks, or for a tightening up of the textbook laws, were criticised by opposition parties and teachers' unions for advocating a return to authoritarianism in education, but were not deterred. This so-called 'patriotic education debate' (*aikokushin kyōiku ronsō*) is worth considering in more detail, since it gave rise to the Japanese media's 'blitz' on textbooks in 1982, which in turn sparked off Chinese and Korean protests. Understanding the nature of the debate also helps to explain the reaction of the Ministry of Education and LDP education-related dietmen to the 1982 Textbook Issue.

The 'patriotic education' debate

The 'patriotic education' debate of the 1980s should be seen within the context of the antagonism between the 'conservatives' (Ministry of Education, LDP) and the 'progressives' (Japan Teachers' Union (JTU), academics, Japan Socialist Party, Japan Communist Party) which has dominated education in postwar Japan. After the war, the conservatives were keen to maintain those elements of the prewar education system that they felt had been successful (for example, the 'traditional Japanese morality' of the 1890 Imperial Rescript). By contrast, the progressives were strongly opposed to any government intervention in education given the 'militarist abuse of the pre-war system', and were ready to fight against any attempts by the government to impose central controls.[26] The Occupation's education reforms, which limited central control of education and laid the foundation for an education system based on democratic control and egalitarianism, gained the full support of the progressives, but were strongly opposed by the conservatives who then made the reversal of the Occupation reforms one of their top priorities. The reduction of teachers' union rights, another policy instigated by the Occupation forces, understandably did not gain the support of the progressives and only served to aggravate the tension between the LDP and Japan Teachers' Union.[27]

Conflict between the two groups has continued ever since the Occupation, with LDP governments trying to limit what they have perceived as the Japan Teachers' Union's Marxist, left-wing influence on the education system, and the JTU in turn trying to block LDP moves to recreate what the former has perceived to be a prewar-style authoritarian education system. A running battle on textbook authorisation and content is just one of the facets of the conflict between the two groups. The first 'crackdown' by the government on JTU influence occurred in 1955, with the Democratic Party's criticism of the content of social science textbooks in a series of reports entitled 'The Problem of Deplorable Textbooks' (*Ureubeki kyōkasho mondai*). The changes in education that ensued marked 'the turning point in the textbook authorization procedure from a relatively free system in the early '50s to an increasingly rigid system by the end of the decade'.[28] The main concern of the government was a left-wing bias in textbooks that was seen to be glorifying Communism and criticising Japan. In 1956 the LDP introduced a bill into the Diet calling for tighter screening of textbooks.

Although the bill was not passed, the government made changes in the Ministry of Education later the same year which involved the expansion of the Ministry's Textbook Authorisation Research Council and the implementation of other recommendations contained in the 'Deplorable Textbook' reports which had the desired result of tightening up textbook screening.[29]

Textbook authorisation became even tougher in 1958 as a result of the introduction of a nation-wide mandatory curriculum (Course of Study, *gakushū shidō yōryō*) which allowed the government to stipulate course content and authorise only those textbooks conforming to the guidelines.[30] In 1977 and 1978, the Course of Study underwent a complete revision and the Ministry of Education also implemented changes to the Standards for Textbook Authorisation. The objectives of the new Course of Study were (1) to raise children who would be 'rich in humanity', or well-rounded human beings, (2) to provide latitude for personal development and expression, and (3) to offer education that emphasised basic knowledge but was also suited to the abilities of individual students.[31] Concrete changes included a reduction in classroom hours, designation of the '*Kimigayo*' as the national anthem, and changes to the curriculum that were implemented in primary schools in 1980, secondary schools in 1981 and high school in 1982. Of particular note was the introduction of a new textbook called 'Contemporary Society' (*Gendai Shakai*) into high school social studies courses which became the target of LDP criticism in 1981. The changes to the Standards for Textbook Authorisation, the first changes in twenty years, involved a number of alterations to the system such as clearer definitions of revision authorisation (*kaitei kentei*) and new authorisation (*shinki kentei*), clarification of the procedures and content of the three stages of authorisation, and clarification of the responsibility of the publisher to submit applications for 'correction of errors' (*seigo teisei*).[32] The changes are significant because the textbooks compiled in accordance with the new Course of Study, and authorised under the new Standards for Textbook Authorisation soon formed part of the second major 'crackdown' on textbook content which began in 1980.

Before focusing on the specifics of the 1980 'crackdown', it is worth explaining the various stages of the textbook authorisation system since this also became a focal point of domestic and international criticism during the Textbook Issue.

The textbook authorisation system

Textbooks in Japanese schools are revised every three years in rotation (see Table 4.1), and must be approved by the Ministry of Education before they can be used in schools. Textbooks do not have to be completely rewritten for the purpose, but both existing textbooks submitted for partial revision or 'revision authorisation' (*kaitei kentei*) and newly-compiled textbooks submitted for 'new authorisation' (*shinki kentei*) must undergo the same authorisation process.[33] In 1982 the process involved three stages (see Figure 4.1), and took three years from submission of the manuscript to the textbooks being used in schools.[34]

In the first stage of the process, authorisation, private publishing companies commissioned teachers and lecturers to produce a manuscript which had to comply with the guidelines set down by the Education Ministry, that is, the Course of Study (*Gakushū Shidō Yōryō*) and Standards for Textbook Authorisation (*Kyōkayō Tosho Kentei Kijun*).[35] Once edited by the publisher, the manuscripts were submitted to the Education Ministry's Textbook Examination Committee (TEC, *Kyōkasho Chōsakan*), which undertook the 'manuscript investigation' (*genkō chōsa*). This meant that the manuscript was assigned to three members of the panel who evaluated the text and passed their results onto the Textbook Authorisation Research Council (TARC, *Kyōkayō Tosho Kentei Chōsa Shingikai*).[36] The appropriate TARC subcommittee appraised the manuscript on the basis of TEC's evaluation, and returned it to TEC with recommendations to either pass, conditionally pass, or fail it. A 'conditional pass' meant that the Ministry had made a number of recommendations or 'suggestions'.[37] 'Suggestions for correction' (*shūsei iken*) referred to changes that had to be carried out if the book was to be approved. 'Suggestions for improvement' (*kaizen iken*) were not compulsory and were left to the author's judgement. The TEC passed the results of this preliminary examination

Table 4.1 Cycle of textbook authorisation

Textbook level	Year					
	1978	1979	1980	1981	1982	1983
Primary	A	S	U	A	S	U
Middle	U	A	S	U	A	S
High (1st year)	S	U	A	S	U	A
High (2nd year)	A	S	U	A	S	U
High (3rd year)	U	A	S	U	A	S

Source: Monbushō, 1986, 3.

Key: A = authorisation; S = selection; U = used in schools; shaded area = textbooks authorised under the new Course of Study.

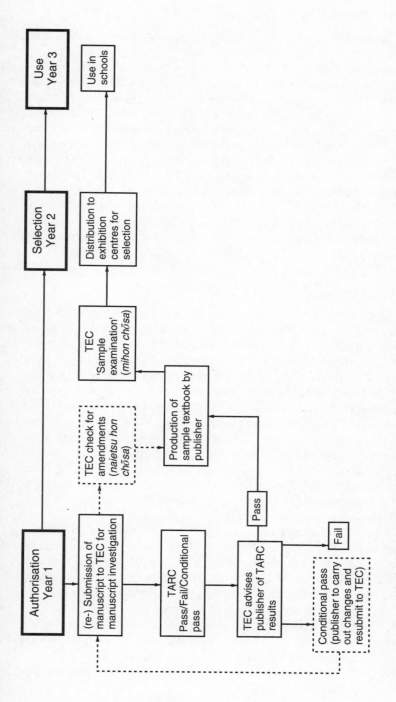

Figure 4.1 Stages of the textbook authorisation system in 1982
Source: Adapted from Kyōkasho Seido no Gaiyō, 1986, 9 and Takahashi, 1988, 55

on to the applicant, who would usually amend the maunscript before re-submitting it.

During the 'private examination' (*naietsu kentei*), the TEC checked the re-submitted manuscript to ensure that any deletions or revisions had been carried out satisfactorily. The TEC then notified the applicant, who, if successful, could proceed with production of textbook 'samples'. Finally, during 'sample examination' (*mihon chōsa*), a sample of the finished textbook was submitted to TEC to undergo a final check on format and binding. Once final approval had been gained, the sample textbooks were then distributed to the 700 nation-wide 'exhibition centres' at the beginning of July for headmasters (of private schools), and local Education Committees (of state schools) to select the textbooks they wished to use. After the selection process, the publishers could begin producing the textbooks ready for use in schools the following April.

'The New Problem of Deplorable Textbooks'

The 1980 campaign was reminiscent of the 'Deplorable Textbooks' debate of the mid-1950s. Indeed, the campaign originated from an article in *Sekai to Nihon*[38] entitled 'The New Problem of Deplorable Textbooks' (*Shin ureubeki kyōkasho mondai*). This was followed by a series of seventeen articles called 'The Bias in Social Studies Textbooks' (*Shakaigaku kyōkasho no henkō*) which appeared in the same journal from March 1980. A similar series entitled 'Textbooks Now – A Proposal for Educational Normalisation' (*Ima kyōkasho wa – Kyōiku seijōka e no teigen*) was carried in the LDP journal *Jiyū Shinpō* from January to August 1980.[39] These articles focused on the problem of primary school textbooks, but criticism soon developed to incorporate middle and high school textbooks also, as these textbooks were the first batch to have undergone authorisation under the new Course of Study.

By the middle of 1980, the target of the so-called 'Biased Textbooks Campaign' (*Henkō kyōkasho kyanpein*) was a middle school social studies textbook, *Civics* (*Kōmin*). In July, Justice Minister Okuno Seisuke criticised the textbook for its lack of patriotism (*aikokushin*). This was followed by similar criticisms from other LDP members, one of whom, Mitsuzuka Hiroshi, was ironically to play a leading role in the negotiations with Korea during the 1982 Textbook Issue.[40] In October 1980, Education Minister Tanaka Tatsuo echoed earlier sentiments in a Lower House Education Committee meeting when he complained that there were few passages relating to patriotism in current textbooks.[41]

Criticism of textbooks came not only from the LDP but also from the bureaucracy, and from the commercial and academic worlds. The complaints from these sources differed from LDP criticism, however, and were not so much focused on the lack of patriotism as on content of passages in the textbooks relating to social problems such as welfare, consumer rights, energy and pollution problems associated with big business.[42] The Science and Technology Agency (*Kagaku gijutsuchō*), for example, filed a complaint about errors contained in the textbooks, which were promptly corrected.[43]

At the end of 1980, the LDP took the 'Biased Textbooks Campaign' one step further by setting up five subcommittees to consider not just the problem of textbook content but reform of the entire education system.[44] The Subcommittee on the Textbook Problem (chairman, Mitsuzuka Hiroshi) met regularly with various groups (LDP, the University of Tsukuba Group, Japan Teachers' Union, academics, etc.) to discuss, amongst other things, problems with the current textbook system and revision of the textbook authorisation system. The results of the Subcommittee's deliberations were announced in June 1981. The report identified a number of problems. For example, the JTU was criticised for putting pressure on local education boards to use only left-leaning textbooks, and on the other textbook publishing companies for commissioning only left-wing scholars to write textbooks.[45] The report suggested a number of proposals to improve and strengthen the textbook authorisation system, including an increase in textbook examiners, a broadening of the selection areas for primary and secondary schools to *todōfuken* (urban and rural prefectures), and an examination of the legal basis for textbook authorisation, selection, production and distribution.[46]

The JTU and the publishing company unions criticised the report for advocating the establishment of a 'quasi-State compiling system' (*kyōkasho no junkokuteika*). The mass media carried daily reports on the textbook problem, investigating the 'actual state of biased authorisation and thought control' by focusing on the *Gendai Shakai* (Contemporary Society) high school textbooks then undergoing authorisation (for use in 1983).[47] According to the publishing unions' annual 'Textbook Report' (1981), the authorisation for all new high school textbooks in 1980–1 had been stricter than in previous years as a result of the LDP's and Keidanren's criticisms. The 'Textbook Report' stated that the *Gendai Shakai* textbooks reflected the attempt to increase control over content. Some of the twenty-one textbooks that underwent authorisation had as many as 200 *shūsei iken* and 400 *kaizen iken*, mainly in the area of economics but also in politics, big business, pollution and the State.[48]

Yet despite this apparently more stringent authorisation, the LDP still continued its criticism of the textbooks. In 1981 these criticisms were of passages relating to political systems, the constitutionality of the Self Defence Forces, citizens' duties and rights, and the Northern Territories issue. The LDP called for revision of 100 textbooks published by five publishing companies.[49] Furthermore, in July 1981 Education Minister Tanaka asked that high school textbook writers and publishers in their preparation of textbooks for the 1983–6 triennium 'soften their approach to Japan's excesses during World War II' and place more stress on patriotism.[50]

The education campaign continued in November 1981, with Education Minister Tanaka's request that the Thirteenth Central Education Council (CEC, *Chūō Kyōiku Shingikai*) carry out an inquiry into three areas: educational content, method and textbooks; diversity and flexibility in middle-school education; and pre-school education. The CEC set up a number of subcommittees of which the Textbook Subcommittee (chairman, Yoshimoto Jirō) met six times between January and April 1982. By the time it was ready to announce the results of its deliberations in July 1982, however, the Textbook Issue had developed into a diplomatic incident, and the decision was taken to revise the report in light of the new developments.[51]

At the party conference in January 1982, the LDP gave an appraisal of its recent education policies:

> In education, in addition to the improvement of the quality of teachers, we have made every effort to demand better textbooks – a problem that could not be overlooked. In the compulsory education curriculum for primary and middle schools the most desirable aim must surely be to cultivate the Japanese spirit and foster national pride. Hitherto, it is a fact that textbooks have often been compiled without these fundamental points in mind, and it is only through dealing with this problem face on that we have gained the approval of many sensible citizens.[52]

In response to this, the opposition parties and JTU declared a 'counter-offensive on education', part of which could be seen during the 1982 Textbook Issue. For those LDP politicians and Ministry of Education bureaucrats who advocated changes to the education system, the 'patriotic education debate' was just another aspect of the general trend of the early 1980s which sought to develop a new national pride (*minzoku no hokori*) and raise Japan's status in international affairs. For opposition parties, the JTU and Asian governments, the changes represented a retrogressive move to a prewar-style authoritarian education system and had to be opposed. The nature of that opposition will be discussed in Chapter 7.

Chinese domestic dynamics

The changes taking place in Japan in the early 1980s were due to a combination of internal and external factors. Important changes were also taking place in China from the mid-1970s to the early 1980s, and consideration of these is equally important to an understanding of the events of the Textbook Issue. This section will therefore examine some of the major changes in Chinese domestic and foreign policies prior to and during 1982.

The rise of Deng Xiaoping

Deng Xiaoping's rise to power after the death of Mao Zedong in 1976 was the result of a power struggle between three main factions: the 'neo-Maoists' led by Hua Guofeng, the 'Old Guard' (or 'elder statesmen') headed by Ye Jianying, and the 'pragmatists' led by Deng.[53] The contest for party leadership between Hua and Deng began in 1977 after Deng was rehabilitated and reinstated, and Hua Guofeng was acknowledged leader of China at the Eleventh Party Congress. Deng gradually managed to oust Hua from power by challenging his legitimacy as Mao's successor, removing his allies from key posts and replacing them with his own.[54] By the end of 1978, Deng was the dominant force in Chinese politics, even though Hua Guofeng retained the titles of Party chairman and State premier. By 1980 Deng's faction represented the majority in the Central Committee and National People's Congress and his overall leadership was unassailable. One of Deng's protégés, Zhao Ziyang replaced Hua as State premier in late 1980, and the 'Resolution' on the history of the Communist Party of China given at the 6th plenum of the Eleventh Central Committee in 1981 represented the final blow to Hua's authority, even though he still remained a member of the Politburo.

By 1982, Hua's faction was in no position to present any sort of challenge to Deng as he prepared to finally consolidate his power at the Twelfth Party Congress in September. However, Deng was still faced with a number of problems, and it is within the context of Deng's search for legitimacy and consolidation of power in the run-up to the Twelfth Party Congress that these problems – and their link to the Textbook Issue – must be viewed.

Reform problems

Deng's problems were related to the set of reforms begun in 1978. Under his leadership, China moved away from the more radical Maoist policies of isolation and self-reliance towards modernisation and 're-entry into the family of nations'.[55] The 'Four Modernisations' of agriculture, industry, national defence, and science and technology[56] and the 'Open Door' policy had huge implications for China's domestic politics, economy, defence and foreign policy, but the policies did not always meet with agreement nor was their implementation trouble-free. Economic policies, for example, were resisted by those who were not so favourable to the idea of market forces and who preferred to exclude foreign (or at least Western) influences. Deng met resistance from the other main faction in Chinese politics, the 'Old Guard', over national defence and foreign policy issues. Finally, he found that opening up to the West brought with it ideological and social problems which further threatened his legitimacy.

In terms of China's economy, Deng and his supporters felt that China's economy had been hindered by Mao's policies of self-sufficiency. Thus, a series of economic reforms was introduced which opened up China to foreign investment, markets and suppliers and allowed market forces to operate in the economy to encourage efficiency and provide incentives. However, as the description of the 'Baoshan Shock' illustrated (Chapter 3), overambitious and unrealistic planning led to the announcement of a series of readjustment measures from 1979. The 'shopping spree' upon which Chinese economists had embarked in 1978 had committed China to billions of dollars worth of contracts which China could not fulfil in the time scale initially given. The result was unilateral plant cancellations, inability to fulfil quotas and so on, which caused problems with the foreign governments with whom deals had been signed. Domestically, the economic reforms did not mean an overnight transformation of the economy, and with declining growth in 1980 and the retrenchment measures that followed, there was a certain amount of cynicism amongst those sectors of society disadvantaged by the reforms (see below).[57]

Despite these problems, Deng remained committed to economic policies which would spur economic growth and modernisation. Deng's economic policies had foreign policy implications as well. Resistance to the economic reforms came mainly from Chen Yun, a pragmatist himself, but whose preference was for a more centrally planned economy and a conciliatory stance towards the Soviet Union. However, Deng's plans for modernisation required import, technology and investment from advanced industrialised nations and therefore drew China closer to the West and Japan.[58] This in turn necessitated a shift away from Mao's 'three worlds theory', which had been the backbone of China's foreign policy throughout the 1970s.[59] The 'three worlds' policy had advocated a united front of Second and Third World countries against First World (potential) hegemons, the Soviet Union in particular. However, by the late 1970s there was a general consensus within the Chinese elite that China should move back into world affairs after years of isolation during the Cultural Revolution. This was facilitated by the changes in the international system and explains China's moves during the 1970s towards rapprochement with the West when diplomatic relations were re-established with USA, Canada, European countries, Japan and Third World countries. After 1980 China appeared to have achieved its aim of moving back into the world, having been accepted into a number of international organisations (such as the World Bank), and generally improving its relations not just with the West but also with ASEAN and India. By 1982, the 'independent foreign policy of peace' was to confirm the rejection of Mao's 'three world' foreign policy line, but was not greeted with enthusiasm by the 'Old Guard' which feared that Deng's policies were leaning too much in favour of the USA. However, the 'Old Guard's' main criticisms of Deng's reforms were in the areas of defence and ideology.

Reforms carried out in the sphere of defence between 1979–80 were aimed at reducing the political role of the People's Liberation Army, at reaffirming party and government control, and at transforming the PLA into a more modern, specialised and professional army. Because of the government's concentration on economic modernisation, the military budget was cut and reforms were attempted which were aimed at removing elderly, unskilled and unqualified personnel.[60] These reforms gave rise to the power struggle between Deng Xiaoping and certain elements of the PLA which culminated in 1982 and which warrants further attention. Joffe describes two groups within the PLA: the professional military and senior military leaders (part of the 'Old Guard'). While the former group was supportive of Deng's military modernisation programmes, the latter spoke out against Deng's policies and 'intruded into political affairs'.[61] The locus of this group was the PLA General Political Department, and the 'ringleader' was thought to be Ye Jianying, an 'archetype of the soldier-politician whose concerns embraced both military and national affairs'.[62]

The power struggle between Deng and the 'Old Guard' was not as confrontational as that between Deng and Hua, but was considerably more complex. While PLA leaders were not contenders for power in the sense of having leadership positions like the Hua group, they were nevertheless keen to influence policy. Furthermore, the prestige they still held meant that Deng had to be careful to take their views into account to at least some extent.[63] Deng was criticised for emphasising 'pragmatism over ideology' (seen as harmful to troop discipline and morale), for reducing the role and prestige of the PLA, and for the personnel reforms (because they forced retirements and limited prospects for promotion).[64] In addition, Teiwes points out that the PLA leadership criticised some of the non-military reforms because they had implications for army prestige (liberalisation in society damaged the army's social prestige), or affected soldiers' relatives (for example, agricultural policies).[65]

The power struggle between Deng and his critics did not manifest itself in open conflict, and perhaps the term 'power struggle' overstates the friction between the two groups. Teiwes, for example, sees the PLA leaders as 'a pressure group concerned with the PLA's institutional interests' who did not interfere in economic policymaking, but did raise objections to ideological and political changes if they were seen as detrimental to their (and society's) interests.[66] In fact, the relationship was marked by a certain amount of compromise and flexibility in their dealings with one another and the common concern for maintaining loyalty from the PLA and political stability and unity in the country.[67] In many ways the relationship was mutually supportive. For example, Deng was protected by members of the 'Old Guard' when he was blamed for the 1976 Tiananmen Square Incident[68] by the Gang of Four, and they helped him in his return to power in 1977. Deng also relied on at least their tacit consent in the removal of Hua Guofeng from key posts in 1980, even though they were formerly Hua's allies.[69] In return, Deng made certain concessions to ease disapproval of his policies and minimise the resistance he faced from these more traditional elements of the PLA.

The importance of their continued support for Deng after 1980 could be seen in Deng's accommodation of the 'Old Guard's' views, which Joffe sees as 'marginal concessions and tactical retreats'.[70] Deng's harder ideological line announced at the end of 1980 is thought to have appeased some of Deng's military critics who felt that ideology was lacking in Deng's policies. In the same year the Party's evaluation of Mao Zedong and the Cultural Revolution (Resolution on CPC History) [71] did not condemn the PLA's actions which were described as having some 'negative consequences' but were 'absolutely necessary'. Finally, in 1981 Deng and Hu Yaobang endorsed the PLA General Political Department's attack on 'bourgeois liberalisation' in literature and art (even though the GPD's criticism also appeared to challenge Deng and Hu's 'soft' attitude towards intellectuals).[72]

Joffe argues that while the 'Old Guard' was a force to be reckoned with during Deng's rise to power, after 1982 their influence was dwindling.[73] Thus the conflict that occurred in 1982 between Deng and the 'Old Guard' must be seen as the culmination of the power struggle between the two factions. This may help to explain in part Deng's motives during the Textbook Issue, and will be discussed in more detail in Chapter 6.

The final major problem facing Deng's reform programme in the early 1980s came not from within the party and army, but from other elements of Chinese society, most notably Chinese youth and intellectuals. The de-emphasis of Mao Zedong Thought and Marxist-Leninist ideology, and the emphasis on a 'consumer culture', had led to the development of a new 'ideology', materialism. For those who did not benefit from the economic reforms, such problems as unemployment brought disillusionment with the system. Increases in crime and juvenile delinquency became causes for Party concern. Dittmer cites the results of an opinion poll conducted at Fudan University in the early 1980s where 'nearly as many students said they believed in nothing at all as said they believed in socialism'.[74] Other opinion polls pointed to young people's lack of faith in the 'superiority of the socialist system', in the success of the Four Modernisations and in 'revolutionary ideals'. Beijing University students listed the most serious problems for Chinese youth as a 'crisis of confidence', 'unemployment' and a 'lack of future prospects'.[75]

There was discontent not only among the Chinese youth, but also among intellectuals[76] who had been encouraged to express themselves freely in the late 1970s, only to have the privilege removed shortly after. Deng had called for a 'liberation of thinking', or 'emancipation of the mind' since this was seen as 'the key to restoring the morale and dynamism of the Chinese people after the experiences of the Cultural Revolution'.[77] In 1978 Deng had even given his blessing to the big-character posters appearing on 'Democracy Wall'. But once 'Democracy Wall' became the outlet for those highly critical of the leadership and their reforms, Deng immediately placed limitations on the extent of 'liberation' by imposing the 'Four Basic Principles'.[78]

For Deng, these problems were the potential source of domestic discord and disorder, and questioned his legitimacy. The growing lack of respect for authority could be seen in old and young, 'literati' and workers alike.[79] To prevent this pernicious trend from developing further, the leadership saw the need for a re-emphasis on ideology. In other words, the pendulum that had swung in favour of 'expertise' with the reforms of the mid-to-late 1970s was beginning to swing back to an emphasis on 'red' ideology by the 1980s. The crackdown on the fledgling democracy movement began in spring 1979 when the leadership adjusted the short-lived concept of 'liberation of thinking' in favour of a more centrally-guided approach. In his speech about 'Problems on the Ideological Front', Deng said:

> Some young people are discontented with certain social conditions today. There is nothing strange about this and it is nothing to be afraid of. But we must guide such young people or they may go astray. It is good that many young writers have emerged in recent years. They have written a number of fine works. But we must admit that among them . . . there are also bad tendencies that have an adverse influence on some young readers, listeners and viewers.[80]

Re-emphasis of the importance of socialist ideology began in earnest towards the end of 1980 with calls for socialist spiritual civilisation. These were followed by the campaign against 'bourgeois liberalisation' which continued until early 1984, culminating finally in the campaign against 'spiritual pollution'.[81] Initially the calls for a return to socialist ideology had come from critics of Deng's reforms, notably Hua Guofeng and those in the PLA who, as noted above, felt that Deng's pragmatist views had veered too far away from Maoist and socialist ideological principles. Ye Jianying talked of the need for spiritual civilisation, in a speech given in 1979 to commemorate the thirtieth anniversary of the founding of the People's Republic.[82] In April 1980, Hua Guofeng, addressing a PLA work conference in an attempt to mount a counter-offensive against Deng, criticised the reforms for placing too much emphasis on economic means. He called on the PLA to ' "promote proletarian ideology and eliminate bourgeois ideology" and to achieve a high level of "spiritual civilisation", unity, and discipline'.[83] Hua's speech left him open to attack from Deng, who later criticised Hua for violating Party discipline by criticising approved policy. Deng, however, did not object to the PLA using the slogans of bourgeois ideology and spiritual civilisation for educational purposes. Indeed, in 1981 Deng 'accorded the PLA a role as national model for the new morality.'[84]

By December 1980 Deng incorporated the concept of socialist spiritual civilisation into his own agenda, providing the 'first authoritative exposition' of the concept:

> The socialist China we are building should have a civilization with a high cultural and ideological level as well as a high material level.

When I speak of a civilization with a high cultural and ideological level, I refer not only to education, science and culture . . . but also to communist thinking, ideals, beliefs, morality and discipline, as well as a revolutionary stand and revolutionary principles, comradely relations among people, and so on.[85]

In the same speech, Deng stressed the need to 'oppose the tendency to worship capitalism and to advocate bourgeois liberalization', and instead to 'encourage patriotism and a sense of national dignity and self-confidence'. He talked of strengthening education in politics, ideology and moral values so that young people would be 'imbued with high ideals and moral integrity, . . . armed with knowledge, . . . physically fit' with good habits, such as 'respecting discipline, observing food manners and safeguarding public interest'.[86]

Thus with the leadership worried about the state of Chinese youth and their lack of knowledge about the history of the Party and army,[87] the Party was called upon in 1981 to develop a sense of 'spiritual civilisation' among young people. The PLA's General Political Department used the slogan of 'four haves, three stresses, and two defy's' in its efforts in 'Strengthening Youth Work in the Army',[88] and stepped up its campaign against 'bourgeois liberalisation' in the first half of 1981.[89] The socialist spiritual civilisation campaign continued throughout 1981, reaching a pinnacle in September 1982 with Hu Yaobang's lengthy and authoritative treatment of the subject in his report to the Twelfth Party Congress. The development of the campaign in 1982 helps to explain some of the events of the Textbook Issue and will be returned to in Chapter 6.

Summary

Pollack talks of a rise in national self-confidence in advanced industrial states in the early 1980s which manifested itself in political, economic and military terms. This could be seen in the adoption of 'narrowly nationalistic' and protectionist policies, for example, US protectionist policies in response to trade imbalances with Japan, and US calls for more burden-sharing amongst NATO countries.[90] Reagan's 'determination to boost American pride and self-confidence' could be seen in his attempts to restore the USA to its position at the top of the world's hierarchy.[91] As suggested in this chapter, similar trends could be discerned in Japan and China (despite the latter not being an 'advanced industrial nation') where both governments were actively encouraging patriotism and national self-confidence. This parallel rise in national

78   *Background to the Textbook Issue*

self-confidence in China and Japan is significant because it helps to explain the actions and reactions of both governments in their respective treatment of the Textbook Issue.

The ethos of the 'Socialist Spiritual Civilisation' campaign with its stress on instilling patriotism and high moral values into young people bears a striking resemblance to the contemporaneous movement in Japan, with the LDP calling for changes in education to help impart a 'love of country' (*aikokushugi*) and greater awareness of duty in the Japanese youth. The movement in Japan was part of a broader debate which focused on the question of how Japan could become more integrated in international affairs and play a more powerful role commensurate with its economic status. Similarly, the youth education campaign in China also formed part of a broader trend in China, aimed at socialist modernisation which, if successful would enable China to a play a greater role in international affairs.[92]

By the end of 1982, both China's and Japan's foreign policy goals had changed, which did indeed indicate that both were seeking to play a greater or at least a different role in international affairs. The shift in China's foreign policy goals was officially announced at the Twelfth Party Congress in September. As will be discussed in Chapter 6, under the new 'independent foreign policy of peace', China's aim was to remain 'neutral', non-aligned to either of the superpowers, and in so doing have greater leverage in international affairs.[93] The manner in which this 'independent foreign policy' was articulated and implemented has been described as 'assertive nationalism',[94] with China introducing an 'emotional and hostile tone to relationships which [were] posited as historically and fundamentally antagonistic'.[95] Examples of this assertive nationalism are to be found in China's reactions to foreign actions such as US arms sales to Taiwan and Japanese school textbook revision, and in the negotiations with the British government over Hong Kong.[96] Japan also appeared to be changing its foreign policy stance in the early 1980s in favour of protecting its national interest and moving away from its dependence on the USA.[97] This trend was to develop still further with Nakasone Yasuhiro's emergence as Prime Minister in November 1982 and the articulation of his 'grand vision'. Nakasone advocated an activist foreign policy instead of the reactive policies of his predecessors. He talked of 'settling postwar accounts' and foresaw Japan as a global leader by virtue of its economic, scientific and technological skills.[98] Although many of Nakasone's grand plans were never fully realised, his appeal lay in his ability to capture the prevailing mood of self-confidence in Japan. While Japan's new foreign policy cannot be described in the same terms as China's 'assertive nationalism' with its 'emotional and hostile overtones', it nonetheless represented a shift towards a *more* assertive stance than in the past.[99]

Viewed in this way, the trends and general mood in both Chinese and Japanese domestic and foreign politics in the early 1980s suggest that an emotive issue concerning different interpretations of history (i.e. the Textbook Issue) was bound to develop (or be easily developed) into an issue concerning not just history books but other, apparently unrelated, factors. This is not to say that the Textbook Issue could have been predicted or even prevented, but by placing it in the broader context of general 'ideological' and political trends in China and Japan, then the actions and reactions of both governments and people are better understood.

5 The Textbook Issue
Outline of events

This chapter will follow the events of the Textbook Issue describing how it escalated from a Japanese domestic issue to an international controversy, and how it was eventually resolved. The issue can be broken up into distinct stages which correspond to the increasing severity of the problem. Table 5.1 indicates the periodisation and outlines the key events of the issue as it developed from a Japanese domestic problem, to a diplomatic issue between China and Japan, to a diplomatic issue between Japan and Korea, to an Asia-wide/international issue, through a period of negotiations, and finally to the August statement and the settlement of the issue in September.

Stage 1: the Textbook Issue as a domestic problem

Given the trends in Japanese education since 1979 described in Chapter 4, with the LDP's 'Biased Textbooks Campaign' and calls for textbooks with more patriotic content, it is understandable that the Japanese press was keen to cover the results of the 1981–2 textbook screening process when they were made public by the Ministry of Education in June. The textbooks that had undergone authorisation in 1981–2 were language, history, geography, economics and politics, maths, English and science textbooks for primary schools and second/third-year high schools. Of particular interest to the media were the high school social studies textbooks. According to reports on Japanese television and in the press at the end of June, the new textbooks had undergone rigorous authorisation and contained wording which seemed to be reverting to a prewar tone.[1] The subtitles of the *Asahi Shimbun* report of 26 June referred specifically to changes that involved 'a watering down of the term invasion (*shinryaku*)' [2] and of 'honorific language applied to Emperors of the pre-Nara era'.[3]

The *Asahi Shimbun* reported that the tendency towards stricter

Table 5.1 Periodisation and key events in the Textbook Issue

Stage	Date	Event
Stage 1: Domestic issue	26–7 June	Japanese press reports on textbooks reverting to prewar tone.
Stage 2: Bilateral issue	20 July	PRC press campaign begins.
	26 July	PRC lodges formal protest.
	26–9 July	Japanese formulate preliminary response.
	28–9 July	Talks between Japanese and PRC governments.
	1–4 August	PRC retracts invitation to EM Ogawa to visit China in September; press campaign stepped up and 'demands' reiterated.
Stage 3: International issue	3 August	ROK lodges formal protest.
	4 August	Issue becomes 'important problem' for Japanese government.
	5 August	PRC upgrades talks to vice-ministerial level.
	9–12 August	Japanese officials to Beijing; formulation of secondary response.
	12 August	ROK reiterates demands.
	15 August	Chinese press campaign intensifies (anniversary of end of war).
Stage 4: MOE/MFA compromise	17 August	Prime Minister Suzuki 'takes charge'.
	18–23 August	MOE/MFA begin to compromise.
	23–5 August	Japanese officials to ROK.
Stage 5: Settlement	26 August	Japanese government statement.
	27 August	ROK accepts statement 'in principle'.
	28 August	PRC rejects statement.
	2 September	Japanese reiterate commitment to statement but provide additional explanation.
	6–8 September	Further talks with PRC and ROK governments.
	8–9 September	PRC and ROK accept secondary explanations; issue 'temporarily' resolved.

authorisation became evident following the LDP's 'Biased Textbooks Campaign' which resulted in an 'authoritarian tone' appearing in the previous year's social studies textbook *Contemporary Society* (*Gendai Shakai*). The report stated that:

> The Ministry of Education, following on from last year, continues to force deletion or revision of descriptions of such subjects as the Constitution, the Security Treaty, Self Defence Forces, the Northern Territories issue, rights and duties, big business and economics. In addition, this year, in passages concerning the Emperor system, Japanese aggression, and 'criticism of the contemporary system', the strict stance on authorisation is particularly conspicuous, and 'the pre-war'[4] [tone] has re-emerged.[5]

According to textbook authors and editors interviewed by the newspaper, the most problematic textbooks had been *History of Japan*, *World History* and *Politics and Economics*. All the books, according to the newspaper's sources, had been subjected to similar instructions from the Ministry of Education. These instructions were:

1   to water down as much as possible descriptions of Japan's prewar aggressive behaviour;
2   to write about the 'democratic nature' of the Meiji Constitution;
3   to use more honorific expressions when referring to pre-Nara Emperors;
4   to explain that the Self Defence Forces were established according to the SDF Law;
5   to stress Japan's right to possession of the Northern Territories;
6   to stress citizens' duties rather than rights;
7   to stress the contribution of big business [to Japan's development].[6]

Although no authors' names, publishers' names or textbook titles were given, the report listed some of the recommendations made by the Ministry of Education relating to descriptions of Japan's actions during the war in order to illustrate the types of changes in wording, and emphasised the way the wording had been toned down. For example 'invade' (*shinryaku*) had been replaced by 'attack/advance' (*shinkō*); 'tyranny' (*kasei*) by 'oppression' (*assei*); 'oppression' (*danatsu*) by 'suppression' (*chinatsu*); and 'rob' (*shūdatsu*) by 'transfer' (*jōtō*).[7]

The inside pages of the *Asahi Shimbun* provided more specific examples of how certain passages had been changed as a result of authorisation. These examples concerned references to Japanese Emperors, imperialism, nuclear power plants, citizens' rights and duties, and Japan's aggression. It was the latter category, which contained details of changes to passages about Japan's invasion of China, the Korean Independence movement, the 'Three Alls' policy and forced labour, that was to cause the Chinese and Korean governments to protest. Table 5.2 sets out the 'before' and 'after' versions of the textbooks according to the *Asahi Shimbun*.[8] The other Japanese newspapers carried similar examples from pre- and post-authorisation textbooks and while there was some discrepancy in details, all the newspapers seemed to agree that the most significant change in the textbooks had been the replacement of 'invasion' (*shinryaku*) with 'advance' (*shinshutsu*).

The Chinese Xinhua news agency remarked upon the textbook changes in a bulletin on 29 June entitled 'Japan's Ministry of Education Distorts History in Textbooks'. However, the report merely commented that 'Japanese newspapers are showing deep concern about distortions of history aimed at beautifying Japan's invasion of China',[9] and did not provide any further analysis. Similarly, a short article appeared in the *Renmin Ribao* (based on the Xinhua bulletin) the following day which commented on the recent Japanese press reports and remarked that the Japanese Ministry of Education's distortion of history and beautification of militarist Japan's invasion of China had been criticised by Japanese public opinion. The article cited reports in the *Mainichi* and *Yomiuri* newspapers to show how the Ministry had altered descriptions of the invasion of China, the Nanjing Massacre and the September 18 Incident.[10] The changes according to the *Renmin Ribao* are given in Table 5.3. It is significant that at this stage neither of these reports by Xinhua and *Renmin Ribao* condemned the Japanese Ministry of Education or government for changing the textbooks; they merely reported the Japanese newspaper coverage of the matter in an objective, non-critical manner.

Between 30 June and 20 July there was no further mention of the textbook matter in the Chinese media. However, the 20 July issue of the *Renmin Ribao* contained an article which condemned the distortion of historical facts in Japanese primary and secondary school textbooks. This 'short commentary' (*duanping*) may be considered the starting point of the media campaign by the PRC against the Japanese government, which then sparked off similar campaigns throughout the region, and developed into what has been described as an 'anti-Japanese movement.'[11]

Before focusing on the events of the Textbook Issue as it developed into a diplomatic incident between China and Japan (Stage 2), it is worth considering the role of the Japanese press in this issue, since as

Table 5.2 Textbook changes according to the *Asahi Shimbun*

	Invasion	Korean independence movement	'Three Alls Policy'
Before authorisation	When Japanese troops invaded North China. . . (*Nihongun ga kahoku o shinryaku suru to*) The all-out invasion of China. . . (*Chūgoku e no zenmen shinryaku*)	Even in Korea which had been placed under strict military rule and where land had been taken away from peasants under the pretext of land survey work, the trend towards independence grew stronger . . . and in Keijo (now Seoul) demonstrations and meetings advocating 'Korean independence' were held and soon spread throughout Korea.	In occupied territory [the Japanese army's] behaviour was tyrannical and exploitative, and [the army] was subjected to criticism for the so-called 'Three Alls Policy' [carried out] on the China front.
After authorisation	When Japanese troops advanced into North China. . . (*Nihongun ga kahoku ni shinshutsu suru to*) The full-scale attack on China (*Chūgoku e no zenmen shinkō*)	Even in Korea which had been placed under the rule of the sabre and where many peasants had lost their right to land as a result of land survey work, the trend towards independence grew stronger, and in Keijo (now Seoul) meetings proclaiming Korean independence were held, and demonstrations and riots spread throughout Korea.	In occupied territory [the Japanese army] practised tyranny and plunder. In opposition to Japan's brutal rule, anti-Japanese resistance movements spread in occupied territories, and the Japanese army was hard pressed to maintain the peace.

Source: *Asahi Shimbun* 26 June 1982, 22.

Table 5.3 Textbook changes according to the *Renmin Ribao*

	Nanjing Massacre	Invasion	The 18 September Incident
Before	When Nanjing was occupied, the Japanese troops killed and committed rape and arson. This Nanjing Massacre received international condemnation. It is said that the number of Chinese sacrificed at Nanjing exceeded two hundred thousand.	The invasion of North China (*qinlüe*). The all-out invasion of China (*qinlüe*).	No examples given.
After	'Rape', 'plunder' and 'arson' deleted; number of deaths deleted; cause of the Nanjing massacre: 'The incident began because the fierce resistance of the Chinese troops incurred huge losses of Japanese troops which caused the Japanese troops to kill many Chinese troops.'	The advance into North China (*jinchu*). The all-out attack on China (*jingong*).	[Japanese troops] blew up the South Manchurian Railway.

Source: *Renmin Ribao* 30 June 1982, 6.

noted in Chapter 1, it was due to erroneous reporting from the Japanese press clubs that the alleged changes to the textbooks were first brought to the attention of the Japanese, then the foreign, public. The next section will therefore examine how the press came to make the errors and how they influenced ensuing events.

Role of the Japanese press

Given the trends in education since 1979, the 'nationalisation' of the textbook problem, and Education Minister Tanaka's 'request' of 1981 to make textbooks more patriotic, it is understandable that the press would cover the results of the 1981–2 textbook authorisation process. When it was discovered that the Japanese press was to blame for sparking off the diplomatic incident, general interest and current affairs journals were soon filled with polemics on the appalling state of Japanese journalism.[12] Yet the fact that the incident was initiated 'by mistake' went largely unnoticed outside Japan. The Chinese press, understandably, made no reference whatsoever to the erroneous reportage, but neither did the Asian or Western press which came down equally hard on the Japanese Ministry of Education. Accounts of the Textbook Issue written in subsequent years have also tended to play down the fact that the whole incident was sparked off by inaccurate reporting, or have otherwise completely overlooked it.

The newspapers that printed reports about the Ministry of Education requesting authors to change *shinryaku* to *shinshutsu* in relation to Japan's war in China were those whose journalists were members of the Ministry of Education Press Club (*Monbu Kisha Kurabu*). The press clubs are associations of reporters assigned to ministries, political parties, courts, economic associations, labour unions or any such institution which the Japanese press regards as sources of newsworthy information. The size of the club depends on the weight given to that institution by the press; for example, when the LDP was in power, opposition party press clubs were smaller than those clubs associated with the LDP. The press clubs are provided with sometimes vast amounts of information from their respective news sources, in addition to offices, furniture and entertainment facilities. Membership is restricted to reporters of member papers of the *Nihon Shimbunkyōkai* (Association of the Publishers and Editors of Japanese Newspapers). Journalists from magazines and foreign papers are not eligible for membership.[13] The press club reporters do not stay with one club permanently, but are rotated every two or three years to help 'create well-rounded, knowledgeable reporters.'[14] The 'group reporting system' used in the press clubs helps to explain the errors that occurred in the 1982 Textbook Issue reportage since 'most new stories are products of the joint efforts of a number of newsmen.'[15]

In line with standard practice, the Ministry of Education gave the Press Club sample copies of the authorised textbooks just one week before the MOE made the results public itself. Given the large number of texts, the Press Club chose to examine the subjects that had caused problems in previous years and divided them amongst its sixteen members. Each journalist then produced a report on the texts assigned to him and the reports were passed around. In 1982, the Press Club received the texts on 16 June and had to produce reports by the 21 June deadline, two days before the MOE was due to publicise the results. The subjects that the Press Club chose to focus on were history and Japanese language. By drawing straws, the *Asahi Shimbun* reporter was allotted *Kōtō Gakkō Nihonshi* (A History of Japan for High Schools), the *Yomiuri Shimbun* reporter was assigned to *Yōsetsu Nihonshi* (An Outline History of Japan), and the *Nihon Terebi* reporter was given the 'problem' book *Sekaishi* (World History) published by Jikkyō.[16]

Since neither the Ministry nor the textbook companies provided the original manuscripts with which reporters were able to compare the final version, the reporters had to check with individual textbook authors about the type of changes that had been made. The *Nihon Terebi* reporter met with one of the authors of *Sekaishi* (Professor Chizuka Tadayumi), who said that the phrase *Kahoku o shinryaku* (the invasion of North China) had been rewritten to *Kahoku ni shinshutsu* (the advance into North China). It seems then that the Nihon Terebi reporter produced his report on the basis of the interview with Professor Chizuka, and when the other journalists read his report, the *shinryaku–shinshutsu* change caught their eye and became the 'catch-phrase' for the ensuing Textbook Issue. The change in wording was seen by the reporters as representative of the general policy of MOE since the 1960s, and more specifically as a materialisation (*gutaika*) of the MOE's recent strengthening of authorisation standards.[17]

The *Asahi Shimbun* is said to have 'led the pack' in the reporting on the Textbook Issue, followed by *Mainichi Shimbun* and *Tokyo Shimbun*. The *Yomiuri Shimbun* had mixed feelings on the issue, while the *Sankei* and *Nikkei* had reservations.[18] While some of the papers differed on certain details (for example, whether the changes had been carried out according to the MOE's non-compulsory 'suggestions for improvement' (*kaizen iken*) or compulsory 'suggestions for correction' (*shūsei iken*), all agreed on the 'fact' that after authorisation *shinryaku* had become *shinshutsu*. The chart published on 26 June in the *Asahi Shimbun* (reproduced in part above) showed how the (unnamed) authorised text-books compared with the 'original manuscripts' in such subject areas as reference to the Emperor, the Meiji Constitution and the 'invasion' (of China). Particular reference was made to the 'softening' of the word *shinryaku*, which, according to the chart, was replaced by *shinshutsu* in the phrase *Nihongun ga kahoku o shinshutsu suru to* ('when the Japanese army advanced into North China'), and by *shinkō* in the phrase *Chūgoku e no zenmen shinkō* (the all-out attack on China).[19] On the same day, the *Tokyo Shimbun* also referred to the substitution of *shinshutsu* for *shinryaku*, and stated that the phrase *kahoku o shinryaku* was changed by compulsory 'suggestion for correction' to *shinshutsu*. The *Hokkaido Shimbun* even stipulated the name of the textbook and publisher. The *Sankei Shimbun* reported on the 27th that in response to a non-compulsory 'suggestion for improvement' (*kaizen iken*) the publishers had changed *shinryaku* to *shinshutsu*.[20]

However, subsequent investigations carried out by both the Ministry of Education and the press discovered that in fact *shinryaku* had not been changed to *shinshutsu* in connection with Japan's war in China in any of the textbooks authorised *that year*. In fact *shinryaku* appeared in a number of textbooks,[21] while in others the words *shinshutsu* and *shinkō* (attack) had been used in the *original manuscript*.[22] Professor Chizuka also said later that he did not even recall discussing such changes with the Nihon Terebi reporter.[23] Nevertheless, the phrase 'Invade Changed to Advance!' (*shinryaku – shinshutsu ni kakikaesaseta*) became the 'epithet' for the issue and remained firmly in place in the ensuing press coverage, soon to be adopted by the Chinese press also.[24]

By the time the error was discovered, or rather made public, both China and Korea had officially protested and regional anti-Japanese sentiment was high. One commentator ascribes to the faith that the MOE had in the *Asahi Shimbun* the fact that they did not question the original June reports.[25] It seems however that some MOE officials knew of the error from very early on. According to Sugiyama, the Head of the Textbook Authorisation Division (Elementary and Secondary Education Bureau) Fujimura Kazuo was well aware of the discrepancy between the newspaper reports and the 'truth' as early as 10 July, but did not 'go public' at a press conference. Nor, it seems, were the higher echelons in the Ministry notified of the discrepancy until much later. According to the Japan Teachers' Union General Secretary Nakakoji, when Education Minister Ogawa met JTU Chairman Makieda on July 23, Ogawa confirmed the 'fact' that *shinryaku* had been rewritten to *shinshutsu*.[26]

The Ministry of Education's attempts to clarify the situation only worsened matters with the many ambiguous, confusing and sometimes contradictory statements issued by its representatives, and in fact the MOE's 'definitive' response to the charges levelled at it by the Chinese government regarding the changes was not formulated until 9 August (see below). Two key events revealed the 'truth' about the changes that were made to the manuscripts during the screening process, although the statements made by Education Minister Ogawa and Bureau Chief Suzuki at the second of these hardly helped to clear up the situation.

The first 'key' event went some way to shedding light on the alleged *shinryaku–shinshutsu* changes. This was the publication in the *Asahi Shimbun* of 29 July of an article detailing the results of the MOE's investigation, which was to form the basis for explanations to the Chinese government. The results appeared to clarify the situation as far as the use of *shinryaku* was concerned, but there was no reference to the other passages which had angered the Chinese government (this was to come in August). The Ministry's investigation revealed that it had looked at three versions of *Nihonshi* and six versions of *Sekaishi* whose manuscripts had contained the term *shinryaku* relating to the Sino-Japanese war. There were fourteen references to *shinryaku* in total in the original manuscripts. After the MOE made its 'suggestions for improvement' (*kaizen iken*), *shinryaku* was deleted or changed in four of the fourteen places as follows, but in the other ten places the wording remained unchanged:

1   A title, *Japan's Invasion of China* (*Nihon no chūgoku shinryaku*), was changed to *The Manchurian and Shanghai Incidents* (*Manshu Jihen/Shanhai Jihen*).
2   The phrase 'The fifteen year war that started with the invasion of Manchuria . . . ' became simply 'The war . . . '.
3   A caption under a map 'Japan's invasion of China' (*Nihon no chūgoku shinryaku*) became 'Japan's encroachment into/invasion of China' (*Nihon no chūgoku shinnyū*).
4   'Mao Zedong . . . fought against Japan's invasion' (*Mō Takutō wa . . . Nihon no shinryaku to tatakau*) was changed to 'Mao Zedong . . . fought against Japan's attack' (*Mō Takutō wa . . . Nihon no shinkō to tatakau*).[27]

So the investigation showed that there had been no substitution of *shinshutsu* for *shinryaku* as the newspapers had claimed, although *shinryaku* had been replaced by *shinnyū* in one place, which can be translated, like *shinryaku*, as invasion, aggression or encroachment. In the ten places where the Ministry of Education had made 'suggestions for improvement', the editors/authors had chosen not to change the wording, leaving *shinryaku* in the text. Many newspapers played down the announcement of the MOE's investigation results, and in some cases even failed to acknowledge it. The *Asahi Shimbun* article from which the above quotes are taken appeared on page 22, while the leading article on the front page was devoted to coverage of the first round of talks between Japan and the PRC. Significantly, the content of the explanations were not covered in great detail, and the results of the MOE's investigation were not referred to at all.[28]

Moreover, it appears that some of the newspapers (the *Asahi Shimbun* at least) were aware of the 'facts' *even before* the MOE's revelations of 29 July that there had been no *shinryaku–shinshutsu* change, yet were careful not to expose their error in too blatant a fashion. Only those readers taking a particularly keen interest would have noticed the slight difference in wording used in, for example, the 27 July issue of the *Asahi Shimbun*. This edition showed a chart of pre- and post-authorisation passages from textbooks, similar to the one in the 26 June issue. This time there were sections relating to the Nanjing Massacre, Korean Independence Movement, forced labour, 'Manchukuo' and 'invasion'. In the latter section, there were no longer any examples of *shinryaku* being changed to *shinshutsu* or *shinkō* as there had been in the 26 June issue. In fact, the only example that was cited of *shinryaku* being changed at all (rather than deleted) was to *shinnyū*, which was in fact one of the changes the MOE admitted to making when it announced the results of its internal investigation on 29 July.[29]

The second 'key' event, the Upper House Education Committee meeting of 29 July, could have been used as an opportunity to deny the allegations made in the Japanese press and in the Chinese representation. Instead, Education Minister Ogawa and Bureau Chief Suzuki only managed to muddy the waters, merely hinting that, according to its investigations, the MOE had found no proof that the alleged changes had been made. Ogawa began by explaining the Ministry's preference of the use of 'advance':

> It is desirable for history textbooks to use unified and objective terms. 'Advance' was used for the Powers (other than Japan), while 'aggression'[invade] was used for Japan. Therefore, we said that 'if the terms are to be unified, advance is objective', and the writers of the textbooks accepted this. We have not the least intention of falsifying historical facts or of reviving militarism.[30]

Thus Ogawa seemed to be admitting to the press allegations that 'invade' had been changed to 'advance'. He then pointed out, however, that not all the recently authorised Japanese history and world history textbooks had changed the wording from 'invasion' in accordance with the TARC's non-compulsory 'suggestion for improvement' (*kaizen iken*). So, although Ogawa admitted that the Ministry had *recommended* that 'invasion' be changed, he failed to clarify what had actually replaced the term in the books that had complied with the *kaizen iken*. He seemed to imply that 'advance' (*shinshutsu*) had been used, but maintained that even where 'advance' was used it was clear from the context 'that it was a war which was waged by Japan against China and that it was an unjustifiable war'.[31]

Bureau Chief Suzuki's statements were equally confusing. He began the meeting by saying:

> In historical facts, there are cases which are assessed as invasion, and cases which are not, and because it was thought that advance (*shinshutsu*) or incursion (*shinkō*) might be more suitable, the descriptions were revised.[32]

Thus he also seemed to be implying that revisions had been made to the textbooks just as the press reports had stated. Yet later on in the meeting he said that 'the MOE's investigations so far have not discovered any examples where invasion was changed to advance'.[33]

Finally, Ogawa confused matters still further by stating that because the textbooks in question were already on display as samples, and soon to be adopted as textbooks, then 'the present stage is not the time for discussing whether they are to be corrected or not.'[34] So despite what Suzuki had said about there being no revisions of 'invasion' into 'advance', Ogawa still implied that there were some textbooks that needed correcting at some point in the future.

In contrast to some of the other newspapers, while its coverage of the MOE's investigation results had been sketchy, the *Asahi Shimbun* did actually carry a report on this Education Committee meeting in its 30 July issues with an outline of the main points raised at the meeting, one of which was Bureau Chief Suzuki's assertion that:

> as the investigations carried out so far have shown, there are no examples of *shinryaku* being changed to *shinshutsu* in this year's screening process, although in 1978 a change was made to the contents page of one version of *Sekaishi* in accordance with a Ministry-imposed *shūsei iken*. Since then however, *shūsei iken* have not been applied [to the word *shinryaku*], only *kaizen iken*.[35]

Despite this, the *Asahi Shimbun* was still careful not to admit or acknowledge that the earlier articles which had alleged that *shinryaku* had been changed to *shinshutsu* had been incorrect. Furthermore, despite being aware of the error at the end of July, the *Asahi Shimbun* continued to refer to *shinryaku–shinshutsu* changes[36] and it took a further month for the newspaper to report the results of its own investigation, a report which still did not admit that mistakes had been made in the early reports, but merely 'confirmed' that the Ministry of Education's investigation had been correct.[37] Other newspapers also continued to overlook the error. The editorial in the 5 August *Mainichi Shimbun*, for example, still contained references to 'the textbook authorisation system which has forced "the invasion of China" to be rewritten to "advance" '.[38]

It should be noted, however, that not all the newspapers were guilty of such misreporting. The *Sankei Shimbun* carried an article in its 28 July issue stating that some textbooks had already contained the problem words *shinshutsu* and *shinkō* prior to screening, and that it seemed that China had 'misunderstood' because of the misleading reports in some Japanese newspapers.[39] The 6 August *Sekai Nippō* (World Daily) contained a chart of pre-authorisation and post-authorisation changes this time supplying the names of the textbooks and publishers, and making clear that some textbooks had contained *shinryaku* both before and after screening. The report concluded that Japanese history textbooks were in reality not changing, and that textbook authorisation had not been strengthened.[40]

In September, the weekly journal *Shūkan Bunshun* exposed the newspapers' erroneous reporting, and some of the October and November current affairs journals criticised the mass media for its 'false reporting' (*gohō*) and for sparking off a diplomatic issue.[41] The *Sankei Shimbun* was the first newspaper to acknowledge the error and it 'apologised deeply' to its readers on 7 September. This caused alarm in the Press Club which called an emergency meeting to decide what to do with the 'errant' *Sankei* reporter. A vote was taken to try and oust *Sankei Shimbun* from the club, but the reporter managed to retain his membership. The *Asahi Shimbun*'s explanation of how the errors arose appeared on 19 September in an answer to a reader's letter asking for the truth about the allegations. The *Asahi Shimbun* admitted that the phrases *kahoku ni shinshutsu suru to* and *chūgoku e no zenmen shinkō* had been used in the original manuscript, but the response was carefully worded. There was an apology to readers for making the error (*ayamari o okashita koto ni tsuite wa dokusha ni owabi shinakereba narimasen*); but the readers were asked to consider whether the incorrect reporting of *shinryaku–shinshutsu* could have been the sole reason for Chinese diplomatic protests, since China had also protested about descriptions of the Nanjing Massacre and the Manchurian Incident.[42] Presumably the logic behind the *Asahi Shimbun*'s reasoning here was that because the *Asahi Shimbun* article of 26 June had not contained any reference to how passages about the Nanjing Massacre and Manchurian Incident had been altered, then the Chinese government must have had other grounds for its protest. These grounds were in the form of articles in other newspapers at the end of June which did contain reference to the Nanjing Massacre and Manchurian Incident; a point which the *Asahi Shimbun* overlooked. Indeed, as Xiao Xiangqian commented, China's protest was based solely on consideration of the Japanese press reports.[43] It seems also that the accuracy of reports relating to some of the other changes in wording must be questioned. Indeed, according to Sugiyama, *shinryaku–shinshutsu* was not the only example of false reporting. For example, the reporter in charge of examining the textbook *Shin Nihonshi* published by Daiichi Gakushusha had stated in his report to the Press Club that the Ministry of Education had issued 'strong instructions' that the phrase the Nanjing Massacre (*Nankin Daigyaku-satsu*) be avoided. According to one of the editors of the textbook (Professor Sakamoto of Hiroshima University) there had been no such instruction from MOE.[44]

Nevertheless, for the media, the matter was clearly one of principle; it did not matter that *shinryaku* had not been changed to *shinshutsu that particular year*. Indeed, Sugiyama quotes one (unnamed) reporter who felt 'it wasn't such a big mistake'.[45] The principle of the matter, for the press, was that over the years the Ministry had gradually been strengthening the authorisation process, and had been trying to replace *shinryaku* with *shinshutsu* (advance), *shinkō* (attack/advance) or *shinshutsu* (encroach); all of which have a less aggressive connotation than *shinryaku*.[46] The *Asahi Shimbun* even showed the 'before' and 'after' of a passage on Japan's 1920s policy in Manchuria in a middle school social studies textbook in use in 1982 which 'proved' that the *shinryaku–shinshutsu* change had occurred in previous years' screening.[47] The attitude shown by the press may help to explain why the MOE never pointed out the incorrect reports. The MOE would still have been censured for its stance on textbook authorisation, especially because, regardless of whether the editors or publishers had followed the Ministry's recommendation, *shinryaku* had after all been subjected to a non-compulsory 'suggestion for improvement' *kaizen iken* in the 1981–2 authorisation process.

It had become customary for the newspapers to cover the results of textbook authorisation, particularly since the 1980 'Biased Textbook Campaign' had brought the issue of textbook content into the open. The determination of some papers to expose the MOE's attempts to strengthen the textbook authorisation system led to 'sensational but inaccurate' reporting which clearly formed the basis of China's diplomatic protest. Furthermore, by continuing to give the 'mistaken impression that the word changes represented a major departure from past policy and practice', the press exacerbated and perpetuated the situation.[48] The Chinese media relied heavily on Japanese press coverage to fuel its anti-Japanese campaign, and the question remains as to whether the Chinese and Korean governments would have made official protests, or at least kept up their press campaigns for such a long time, had the Japanese media not made this 'blooper'.[49] Some observers thought it more than coincidental that very shortly after the *Shūkan Bunshun* published its 'revelation' in early September, the PRC – with its basis for the campaign now gone – decided to accept the Japanese government's measures and consider the matter resolved.[50]

Stage 2: bilateral issue

As described above, by the time the error was made public, the Textbook Issue had already developed into a diplomatic incident. The way in which this happened is described in this section which outlines the beginnings of what can be seen as an officially directed Chinese press campaign (to be discussed in more detail in Chapter 6), the actions of the Chinese and Korean governments, and the preliminary responses of the Japanese government.

China's diplomatic protest

The 20 July *Renmin Ribao* article, entitled 'We Must Bear in Mind This Lesson', began the two-month press campaign in China. It explained how certain words and phrases in passages describing the events of the Sino-Japanese war had been exchanged for euphemistic terminology which served to 'blur Japan's war responsibility' (*Renmin Ribao* quoting unnamed Japanese newspaper). According to the article, Japan's Ministry of Education had ordered that passages relating to the Nanjing Massacre be reworded, with the result that the responsibility for the killings lay with the Chinese army due to its 'tenacious resistance' to the Japanese army. It also mentioned the passages relating to the Japanese army's 'invasion into North China' and 'full-scale attack on China',[51] and the 'September 18 Incident'[52] which was described merely as a 'bombing of the South Manchurian railway by the Japanese army'. The report warned about the possibility that some Japanese people were 'cherishing the spirit of Japanese militarism'.[53]

On 23 July, *Renmin Ribao* carried reports concerning statements made by PRC mass organisations such as the China–Japan Friendship Association, the China Education Society, the All-China Youth Federation and the All-China Student Federation, all of whom expressed 'extreme dissatisfaction' and 'indignation' at the distortion of Japan's history of aggression against China, and called for Japan's Ministry of Education to correct the textbooks. In addition, the major Beijing newspapers – *Guangming Ribao*, *Jiefangjunbao*, *Gongren Ribao* and *Zhongguo Qingnianbao* – all contained articles protesting against Monbusho's 'distortion of historical facts.'[54]

An article in the *Renmin Ribao* on 24 July ('History of Japanese Aggression Against China Can Never Be Distorted') continued to condemn the distortion of history in Japanese textbooks. Furthermore, the article also referred to comments made by some Japanese politicians who had said that changing the content of textbooks (in response to Chinese criticisms) would be 'intervention in Japan's domestic affairs'. The *Renmin Ribao* stated that the distortion of the history of Japanese aggression could not be considered an internal affair, and claimed that changing the word 'invasion' (Chinese, *qinlüe*; Japanese, *shinryaku*) to 'advance' (*jinchu*, *shinshutsu*), and describing the Nanjing Massacre as an event resulting from the 'stubborn resistance of the Chinese army' was an attempt 'not only to mislead the younger generation of Japan but also to bring great humiliation upon the Chinese people'.[55]

Although the names of the Japanese politicians were not given, it is likely that the article was referring to comments made on 23 July by Education Minister Ogawa Heiji and the Director General of the National Land Agency, Matsuno Yukiyasu. Ogawa was alleged to have said during a meeting with Japan Teachers' Union Chairman Makieda Motofumi that he regarded the matter as an internal problem, not a diplomatic one.[56] Director General Matsuno had said that 'the South Korean requests regarding the content of passages in textbooks, depending on the situation, could become interference in domestic affairs'.[57] Similar comments by prominent LDP politicians were to continue to provoke angry responses by the Chinese and Korean governments and media throughout the duration of the Textbook Issue.

South Korea was not too far behind China in its response to the issue. Japanese newspapers reported on 21 July that the South Korean press had begun to criticise the content of Japanese high school textbooks, in particular the 'rationalisation of [Japan's] imperialist and colonialist past' and the 'beautification and falsification of history'. The Korean newspapers called for 'correction through diplomatic routes' and for 'joint efforts of both countries to revise the textbooks'.[58] On 25 July, perhaps prompted by Ogawa's and Matsuno's remarks, the ROK government took action by instructing its embassy in Tokyo to investigate the matter, and announced that action would be taken later to urge Japan to take 'corrective measures'.[59]

The Textbook Issue became a diplomatic issue between the Japanese and Chinese governments (at least as far as the PRC was concerned) on 26 July when Xiao Xiangqian, Director of the Chinese Foreign Ministry's First Asian Affairs Department, met with Watanabe Kōji, Minister at the Japanese Embassy in Beijing. Xiao stated that the attitude of Japan's Ministry of Education in its screening of this batch of textbooks 'makes one suspicious of their true intentions.' He regarded the actions of the MOE in changing Japan's history of the invasion of China as a distortion of historical facts to which the Chinese government could not agree. Furthermore, Xiao stated that:

> In view of the fact that this incident represents a departure from the spirit of the Joint Statement and Treaty of Peace and Friendship, is detrimental to the consolidation and development of peace and friendship between the two countries, and hurts the feelings of the Chinese people, the Chinese government can not but express extreme concern.[60]

Xiao then demanded that the Japanese government rectify the errors in the textbooks, referring in particular to the passage that replaced the 'invasion of North China' with 'advance into North China'; to the exchange of 'all-out invasion of China' for 'all-out advance into China'; and to the passage that attributed the Nanjing Massacre to the 'stubborn resistance of Chinese troops'.[61]

Japan's preliminary response

In response to China's representation, the Ministry of Education held a joint conference with the Ministry of Foreign Affairs on the same day (26 July), after which Education Minister Ogawa was quoted as saying that 'as might be expected, although we do not intend to change the textbook authorisation policies, we will explain our true intentions and resolve both countries' [Chinese and South Korean] misunderstandings.'[62] The first official statement from the MOE was issued by Elementary and Secondary Education Bureau Chief Suzuki Isao, who said 'the Japanese government will listen humbly to Chinese opinion and would like to explain the situation fully'.[63]

It is interesting to note that at this point, the Japanese government was treating the 'textbook problem' not as a diplomatic matter, but as 'a purely domestic educational matter',[64] and moreover, Prime Minister Suzuki was keen to ensure that it did not develop into a diplomatic problem.[65] The Ministry of Education was therefore entrusted with handling the matter, with the Ministry of Foreign Affairs being used as a channel of communication with the Chinese government.

On 27 July the Textbook Issue became the subject for discussion at a number of Japanese governmental meetings. After talks between Prime Minister Suzuki, Education Minister Ogawa and Chief Cabinet Secretary Miyazawa Kiichi in the morning, and later a joint MFA–MOE meeting, the decision was taken to explain the Japanese position through diplomatic routes.[66] However, the government was by no means united on how to handle the issue. Education Minister Ogawa indicated at a Cabinet meeting on 27 July that his Ministry, though willing to listen to Chinese protests and explain the system of textbook authorisation, was not willing to change the 'results of the examination and approval [process], because of a protest from another country.'[67] The Ministry of Foreign Affairs view was different, however; MFA leaders were reported as saying on the 26th that 'it is fundamental that our country deeply reproaches itself for its past history, and has restored relations with China and Korea. . . . As for the expressions causing the problem, the truth must be described as the truth.'[68]

The *Asahi Shimbun* took this as an indirect expression of the MFA's doubts about the changes to historical facts brought about by the MOE's strengthening of textbook authorisation.[69] Moreover, according to a Korean press report of 28 July, it seemed that the MFA was in favour of correcting the textbooks in line with China's request, since the MFA had expressed its willingness to the Korean Embassy to recommend correction of the textbooks to the Ministry of Education.[70]

The contrast between the MOE's reluctance to do anything but 'listen and explain' and the MFA's apparent willingness to see the textbooks corrected represented the earliest indication of an emerging conflict of opinions between the two ministries on how to deal with the textbook problem. Yet whatever MFA spokesmen were saying to their Korean counterparts or alluding to in press conferences, the official position of the MFA had yet to be clarified. One of the main worries within the MFA was whether the passages in the textbooks did in fact represent a violation of the Sino-Japanese Joint Statement and Treaty of Peace and Friendship as the Chinese government claimed. The MFA was also worried that the Textbook Issue was not just a historical issue, but reflected a general adverse trend in Chinese and Korean policies and postures towards Japan. There was also the view within the MFA that the international situation surrounding Sino-Japanese bilateral relations should be taken into account, in particular China's cautiousness about recent regional trends such as US arms sales to Taiwan and Japan's Esaki trade mission to Taiwan (see Chapter 6).[71] Nonetheless, the MFA was in no position to comment on how the MOE should handle the problem. Foreign ministry leaders admitted that there was nothing they could do since textbook authorisation was within the jurisdiction of the MOE, and the matter had, after all, been entrusted solely to the MOE.[72] In fact, oddly, the MFA even appeared to support (albeit briefly) the MOE's stance when, at a Foreign Affairs Committee meeting in the Lower House on 30 July, Chief Cabinet Secretary Miyazawa Kiichi (in his capacity as acting Foreign Minister) echoed the MOE's view that 'textbooks are basically produced by the private sector' and stated that requests for revision of the problem passages could not be responded to.[73]

In stark contrast to the initial responses of both the MOE and the MFA, some Liberal Democratic Party dietmen were quick to express their outright rejection of Chinese and Korean requests as interference in domestic affairs. Three dietmen in particular voiced such opinions during the cabinet meeting of the 27th. Director General Matsuno Yukiyasu, who had already incurred the anger of the Chinese government with his earlier remarks, was joined by Director General of the Science and Technology Agency Nakagawa Ichirō, and Minister for Posts and Telecommunications Minowa Noboru, in criticism of China's requests. Matsuno was quoted as saying that 'changing the wording in textbooks according to a foreign request is interference in Japan's domestic affairs. To change advance into invade would be a distortion of facts and children would lose respect for their forefathers.'[74]

Minowa said that changing 'invade' into 'advance' could not be called a distortion of history, and Nakagawa queried why there was 'so much dissatisfaction about some slight change in wording about historical facts'.[75] At a press conference after the Cabinet meeting, Matsuno was also quoted as saying that:

> At the time that Japan advanced into China, it had the view that the whole nation was united into one, and no-one thought of it as aggression. It should be set forth, specifically, that we did not think of it as aggression in the past, and that today, it is the same way.[76]

This opinion was probably widespread in the LDP, as Chapter 7 will elucidate, but could clearly not be seen to be the 'official' line and was criticised by other less hawkish LDP dietmen and bureaucrats. Miyazawa made it clear that the opinions expressed by Matsuno, Nakagawa and Minowa were the personal views of individual cabinet ministers, and they did not represent the government view as expressed to China.[77] Education Minister Ogawa also expressed the view that it was not desirable to take such a 'high-handed attitude', and MFA Asian

Affairs Bureau Councillor Hasegawa argued that the requests did not constitute interference in domestic matters because China was not seeking corrections compulsorily.[78]

Nonetheless, the Chinese press picked up on Matsuno's comments and those of other 'certain high-level officials' in a short commentary on 30 July, which criticised the politicians for 'spouting empty rhetoric and vigorously defending the Japanese Ministry of Education's conduct of beautifying militarism.'[79] Referring specifically to Matsuno's remarks, the article commented that:

> The handful of Japanese militarists who invaded China did not represent the Japanese people or their forefathers. How can it not be a good thing to let Japanese children know that there was a handful of scum among their forefathers who plunged the Japanese people and the people of neighbouring countries into catastrophe, and thereby help the children to draw a lesson and make them more vigilant.[80]

On 28 July, Minister Watanabe Kōji met with Director Xiao Xiangqian in Beijing to officially explain the Japanese government's stance. Watanabe stated that the Japanese government's view concerning the war, as made clear in the preamble to the Sino-Japanese Joint Statement, had not changed in the slightest; that although this awareness was reflected in school education, the Japanese government humbly acknowledged the Chinese government's representation on the matter; and that Japan's textbook screening system would be explained fully to Chinese Embassy representatives in Japan.[81] Both Prime Minister Suzuki and Chief Cabinet Secretary Miyazawa also stated on 28 July that the Japanese government would like to explain its position and was willing to do so in a couple of days.[82]

In fact, explanations were carried out the following day when Bureau Chief Suzuki Isao met with Chinese Ambassador to Japan, Wang Xiaoyun. Suzuki first expressed regret over the misunderstanding caused by descriptions in Japanese textbooks, but reassured the Ambassador that the books did contain information on the Joint Statement, the Treaty of Peace and Friendship, and on the damage inflicted on China by Japan. But Suzuki went on to stress that 'textbooks are produced based on private initiative, and government participation is limited.'[83] The explanation of the textbook authorisation system which was to anger the Chinese government was as follows:

> Japan's textbook authorisation system is limited to checking privately written and edited manuscripts for their suitability as text-

books; the opinions given by the government during screening are for reference, and specific action is entrusted to authors; the problematic term 'invasion' (*shinryaku*) was changed to another expression as a result of this screening system.[84]

In response, Wang Xiaoyun immediately expressed his personal disapproval of the explanation, saying that in his view the revisions to the textbooks had been based on governmental direction, and the screening system opposed the spirit of the Joint Statement and the Treaty. Furthermore, there had been no specific explanation as to *why* 'invasion' (*shinryaku*) had been changed during screening.[85] Suzuki's explanation was regarded by the Chinese government and press as an attempt to shirk responsibility and to pass the blame on to authors and publishers. On the evening of 29 July, Xinhua issued a commentary entitled 'Sincerity Should be Verified by Actions', which called for concrete action such as correction of the sections of the textbooks that hurt the feelings of the Chinese people. It also warned that 'if the Japanese government does not show its sincerity by rewriting the parts that hurt Chinese feelings, then the Chinese people and public opinion will not be able to be silenced'.[86] China's strong disapproval of the Japanese government's first round of explanations was an indication that the Textbook Issue was set to develop further. In addition, the Japanese government's 'wait-and-see' attitude was greeted with increasing criticism at home.[87]

As described earlier, at the meeting of the Upper House Education Committee on July 29, Education Minister Ogawa and Bureau Chief Suzuki Isao were questioned about the changes in wording in history textbooks and attempted to clarify the situation. Yet despite the results of the MOE investigation, which had found *no* examples of 'invasion' (*shinryaku*) being changed to 'advance' (*shinshutsu*) as alleged by the Japanese press and Chinese government, neither Ogawa or Suzuki took the opportunity to set the record straight once and for all, or reprimand the press for printing incorrect information. In fact, as we have seen, their responses seemed somewhat contradictory and only served to confuse the issue even more.

Nonetheless, the question of whether or not there were any textbooks in need of correction quickly disappeared amidst mounting pressure on the government from opposition parties demanding quick action. At a meeting of the Lower House Education Committee on 31 July, opposition parties criticised the government's handling of the issue and the Shakaito (Japan Socialist Party) 'urged' the government to 'amend all the passages in the textbooks in which the word invasion was changed to advance.'[88] On 2 August, representatives of the Kōmeitō (Clean Government Party) demanded that the Japanese government correct the history textbooks in the interest of friendly relations between Japan and China.[89] Public opinion in Japan joined the opposition parties in criticising the government's handling of the matter with protests coming from academics, and religious and cultural groups.[90]

On 1 August, Li Tao, Director of the Chinese Education Ministry's Foreign Affairs Bureau called a meeting with Minister Watanabe Kōji and retracted an invitation to Japanese Education Minister Heiji Ogawa to visit China in early September. In light of Bureau Chief Suzuki's explanation of 29 July, that is, his defence of the content of the textbooks and attempt to shift responsibility on to the publishing companies and non-governmental circles, the Chinese government considered a visit by Ogawa to be 'inappropriate'.[91] Ogawa responded to the retraction at a press conference the following day, agreeing that conditions were not suitable for a visit to China but stating that he wanted to continue to try and reach an understanding with the Chinese government. He also stated that the Ministry of Education had no intention of shifting responsibility on to the private sector but if that was the Chinese understanding of the MOE's explanation, then there was still room for further explanations. He said he hoped that the issue could be resolved by September, that is, before Prime Minister Suzuki's planned visit to China, and would do all in his power to that end.[92]

In the meantime the Chinese press and media had stepped up criticism of the Japanese government and its handling of the matter. Descriptions of the Sino-Japanese war and the actions of Japanese troops began to appear, and the trends in Japanese textbooks began to be seen in a broader context as evidence of a revival of militarism in Japan. A report issued by Zhongguo Xinwen She on 31 July warned that the Japanese Ministry of Education's tampering with history represented an attempt by some people in Japan to revive militarism and the 'old dream . . . of the "Greater East Asia Co-prosperity Sphere" '.[93] An article in the *Renmin Ribao* of 1 August, entitled 'It is Better to Be Honest', criticised the MOE's explanation, and a television programme shown in China on the same day to celebrate Army Foundation Day described atrocities committed by Japanese troops during the War of Resistance.[94] Photographs depicting Japanese cruelty during the Nanjing Massacre appeared in the *Renmin Ribao* and *Guangming Ribao* on 2 August, and the *Renmin Ribao* also carried reports on the reaction of Japanese opposition parties, religious groups and academics, on the protests of the Okinawan people over the Textbook Issue, and on articles in Korean, Hong Kong and Southeast Asian newspapers, all of which joined the PRC in denouncing the Japanese government's attitude.[95] The *Jiefangjunbao* contained an article in its 2 August edition calling for vigilance over a revival of militarism in Japan, and criticising the remarks made by Director General Matsuno Yukiyasu.[96]

Stage 3: international issue

The problem escalated still further when the South Korean government made its first official protest to the Japanese government on 3 August. The Korean Foreign Minister met with Japanese Ambassador in Seoul, Maeda Toshikazu, and requested that the Japanese high school textbooks be corrected.[97] This was not expected by the Japanese government, which had been assured by Minister Lee Sang Chin of the Korean Embassy during talks with Bureau Chief Suzuki on 30 July that the ROK government wished 'to avoid it developing into a diplomatic problem'.[98] According to the *Asahi Shimbun*, the Korean government had three reasons for wanting to avoid escalation of the issue: firstly, the Korean government did not want to jeopardise economic relations with Japan, especially the $6 billion loan to Korea that the two governments were negotiating; secondly, the Korean government did not want to come to blows with those pro-Korea LDP dietmen who admittedly were against revision of the textbooks, but who were in favour of a Korean 'security pact';[99] and thirdly, the Korean government was worried that the rising anti-Japanese feeling within Korea could develop into anti-government feeling and social unrest. According to the *Asahi Shimbun*, however, the strength of Korean public opinion was such that by the beginning of August the Korean government had no alternative but to lodge a diplomatic protest.[100]

The Korean government's official protest appeared to shock the Japanese government into taking the matter more seriously. In response to Seoul's official protest, Bureau Chief Suzuki issued the routine statement that the government would listen humbly to Korean opinion, and make efforts to reach an understanding. However, a series of meetings of all levels held on 4 and 5 August suggested that the Japanese government (or rather the Prime Minister) now considered the issue to be a 'full-scale diplomatic problem' and was keen to resolve it as quickly as possible.[101]

The Textbook Issue becomes an 'important problem'

The Japanese government acknowledged that it was facing a serious diplomatic problem on August 4 when it announced that its policy in dealing with the Textbook Issue would be based on the principle of reconfirming the spirit of the Joint Statements signed between Japan and China in 1972 and between Japan and South Korea in 1965. Furthermore, Prime Minister Suzuki instructed the Ministry of Foreign Affairs and Ministry of Education to confer on a response to Chinese and Korean diplomatic representations in order to reach an early settlement.[102]

The *Asahi Shimbun* saw these moves as evidence that it would be necessary to solve the issue on the basis of a 'political judgement', that is, with the involvement of top-level decision makers, since dealing with it at an administrative level had not been successful.[103] It is possible also that the moves were taken with the knowledge that the PRC was about to 'upgrade' the issue by involving Chinese Vice-Foreign Minister Wu Xueqian. At his meetings throughout the day with MFA Administrative Vice-Minister of Affairs Sunobe Ryōzō and Asian Affairs Bureau Chief Kiuchi Akitane, the Prime Minister called for a united party and government stance and stated that 'I am thinking of this as an important problem. As a peaceful nation we have worked for friendship with our neighbours. It is not desirable to receive criticisms from our neighbours.'[104]

In spite of this more positive approach, however, the government announced no specific measures, and with a growing difference of opinion between the MOE and MFA, it seemed unlikely that a 'united view' would be quick to emerge from their joint consultations. Problems were compounded when on 5 August, the Chinese government upgraded talks with the Japanese government to Vice-Ministerial level, reconfirming that the Chinese government was also treating the matter as a serious issue, or in their words, 'an important matter of principle in the development of Sino-Japanese relations'.[105] Chinese Vice-Minister of Foreign Affairs Wu Xueqian met with Japanese Ambassador to China KatoriYasue in order to reiterate China's stance on the Textbook Issue. Wu Xueqian's comments represented the Chinese government's 'official response' to Bureau Chief Suzuki's explanations of 29 July, even though Wang Xiaoyun, the Chinese Education Ministry and the Chinese press had already indicated their disapproval. Vice-Minister Wu told Ambassador Yasue that the Chinese government could not help but disagree with the way the Japanese Ministry of Education had attempted to defend the textbook authorisation process and shift the blame. Referring to the comments of 'top-level officials' who had criticised China for interfering in domestic matters, Wu said that the issue could not be called a Japanese domestic problem, because having suffered invasion, China had a legitimate right to express an opinion and demand the correction of errors that falsified the history of that invasion. Wu Xueqian reiterated that the 'Chinese government demands that the Japanese government takes the necessary measures and corrects the errors made by the Ministry of Education in the process of textbook authorisation'.[106]

Japanese government deliberations continued on the 5th with various meetings. The outcome of a meeting of the MOE and MFA Administrative Vice-Ministers (Misumi and Sunobe) on the morning of the 5th only served to confirm the difficulty of finding a solution to which both ministries could agree. The *Asahi Shimbun* reported that while both men had said they agreed that an early settlement was essential, they had not managed to agree on a concrete policy for dealing with the issue and they considered it would be difficult to find a way of 'calming the situation'.[107]

At an Upper House Education Committee meeting, the MOE rejected the possibility of correcting the textbooks by 'revision of error' (*seigo teisei*), the only method available that allowed immediate revision of authorised textbooks that contained incorrect or outdated information. Japan Socialist Party Dietman Kasuya Terumi queried Bureau Chief Suzuki's announcement that the MOE 'could not respond to the requests using the "revision of error" method', especially when in previous years the MOE had used that method to change passages in textbooks relating to the dangers of nuclear power.[108] Suzuki responded that in the case of descriptions about nuclear power the Ministry had not attached any recommendations during authorisation, and it was the textbook authors who applied for 'revision of error' to be carried out after the textbooks had been authorised. The 'revision of errors' method could only be considered then if, firstly, the passages concerned had not been changed as a result of the Ministry's recommendations during authorisation, and secondly, if the authors themselves applied for revision to be carried out. Neither of these was the case in the Textbook Issue.[109] Yet this 'policy' was clearly at odds with previous years' practice when, for example, in 1980 the MOE responded to complaints from the Science and Technology Agency by revising passages on nuclear power using the *seigo teisei* method.[110]

By 5 August the Ministry of Foreign Affairs had abandoned its earlier view that the Textbook Issue was a domestic as opposed to an intergovernmental matter, and was becoming increasingly concerned about the consequences of the Textbook Issue if it was handled incorrectly. Furthermore the MFA became critical of the MOE's handling of the issue. At a parliamentary vice-ministers' meeting for example, MFA Parliamentary Vice-Minister Tsuji Hideo said that the MOE's defence of the problem as an internal matter and explanation that words in textbooks were changed on the basis of private-sector 'intention' (*minkan ishi*) was 'strange'. As the conflict between the two ministries developed, the MFA accused the MOE of taking a narrow view of the issue, while the MOE criticised the MFA for 'fawning upon' foreign governments.[111]

In the evening, Prime Minister Suzuki held talks with Chief Cabinet Secretary Miyazawa, Education Minister Ogawa, Education Administrative Vice-Minister Misumi, and Bureau Chief Suzuki. Ogawa remained firm in his stance that the MOE would not change the texts as the Chinese and Korean governments had requested because it would rock the basis of a system developed over many years. He said he wished to continue with the policy of explaining the government's true intentions in order to reach an understanding, and added that he thought there should be an explanation of the particular passages under criticism.[112]

By the evening of 5 August it seemed that the MOE and MFA had been able to agree that the MOE would give second-stage explanations to the Chinese and Korean governments which would describe in more detail the process of examining and authorising those sections of the textbooks in dispute.[113] The Japanese government proposed to send top MFA and MOE officials to China and Korea in order to carry out the second-stage explanations, and find out directly from both the Chinese and Korean governments their thinking on the issue.[114] However, the Korean government rejected the proposal on the morning of 6 August, stating that it would not accept any Japanese envoy without a definite promise from the Japanese government that the history books would be corrected.[115] The Chinese government, on the other hand, agreed to accept a visit by the MFA's Public Information and Cultural Affairs Bureau Chief, Hashimoto Hiroshi, and the MOE's Science and International Affairs Bureau Chief, Osaki Hitoshi, from 9–12 August.[116]

Development of Japanese inter-ministry conflict

At a Cabinet meeting held on 6 August, both the Foreign and Education Ministers clarified their respective positions and in so doing revealed the growing conflict between their ministries. The Foreign Minister talked of the necessity to 'cope seriously with the problem of textbook examination and authorisation', but admitted that the MFA could not 'devise any effective measures'.[117] The Education Minister favoured the policy of continuing to 'explain Japan's true intentions and to seek an understanding'.[118] The MOE's position was clearly stated in a document published on 9 August which indicated that the Ministry would not be persuaded to make any changes to the textbooks. The document, the MOE 'view' (*kenkai*), set out the Ministry's opinion on the Chinese and Korean governments' criticisms of such points as changing the word 'invasion', the number of Japanese and Chinese casualties of the Nanjing Massacre, and descriptions of the Korean independence movement.

The *kenkai* explained the use of the words 'invasion' and 'advance' which helped to clarify some of the earlier confusing statements:

> The examples cited by China and given in the Japanese press of invasion (*shinryaku*) being changed to advance (*shinshutsu*) did not appear in the most recent textbook screening in reference to China, although in past years it is likely that there were such examples. Last year there were examples of invasion (*shinryaku*) being changed to attack (*shinkō*) or invasion (*shinnyū*). In reference to Southeast Asia, there were examples of invasion (*shinryaku*) being changed to advance (*shinshutsu*) in the most recent textbook screening.[119]

Regarding descriptions of the Nanjing Massacre, the document stated that there was 'insufficient historical material' on the number of casualties, and that estimates of casualties varied greatly, ranging from as low as ten or twenty thousand to as high as several hundred thousand. In textbook screening therefore, the document stated that the ministry recommended, by compulsory *shūsei iken*, that descriptions of uncertain numbers be avoided. The document also stated that:

> At the time of the occupation of Nanjing we were engaged in a violent war, and such was the chaos that it was not easy to distinguish between the military and non-military. When describing the Nanjing Incident in textbooks, there is a recommendation (*shūsei iken*) that sufficient consideration is given to the circumstances surrounding the incident that it can be fully understood.[120]

On descriptions of the Manchurian Incident, the document stated that the opinion of the Chinese government was not clear and that the authorised textbooks contained detailed accounts of how the incident was started by the Kwantung Army, which blew up a section of the Manchurian railway line but blamed it on the Chinese side. According to the document, there had been no recommendations attached to the descriptions of the Manchurian Incident during the textbook screening process.[121]

The *kenkai* would form the basis of the second round of explanations to be given to the Chinese (by Hashimoto and Osaki) and Korean governments, and the ministry expected that through these explanations an understanding could be reached.[122] The *kenkai* contained no indication that the textbooks would be revised however, and at a Lower House Foreign Affairs Committee Meeting held on 9 August, Bureau Chief Suzuki 'stressed that his ministry remained firm in its stand of not accepting corrections to the textbooks and would not entertain requests by publishers and authors to revise wording'.[123]

In sharp contrast to the MOE's stance was the MFA view. At the Lower House Foreign Affairs Committee Meeting on 9 August, Foreign Minister Sakurauchi stated that it was essential that measures be taken to revise the textbooks in order to settle the issue, and that the MFA would request the MOE to carry out those measures. Sakurauchi further stated that the Japanese government must recognise that the international community has criticised Japan for its war of invasion, thereby acknowledging that Chinese and Korean criticism was justified. He also stressed the need for certain people in government (that is, the Education Minister) to take action in accordance with the Sino-Japanese Joint Statement. Sakurauchi reiterated these views at the Upper House Security Treaty Special Committee meetings the following day, adding that although textbook authorisation was the responsibility of the MOE, it was the MFA's responsibility to pass on any criticisms from foreign countries and ensure that the criticism is correctly replied to.[124]

The MFA's view was put in writing in the form of a *kenkai*, published on 12 August, which stated that the MFA was awaiting the return of Hashimoto and Osaki from Beijing to decide on a response to the textbook problem, but that it would be necessary to revise the textbooks. According to Foreign Minister Sakurauchi, who stressed that the *kenkai* was his own personal view and not that of the Japanese government,[125] the key was how to persuade the MOE and those in the LDP opposed to revision of the textbooks to change their opinion. The Foreign Minister's *kenkai* incensed the MOE, which expressed extreme dissatisfaction at the way the MFA had announced its wishes to revise the textbooks without first notifying the MOE.[126] On the following day, Education Minister Ogawa said that his stance against correction of the textbooks remained unchanged.[127]

In the meantime, the LDP hawks were still expressing their views despite requests by LDP Secretary General Nikaido Susumu to refrain from expressing their private opinions in public.[128] At the Cabinet meeting of August 6, Director General Matsuno Yukiyasu once again criticised the Chinese and South Korean governments and reiterated the opinion that their demands represented interference in domestic affairs.[129] Furthermore, he criticised the content of Korean textbooks, saying that Korean history books depict Itō Hirobumi as a 'ringleader of aggression against Korea', and Itō's assassin as a national hero who was justified in his action. Unlike his previous comments on the subject, this one was met with strong criticism by the MFA when a MFA spokesman later criticised Matsuno saying that Cabinet members should consider the effects their personal views might have before making any statements.[130] In Nagoya on 9 August, Matsuno defended his comments of 6 August which had since prompted severe criticism from South Korea. He denied having said 'let's forget the past', explaining that his comments had been misquoted. Yet he then went on to say that each country has its own view of history and that it would be better if countries did not examine each other's past too deeply. He also said that no country teaches about the bad things it has done. These remarks prompted the Education Minister to condemn Matsuno, saying that his 'regrettable remarks' had added to the problem and were hindering the amicable settlement of the Textbook Issue.[131]

Second-stage explanations

On August 13 Director Generals Hashimoto and Osaki reported to Prime Minister Suzuki, Foreign Minister Sakurauchi and Education Minister Ogawa on their three days of talks with Xiao Xiangqian, Li Tao and other Chinese Education and Foreign Ministry representatives. There had been three meetings between the two Japanese representatives and their counterparts in Beijing on 10-12 August. The general outcome of the discussions according to Hashimoto and Osaki was that 'the Chinese side's severe stance [had] not changed at all'. [132] The details of the talks are not known, partly because the Chinese government had requested that the content of the talks be kept private. But at a press conference held on their return, Hashimoto and Osaki explained that the purpose of going to China had been to explain in detail the Japanese government's view on the Textbook Issue and to talk directly and frankly with the Chinese government. Hashimoto said that the Chinese side had not been satisfied that Japan's self-reproach (for wartime actions in China) had been fully reflected in the textbooks. Nonetheless, according to Hashimoto the Chinese government had expressed the hope that the issue could be settled amicably and he confirmed that some success was achieved in understanding each other's viewpoint.[133]

In light of the Beijing talks, and of Korea's reiteration on 12 August of requests for correction of the textbooks,[134] the Japanese government decided to treat the issue on two levels: firstly, to reiterate Japan's acknowledgement of its war responsibility to China and Korea and its reflection on the past in the form of a statement by the Prime Minister the following week; and secondly, to entrust the problem of how to deal with revision of the textbooks to the Japanese government.[135]

Over the next few days, the MOE and MFA held separate meetings to discuss the new strategy,[136] but while these discussions were taking place the anti-Japan campaign in the PRC media and mounting anti-Japanese feelings and demonstrations in the ROK added to the pressure on the Japanese government to find a more speedy solution to the Textbook Issue. The thirty-seventh anniversary of Japan's surrender in the Second World War was marked on 15 August. The *Renmin Ribao* carried an article entitled 'Past Experience, if Not Forgotten, is a Guide to the Future'. Most of the article was given over to a recollection of the history of Japan's expansion from 1894 and the war with China. It also described how China and Japan had managed to develop friendly, cooperative relations since the war, but warned that some Japanese were attempting to revive militarism and the 'Greater East Asia Co-Prosperity Sphere'.[137] Other Chinese regional papers also carried reports in the run-up to 15 August, recalling, for example, bombings of Chinese cities and atrocities committed by Japanese troops.[138] There were also reports about seminars and forums at which Japanese actions were denounced,[139] and about exhibitions of Japanese war crimes held in Changsha and Guangzhou.[140] In Japan 15 August was also commemorated, most notably with a memorial service and a visit by Prime Minister Suzuki and his Cabinet to the Yasukuni Shrine to pay homage to Japanese war dead. This was also reported in the *Renmin Ribao*, which regarded the Yasukuni visit as an activity 'of some people in Japan who have ulterior motives to whip up opinions for the revival of militarism'.[141]

In Korea, anti-Japanese feeling had been steadily growing as the problem developed. By 10 August there were reports of vandals in Seoul destroying a monument commemorating the building of a bridge by the Japanese during Korea's period of colonialisation. Taxi drivers were refusing to take Japanese passengers and some shops were barring Japanese customers and boycotting Japanese goods.[142] On 13 August the Korean government postponed, in effect cancelling, that year's Japan–South Korea junior exchange athletics meeting due to be held in the summer, because of the high-level of anti-Japanese sentiment in South Korea.[143] In Seoul, a rally was held on 15 August to mark the anniversary of Japan's defeat and to protest against Japanese textbooks.[144]

International reaction

The continued anti-Japan campaigns in China and South Korea were a clear indication that the measures taken by the Japanese government had not gone far enough to appease either the Chinese or Korean governments. Furthermore, the issue was attracting attention throughout the region, as well as in the Western press. By mid-August, the press and governments in neighbouring countries had begun to comment on the issue. A survey carried out by the *Ajia Keizai Kenkyūjo* showed that the major newspapers of Singapore and Hong Kong carried more coverage than did the PRC press, though less than ROK.[145] The Macao, Indonesian, Thai and Taiwanese press also contained more than fifty articles each relating to the Textbook Issue.[146] The issue was covered to a lesser extent in Malaysia, the Philippines, North Korea Burma and elsewhere.[147] Further afield, the issue attracted the attention of, amongst others, the American and British press. The coverage in the British press tended to be analytical, commenting for example on the way the issue was being used by the Chinese as a means of diverting attention away from 'tricky' problems between the USA, China and Taiwan.[148] The *New York Times* followed the issue as it developed, noting in particular the reactions of the Korean people and the 'disturbing' response of the Japanese government.[149]

While the media in the Asian countries did not carry out such well-directed campaigns as those in China and South Korea, they all contained warnings about a possible revival of Japanese militarism, and criticised the tendency of Japanese textbooks to emphasise the Japanese as victims of the nuclear bomb without questioning why the bombs were dropped.[150] The Japanese press frequently reported upon on the increasingly high-profile nature of the issue in the neighbouring countries, a matter which would not have gone unnoticed by the Japanese public or the government. Furthermore, the Taiwanese authorities issued a memorandum to the Japanese government at the end of July requesting the Japanese government to take 'suitable measures' and stating that the 'Ministry of Education's forced re-writing of textbooks not only ignores the feelings of the Chinese (Taiwanese) people, but ignores the wish of the Japanese and Chinese people to pursue peace.'[151] The Taiwanese authorities appeared to take the matter no further. The issue became a diplomatic one only between Japan, China and Korea, but one which the Japanese government was increasingly keen to resolve. Yet resolution of the issue did not appear imminent, given the lack of consensus within the Japanese government. Although press reports of 16 August stated that the Japanese government was moving closer to a 'basic opinion' (*kihon kenkai*) on the Textbook Issue, they also pointed out that, due to the continuing difference of opinion between the MFA and MOE, government leaders acknowledged that it would be difficult to reach a unified view and a resolution would ultimately be based on the Prime Minister's 'political judgement'.[152]

Stage 4: MOE/MFA compromise

According to reports on 17 August, Prime Minister Suzuki said that 'Japan should accept criticism from its Asian neighbours of school textbooks termed as "distorting" Japan's actions before and during the Second World War' but that 'it is important to maintain Japan's textbook screening system'. His remarks were considered an indication of 'his readiness to change the textbooks within the framework of the screening system'.[153] Faced with increasing pressure from the Prime Minister and the Ministry of Foreign Affairs, the Ministry of Education appeared willing to start making concessions. On 17 August, for example, the Ministry announced its decision to 'restore such descriptions as Japan's wartime "invasion" instead of "advance" into China, and the South Korean "independence movement" instead of "riots" when the ministry screen[ed] school textbooks for use from fiscal 1984'.[154] In other words, the textbooks then undergoing, or about to undergo, screening (for selection in 1983 and use in 1984) would not have any suggestions for correction or improvement attached to words like 'invasion'.[155]

Regarding the 'problem' textbooks, the MOE proposed on 19 August to bring forward by one year (to 1983) the normally triennial 'revision authorisation' (*kaitei kentei*).[156] This would mean that even though the 'problem' textbooks would still be used in classrooms from April 1983, they would undergo revision in 1983, for selection in 1984 and use from April 1985. The view in the MOE was that by making this concession the Ministry would avoid having to revise the textbooks *immediately*, yet at the same time would be able to show that it intended to revise the textbooks, and could thereby gain the understanding of the two governments. Furthermore, the MOE would be able to avoid criticism of those in the LDP who were strongly opposed to revision on the grounds that it was interference in internal affairs, because it would be the responsibility of Japanese *textbook companies* to submit independent applications for revision (rather than the Japanese government issuing a formal request to the MOE in response to demands from a foreign government).[157]

The MOE was confident that with this sort of concession it could reach an agreement with the MFA, and that a public announcement could soon be made.[158] In the meantime, however, Foreign Minister

Sakurauchi had reiterated the view, during an Upper House Foreign Affairs Committee meeting on the afternoon of 19 August, that the spirit of the Sino-Japanese Joint Statement ought to be reflected in school textbooks, and that it was necessary to revise the textbooks immediately.[159] The MFA's response to the MOE's proposal was therefore not as favourable as the MOE had hoped, because the proposal would mean that the unrevised textbooks would be in use in schools for two years before being replaced by revised versions in 1985. The MFA therefore pressed for further concessions on the morning of the 20th at a joint MFA and MOE meeting, asking that 'revision authorisation' be brought forward two years as opposed to one. The MOE objected to this request because it would mean that notification of revision, which had to be given one year prior to submission, would have had to be forgone. The MOE felt that if this was allowed, it would cause the system to collapse and stressed that bringing revision forward by one year was the biggest concession it could make.[160]

At a meeting on the evening of the 20th, the MFA, still on the offensive, suggested that if the MOE could not revise the textbooks immediately, then it should take such measures as issuing notices instructing schools not to use those textbooks, or instructing teachers to correct the word 'advance' to 'invade' during lessons. Angered by the MFA's badgering, the MOE then withdrew its offer completely, blaming the MFA for 'sending the proposal back to the drawing board'.[161]

Despite this setback, both Ministries did manage to agree that the government view (*kenkai*) would incorporate revision of the textbooks 'in some form'. Chief Cabinet Secretary Miyazawa instructed the Ministry of Education to look into the timing and form that revisions should take, and asked that further co-operation take place between the two ministries in time for Prime Minister Suzuki's press conference planned for 23 August.[162] At the press conference, the Prime Minister set out the government's basic position on the Textbook Issue and an outline of how the government planned to respond. He also said that efforts would be made to produce the government's unified view before Foreign Minister Sakurauchi's departure for India on 27 August, and that he definitely wanted the matter to be settled before his visit to China.[163] Prime Minister Suzuki's main comments were that:

1   it is natural that we reflect in the textbooks our awareness of the self-reproach and responsibility we feel for the suffering inflicted on neighbouring countries in the past war;
2   we will make efforts to improve textbook descriptions to make them more appropriate;

3   we are investigating ways to gain China's and Korea's under-
    standing.[164]

   The *Asahi Shimbun* commented that although the Prime Minister did
not refer directly to 'revising the descriptions', this was a further indication that the government was intending to comply with requests for
correction of the textbooks and settle the matter as soon as possible.
Furthermore, on the matter of 'co-ordination work' (*chōsei sagyō*)
between the Ministry of Education and Ministry of Foreign Affairs, the
Prime Minister stated that he would 'take final responsibility' for
bringing the matter to a conclusion.[165]
   In the meantime it seemed that the MOE and MFA had finally
managed to reach a compromise. According to the *Asahi Shimbun*,
agreement had been reached on the following points:

1   that the problem textbooks, due for use in 1983, would undergo
    'revision authorisation' one year earlier than normal and would be
    ready for use from 1985;
2   because the unrevised textbooks would be used in the classrooms
    for 1983 and 1984, the MOE would issue a 'bulletin' to all schools
    recommending that history tuition should stress friendly relations
    with neighbouring countries;
3   starting with new textbooks due to undergo authorisation in the
    remainder of 1982, textbook authorisation would no longer contain
    suggestions for improvement or suggestions for correction (*kaizen
    iken, shūsei iken*) that sought to change 'invade' to 'advance'.[166]

The *Asahi Shimbun* considered that these points would form the backbone of the government view, but the report said that it remained to be
seen whether the Chinese and Korean governments would accept the
measures. Moreover, the final version of the government view would not
be produced until Mitsuzuka Hiroshi and Mori Yoshirō had returned
from talks with the Korean government, which had eventually agreed to
Japan's proposition to send Japanese representatives to Seoul to explain
their position.[167]
   Despite the fact that the MOE and MFA appeared to have reached a
compromise by 23 August, the Education Minister still had reservations
about the handling of the Textbook Issue, fearing that the principles of
education policy might be allowed to slip if the matter was dealt with as
a purely diplomatic one. In a meeting with Prime Minister Suzuki on the
24th, Education Minister Ogawa asked that the Ministry of Education
be allowed to take responsibility for and handle the Textbook Issue

henceforth, warning that if promises made by the Japanese government were not be fulfilled, a serious international problem might ensue. At a press conference after the meeting, Ogawa said that the Prime Minister fully understood the MOE's position and he expected the Ministry's viewpoint to be reflected in the government view.[168]

On 25 August, on their return from talks with Korean government leaders, the Chairman of the Subcommittee on the Textbook Problem, Mitsuzuka, and the former chairman of the Education Committee, Mori, met with Chief Cabinet Secretary Miyazawa and the Foreign and Education Administrative Vice-Ministers, Sunobe and Misumi, at the Prime Minister's residence to discuss Korea's position. Mitsuzuka's report stated that the anti-Japan atmosphere in Korea was very strong, and the Korean government wanted the Japanese government to settle the problem quickly and make every effort to correct the textbooks.[169] In response to the report, Miyazawa promised to draw up the government statement as soon as possible.[170]

Stage 5: settlement

On 26 August, CCS Miyazawa issued the 'unified' government statement on the Textbook Issue. Paragraph 1 reaffirmed Japan's unchanged awareness of its past actions, quoting sections from the Joint Statements signed with Korea and China that referred to Japan's contrition and deep reproach for the suffering inflicted upon Chinese and Korean people. The second paragraph stated that the spirit of the Joint Statements should be reflected in Japanese education and textbook authorisation, and in light of the criticisms from Asian countries about descriptions in Japanese textbooks 'the Japanese government [would] pay full heed to this criticism in promoting friendship and goodwill with the nearby countries of Asia, and the government [would] undertake on its own responsibility to make the necessary amendments.'[171] Paragraph 3 referred to textbook authorisation, stating that:

> [In order to carry out the amendments] in future textbook authorisation, the authorisation criteria will be revised by the Textbook Authorisation Research Council and care will be taken that [the spirit of PRC–Japan and ROK–Japan Joint Statements] is fully realised. For textbooks which have already been authorised, measures will be taken to realise [the spirit of the Joint Statements] quickly, but in the meantime the Minister of Education will issue a policy statement and will ensure that the essence of Section (2) above is fully reflected in the classroom.[172]

The final paragraph reaffirmed Japan's desire to continue to develop friendly, cooperative relations with neighbouring countries, to promote mutual understanding and contribute to Asian and world peace and security.[173]

At a press conference held later the same day, Education Minister Ogawa clarified when and how the textbooks would be changed, and the process for revision of the criteria for textbook authorisation:

1 the TARC would carry out an inquiry into the revision of textbook authorisation criteria, and would produce a report in one or two months time;

2 the new authorisation criteria would be applied to the textbooks due to be authorised in 1982 (for use in 1984) in response to Chinese and Korean criticism;

3 the textbooks currently in dispute (for use in 1983) would undergo revision authorisation (*kaitei kentei*) one year earlier than usual ready for use in 1985;

4 as an interim measure for the unrevised textbooks in use in 1983 and 1984, an MOE 'bulletin' based on the report of the TARC would be dispatched to all schools.[174]

With regard to the TARC inquiry, the Education Minister said that the MOE would probably ask TARC to consider adding a clause to the textbook authorisation criteria which would lay greater stress on friendly relations with neighbouring countries.[175]

Chinese and Korean response

Within Korea there was widespread criticism of Miyazawa's statement, with opposition parties, academics, students and the general public all voicing their strong disapproval of the Japanese government's proposals. The general feeling seemed to be that although the Japanese government had appeared to make every effort to solve the matter, in fact they had done nothing at all. Nonetheless, the Korean government indicated on 27 August that it was willing to accept in principle the Japanese statement on the textbooks, although it made it clear that it was not completely satisfied with the response and 'would continue diplomatic efforts to see that Japanese history textbooks [were] corrected soon and that Japan accepted repeated South Korean requests.'[176]

The Chinese government, however, rejected the statement. On 28 August Vice-Foreign Minister Wu Xueqian met with Ambassador

Katori Yasue to express on behalf of the Chinese government his dissatisfaction with the Japanese government's statement on the Textbook Issue, and requested that effective measures be taken to correct the errors. Wu Xueqian told Katori that after careful consideration of the statement the Chinese government felt that even though the Japanese government had listened humbly and offered to take responsibility to amend the textbooks, the statement lacked clearness and specific reference to the measures that would be taken to correct the textbooks. Because the statement fell short of the Chinese government's demands, Wu Xueqian said that the Chinese side felt disappointed and neither the Chinese government nor people could agree to the Japanese government's statement. Finally, Wu reiterated that (Japan's) acknowledgement of the history of Japan's militarist invasion of China was an important matter of principle, and the Chinese government could not agree to the Japanese government's using the maintenance of the textbook authorisation system as an excuse not to take decisive measures and correct the errors in the textbooks.[177]

Over the next few days, both the Chinese and Korean governments kept up their pressure on the Japanese government by calling for an indication that specific measures would be carried out promptly. An article in the *Renmin Ribao* on 30 August criticised the Japanese government's slow and ambiguous response to Chinese demands. Furthermore, it explained how neither the Chinese nor Japanese people could accept the statement of 26 August because it failed to stipulate concrete measures, and revealed the Japanese government's apathetic attitude.[178] On 31 August, in a meeting with Chinese State Councillor Gu Mu, a delegation of representatives of the Lower House Communications Committee were told that the Japanese government's unified view on the Textbook Issue failed to stipulate when and how 'advance' would be corrected to 'invasion'. On the same day the Korean Foreign Ministry, via the Japanese Embassy in Seoul, demanded that the Japanese government quickly carry out 'concrete measures'. On 4 September, Korean newspapers reported that the Korean Foreign Ministry was planning to send the Japanese government a document listing in detail the corrections it wanted the Japanese government to carry out.[179]

China's reaction appeared to take the Japanese government by surprise. Miyazawa met with the Education and Foreign Ministries on 28 August to discuss China's reaction to the statement. China's rejection was met with confusion in the MOE and surprise in the MFA.[180] An MOE internal document stated that 'the three points of "invasion", "the Manchurian Incident" and the "Nanking Incident" are mentioned as examples [of] what China pointed out, but it is not known whether its demands for correction are limited to these three points.'[181] The Japanese government as a whole was also puzzled by China's response. Miyazawa stated on 28 August that the Japanese government would like to 'verify China's real wishes',[182] and Minister Watanabe Kōji was called back from Beijing to shed some light on the nature of China's demands.[183]

A number of meetings were held over the next few days to discuss how to respond to China's rejection of the 26 August statement. Various suggestions were put forward. For example, the MFA and MOE both proposed sending a special envoy to China to sort out the matter through diplomatic routes, but the government concluded that the policy put forward in the statement represented the optimum course of action based on the present textbook screening system and that additional measures were not possible, although every effort would be made to reach an understanding with China.[184]

On 31 August, after a meeting between the two ministries, the following decisions were taken:

1 to enforce the measures announced in the statement of 26 August;
2 to obtain as soon as possible a conclusion from the Textbook Authorisation Research Council concerning the revision of textbook authorisation criteria;[185]
3 to explain once again to both countries that the quickest method of correcting the textbooks while maintaining the present textbook screening system was to follow the conventions set down by the TARC.[186]

A joint conference of the LDP Education Committee and the Education System Research Council reached similar conclusions on the following day (1 September), that is, that the measures contained in the government statement represented the maximum concessions, and that the government should continue to explain the meaning of the statement to the PRC and ROK governments through diplomatic routes.[187]

In his report to Chief Cabinet Secretary on 2 September, Minister Watanabe explained that the biggest question for the Chinese government was whether, and why, it would take as long as two years before the offending descriptions were corrected. There were also questions about how the Japanese government would correct the textbooks. In addition, Watanabe reported that the Chinese side was unclear as to when the TARC inquiry would begin, and whether the Council's report would differ from government aims (in other words, whether the Council was an independent body). Finally, the Chinese side queried the amount of influence the Education Minister's 'bulletin' would have in the class-room.[188]

Supplementary explanations

On 2 September, the government announced after a meeting between the MFA and the Cabinet Secretariat that based on the report by Minister Watanabe Kōji concerning the situation in China, the Japanese government would once again explain to the Chinese the following week the content of the statement of 26 August. While Japanese press reports mentioned only that the Japanese government would 're-explain' (*zaiset-sumei*) the 26 August view,[189] according to Chinese reports, Ambassador Katori met with Vice-Minister Wu on 6 September and stated that 'after reconsideration the Japanese government had decided to take *further measures* to settle the textbook question on Prime Minister Zenkō Suzuki's instruction for an early settlement of the issue'[190] (emphasis added). It seems from Japanese press reports that 'further measures' did not refer to any new concessions but to a more detailed explanation of the proposals put forward in the statement of 26 August. On 8 September, Ambassador Katori Yasue once again met with China's Vice-Minister for Foreign Affairs Wu Xueqian. On revision of the criteria for textbook authorisation, the content of this final round of explanations was as follows:

1   the inquiry of the Textbook Authorisation and Research Council into the revision of criteria of textbook authorisation would begin on 14 September and produce its report approximately two months hence;
2   TARC would deliberate fully on the government's aims as expressed in the 26 August statement, but the government's view would not infringe upon the Council's jurisdiction;
3   TARC's report would probably recommend inclusion of a new paragraph on authorisation of social studies textbooks which would perhaps read 'it is necessary to take into consideration friendly relations with neighbouring countries'.

On revision of textbooks the explanation was:

4   textbook authorisation for the 1982 fiscal year (for use from 1984) would be delayed pending the results of the TARC inquiry, and the textbooks would then be screened according to the new criteria;

5   textbooks currently in use (authorised in 1980–1) and due for revision (*kaitei kentei*) in 1983 (for use from 1985) would undergo revision according to the new criteria;

6   the textbooks causing the current problem for use from spring 1983 (authorised 1981–2) would undergo 'revision authorisation' (*kaitei kentei*) one year in advance in 1983–4 (for use from 1985);

7   Revision of all textbooks would be completed by 1985. Regarding the textbooks awaiting revision but still in use in 1983 and 1984, an MOE bulletin would be distributed to schools nationwide as soon as TARC's deliberations are completed. The bulletin would set out the Minister's view and the purport of TARC's report.[191]

Similar explanations were also given in Seoul on the following day and as result of both rounds of explanations, the MFA and government leaders were optimistic that the matter would be solved imminently.[192] As anticipated, the Korean government 'expressed its appreciation of the Japanese government's efforts,'[193] and the Chinese government also accepted the supplementary explanations, acknowledging the determination of Prime Minister Suzuki and the Japanese government to resolve the matter.[194] Vice-Minister Wu Xueqian responded to the explanations, saying:

> Although there are still some ambiguous, unsatisfactory points about the concrete measures proposed by the Japanese side to correct the mistakes, it is a step forward compared with the explanations previously made.[195]

In a statement made at a press conference on 9 September, Miyazawa announced that 'the Chinese side has evaluated the [Japanese] Prime Minister's judgement and the government's policy of taking responsibility for the corrections, and with that in mind the problem between China and Japan has been controlled diplomatically.'[196]

For the Chinese and Korean governments, however, the matter was not completely resolved and both governments expressed concern as to whether the Japanese government would carry out the necessary revisions quickly and sincerely, and indicated that they would be observing the Japanese government carefully.[197] Wu Xueqian stated that: 'We will judge whether the Japanese side conscientiously corrects the mistakes in the textbooks by its concrete actions and their results. We reserve our right to comment on this matter.'[198] An unsigned commentator article (*pinglunyuan*) in the *Renmin Ribao* on 9 September represented the last authoritative commentary on the Textbook Issue in the Chinese press.

The article ('It is Hoped that the Japanese Government will be True in Word, Resolute in Deed') warned of the dangers of distorting historical facts, urged vigilance against an 'adverse undercurrent' (Japanese militarism) but stated that the Textbook Issue had nonetheless been brought to a close.[199]

This chapter has described *how* the events of the Textbook Issue unfurled and how the matter was concluded to the apparent satisfaction of both the Chinese and Japanese governments. Yet there are a number of questions raised by the Textbook Issue that require further explanations as to *why* the Chinese and Japanese governments acted in the way they did. Why, for example, did the Chinese government choose to take the unprecedented step of protesting about Japan's textbooks on the eve of the tenth anniversary of normalisation? Why had the PRC not complained in previous years about the state of Japan's policies on history education? What factors explain the response of the Japanese government to the Textbook Issue?

To find the answers to these questions it is necessary to look in more detail at some of the changes, discussed briefly in Chapter 4, that were taking place in the domestic and international environment. The next two chapters will therefore consider the reasons behind the actions and reactions of both governments in order to establish whether the Textbook Issue was concerned solely with the matter of history or whether other factors were involved.

6   The Textbook Issue
China's response

Chapter 5 provided a detailed account of the events of the Textbook Issue and showed how the issue was resolved. However, the account did not help to shed any light on the reasons behind China's decision to make a formal diplomatic protest in the first place, nor did it account for the way the Japanese government reached its 'unified' view. To find answers to these questions, it is necessary to return to the organising framework discussed in Chapter 2 and consider the relative influence of the internal and external factors on the decision makers of both governments. This and the next chapter consider in more detail the linkage between the domestic political and international situations at the time of the Textbook Issue.

This chapter looks first at the arguments for and against considering the Textbook Issue as purely an issue about the interpretation of history, and questions China's motives for pressuring the Japanese government to adopt a 'correct view of history'. The second section describes the nature of the anti-Japan media campaign because this helps not only to establish the extent to which the campaign was centrally controlled (and therefore not a spontaneous response), but also to identify the issues that the Chinese leadership were genuinely concerned about. Comparison of the 1982 campaign with those of previous years also provides evidence of a pattern of behaviour in Sino-Japanese relations and illustrates that the PRC has used a similar device in the past for similar reasons. The third section presents some of the arguments that have been put forward to explain the Chinese leadership's reasons for raising the Textbook Issue to a diplomatic level. The final section considers some of the internal and external influences described in Chapter 3, such as the power struggle with the 'Old Guard' and changes in China's foreign policy, which cast further doubt on the idea that that the Textbook Issue was purely and simply about history.

A matter of history?

As described in the previous chapter, the Textbook Issue was treated as an 'important matter of principle' by the PRC in response to what the Chinese government saw as a violation of the spirit of the Sino-Japanese Joint Statement and the Treaty of Peace and Friendship. The 1972 Joint Statement had brought an end to the 'abnormal state of affairs', but the failure to address issues left over from the Sino-Japanese war – as Chapter 3 described – gave rise to problems in later years. Even during the negotiations leading up to the signing of the Joint Statement in 1972 there was a 'sign of things to come', when, at a welcome banquet hosted by Zhou Enlai, Prime Minister Tanaka Kakuei stated that:

> It is regrettable that in the past seventy to eighty years Sino-Japanese relations have experienced an unfortunate process (Chinese, *buxin de guocheng*; Japanese, *fukō na katei*) and our country has caused the Chinese people a lot of trouble (*tian le hen da mafan*, *tadai no gomeiwaku o kakeshita koto*).[1]

The following day Zhou Enlai made it clear in a meeting with Tanaka that referring to Japan's invasion of China as merely 'causing trouble' was unacceptable and could only provoke strong aversion.[2] In the final stages of the negotiations the Chinese government indicated that it wanted some reference to Japan's wartime responsibility to be included in the preamble of the Joint Statement. Nagano suggests that the Chinese side were seeking an official apology from the Japanese government for Japan's invasion of China. Since inclusion of an apology would have 'required a political judgement of the Tanaka cabinet', Foreign Minister Ōhira suggested that the wording should read 'the Japanese side keenly feels the responsibility for the enormous suffering inflicted on the Chinese people through Japan's past war, and deeply reproaches itself.'[3] The Chinese side agreed to this wording.[4]

The Chinese government's main argument in the Textbook Issue was that the new set of Japanese history textbooks did not uphold the spirit of the Joint Statement; that is, the textbooks did not reflect the Japanese government's 'keen responsibility' or 'deep reproach' for the suffering of the Chinese. As the Chinese government and press reiterated throughout the Textbook Issue, Japan's aggression during the Sino-Japanese war and the suffering inflicted upon the Chinese people constitute historical facts that cannot be distorted. That newly-authorised Japanese textbooks contained distortions of the truth about a war in which many Chinese people suffered was a matter of grave concern to the Chinese government, and could not be considered a purely Japanese domestic matter. As Carol Gluck has pointed out:

> When it comes to war, national history is clearly an international affair. Revising one's own history is one thing; revising another country's history is something else altogether. The Rape of Nanking, after all, belongs at least as much to China as to Japan.[5]

Furthermore, China protested about the distorted textbooks because not only did they represent a violation of the Joint Statement, but they also indicated that there was a debate in Japan about the events of the war, whereas for China there had never been room for discussion on the Nanjing Massacre and Japan's invasion of China. For the Chinese these events represent the truth and *any* debate that seeks to question this truth is anathema to the Chinese government and people. In this sense, then, the protests from China (and other Asian countries) about Japan's history textbooks were justified; after all, there is similar outcry in Europe and America when attempts are made by right-wing groups and politicians to whitewash Hitler's actions or to dismiss the Holocaust as a myth created by the Jews as a way of extracting money from the Germans.[6] As Buruma points out, the Nanjing Massacre held the same significance at the Tokyo War Crimes Trials as did Auschwitz in the Nuremberg trials.[7]

The Textbook Issue has been explained purely in terms of China's dissatisfaction with the Japanese Education Ministry's interpretation of Sino-Japanese history and as an attempt to have the errors in the textbooks rectified. Furukawa Mantarō, for example, explains that the Chinese government and public opinion alike treated the Textbook Issue as a serious problem which struck at the very basis of Sino-Japanese relations. Furukawa argues that the attempts of the 'great powers', especially Japan, to colonise China and the sacrifices the Chinese people suffered as a result have produced a determination that such humiliation and sacrifice will never recur, and a constant vigilance against its Eastern neighbour. Any indication that Japan is attempting to revert to its prewar methods is therefore greeted with alarm in China and, as Chapters 1 and 3 illustrated, there have been many occasions when the PRC has accused Japan of attempting to revive militarism.[8] For the Chinese government, the newly-authorised textbooks were a sign that some elements in Japan were once again seeking to revive militarism, and it was therefore China's right and duty to prevent this trend from developing any further. Furukawa argues that the seriousness with which the Chinese government treated the Textbook Issue was demonstrated by the fact that both Deng Xiaoping and Hu Yaobang referred to the matter (albeit indirectly) in their speeches to the Twelfth Party Congress in September.[9] In his opening speech to the Congress, Deng said:

> While we Chinese people value our friendship and cooperation with other countries and other peoples, we value even more our hard-won independence and sovereign rights. No foreign country can expect China to be its vassal, nor can it expect China to accept anything harmful to China's interests.[10]

Hu Yaobang referred specifically to Japan in his speech, warning that 'some forces in Japan are whitewashing the past Japanese aggression against China and other East Asian countries and are carrying out activities for the revival of Japanese militarism'.[11] Murray Sayle, writing during the Textbook Issue, considered China's protests to be a matter of history only, and that the Chinese simply wanted 'the Japanese to own up to their sins of the past and teach this message to Japanese children.'[12] The Japanese media, public opinion and many of the opposition parties were of the same opinion, regarding the Chinese protests as wholly justified and talking of the necessity to teach the truth about the war to future generations of Japanese children.

Whiting's analysis of the Textbook Issue also concluded that China's reaction was 'automatic', a knee-jerk reaction to memories of China's history of colonisation and suffering at the hands of the Japanese and fears that history could repeat itself. Whiting argues that a 'stimulus-response' pattern has emerged in Sino-Japanese relations which 'generates a loop of political interaction beyond the control of top policymakers in both countries.'[13] With such problems as textbooks, visits by Prime Ministers to the Yasukuni shrine and inflammatory comments of Cabinet ministers, Whiting's argument goes, Japan provides 'ample fuel to ignite [Chinese] popular sentiment against Japan'. The angry, bitter reaction of the Chinese in response to the Textbook Issue was shared by young and old alike, with portrayals of the war in the Chinese media having an 'unanticipated impact on the subjective perceptions and attitudes of the younger generation in China'.[14]

While not denying that the Chinese government was to some extent interested in seeing the Japanese textbooks corrected, there are a number of questions that remain unanswered if one accepts the argument that the issue was 'beyond the control' of the Chinese government, or that the government was concerned solely with Japan's interpretation of history. First, there is the question of why Japanese history textbooks had never before become a Sino-Japanese intergovernmental issue, especially in view of the long-running battle in Japan between the Japan Teachers' Union and the Ministry of Education on the question of 'authoritarian' education. Second, there is the question of the Chinese government's so-called 'spontaneous' response to the initial reports in Japanese newspapers, which actually took nearly a month to develop. Third, there is the question of timing and why the Chinese government decided to take up the issue on the eve of Prime Minister Suzuki's visit to China to celebrate ten years of normalisation. These questions require some consideration because they indicate that there was in fact far more to the Chinese government's actions on the Textbook Issue than first appears.

The first question – why the issue had not been raised prior to 1982 – relates to the state of Japanese textbooks prior to the Textbook Issue, and to Japan's domestic debate on history. Studies show that history textbooks had frequently contained such euphemistic wording as 'advance' in previous years, yet this had not before triggered a response from China. Indeed, the Japanese Ministry of Education openly admitted during the Textbook Issue that in previous years 'advance' (into China) had been used instead of invade.[15] Nor was such euphemistic terminology restricted to the word 'advance', since the whole tone of descriptions of Japan's activities during the war had often been watered down.

A study by Yoneda Nobuji of history and geography middle and high school textbooks revealed that textbooks of the 1970s frequently contained the word 'advance' with regard to descriptions of Japan's actions in China. In a survey of middle school textbooks for use from 1973, Yoneda found that most of the books contained descriptions of the Manchurian 'Incident' (as opposed to Japan's invasion of Manchuria) and the China–Japan 'Incident' (as opposed to the Sino-Japanese War) which played down the role of the Japanese government and laid the blame at the feet of the Japanese army. In addition, the textbooks tended to cover-up the aggressive nature of the war and attributed Japan's 'advance' (*shinshutsu*) into China to growing anti-Japanese resistance in China.[16]

Yoneda's study of high school textbooks found a similar pattern, although in some of these books there *were* references to Japan's 'invasion' (*shinryaku*) of China. On the whole, though, the high school books tended to play down 'aggression' and blamed both 'stubborn Chinese resistance' and the Japanese army for the Manchurian 'Incident'. Descriptions of the Sino-Japanese war were ambiguous on the causes of the war and on the 'concrete facts of Japanese aggression and barbarity'. Of the eleven 'World History' textbooks examined by Yoneda, only two referred to 'the massacre of Nanjing by the Japanese army' and to the fact that 'during this war the Chinese side paid enormous sacrifices'.[17] That these textbooks were being used in schools shortly after Sino-Japanese normalisation in 1972 reflected the fact that, according to Yoneda, the spirit of the Joint Statement was not being adhered to even then. Moreover, aside from updating information in the textbooks about the new 'normalised' state of Sino-Japanese relations, it seems that MOE officials in the early 1970s saw no need to make further changes to textbooks.[18]

Another aspect of the history debate in Japan was the series of high-profile court cases between historian Ienaga Saburō and the state, which exemplified the struggle between the 'progressives' and conservatives concerning postwar education. Since 1965, Ienaga had been involved in a number of long-running legal battles with the Ministry of Education, which he was attempting to sue on the grounds that the authorisation system violated constitutional freedoms of expression, academic freedom and children's right to education. Ienaga brought his first case against the Ministry over the authorisation of his high school history textbook *Shin Nihonshi*, which the MOE textbook examiners had initially failed on the grounds of 'doubtful accuracy' and 'dubious content selection'.[19] Ienaga sued for compensation for 'mental distress and royalty losses', and argued that the textbook authorisation system was illegal. He brought a second suit against the Ministry in 1967, this time seeking a reversal of changes made to the 1966 revised version of the textbook, again contending that the textbook authorisation system was unconstitutional. These cases went up and down the court system throughout the 1970s with various judgments, followed by appeals, followed by nullifications of previous judgments.[20] The court cases were followed avidly by the press, and Ienaga's 'cause' attracted increasing attention and support as he continued his fight into the 1980s and 1990s. It is unlikely that the textbook trials went unnoticed in China, yet it was never raised as a diplomatic matter. Nor had China become involved in the debate in Japan that began in the early 1970s that centred on the 'truth' about the Nanjing Massacre.

The debate about the Nanjing Massacre was conducted in the current affairs journals after journalist Honda Katsuichi published a series of articles, followed by a book entitled *Journey to China* (*Chūgoku no tabi*) in 1972. Honda's book documented the cruel behaviour of the Japanese army in China after the Manchurian Incident and was said to shock the general public with its frank descriptions. To counter Honda's argument, right-wing journalists and intellectuals (in particular Suzuki

Akira, Yamamoto Shichihei and Tanaka Masaaki) wrote books and articles that described the Nanjing Massacre as 'myth' (*maboroshi*).[21] The Chinese government made no official protest about the 'Nanjing Debate' even though, as Buruma points out, those who denied the massacre could not be dismissed as an 'extremist fringe', enjoying as they did the support of a large audience and powerful right-wing politicians.[22] Fujiwara explains that China's lack of response to this debate was due to the fact that until 1982 the Chinese government had taken the view that although Japanese militarism had been bad, the general public in Japan were not to be blamed and the past should not be mentioned if at all possible.[23]

Thus, even though words like 'advance' were commonly in use in textbooks in the early 1970s, the issue of history writing had been popularised by the Ienaga textbook trials, and the Nanjing Massacre had become a heated topic of debate in Japan, the Chinese government took no action until 1982. Indeed, according to Buruma, Chinese survivors were only called upon to provide the newspapers with eyewitness accounts of the Nanjing Massacre for the very first time in 1982. Before 1982, 'no official notice had been taken of them'.[24] Only after 1982 were various memorials, including the Nanjing Museum, erected, and only after 1982 was any historical research carried out by Chinese scholars.[25] Buruma accounts for the lack of PRC interest in the Nanjing Massacre before 1982 by explaining that at the time of the Nanjing Massacre, Nanjing was Guomindang-held territory and the victims were on the Nationalist side. The events of Nanjing therefore 'did not fit into Chinese communist lore',[26] until, that is, they could prove useful to the Chinese government. This could explain why, prior to 1982, the Chinese government was not greatly concerned with what was going on in Japanese government and journalistic circles about textbook authorisation, or Sino-Japanese history. Although it is possible to argue that the Nanjing Massacre debate was a Japanese domestic matter and therefore proscribed Chinese intervention, the same argument could also be applied to textbooks and textbook authorisation – the view taken by many in the LDP and MOE during the Textbook Issue – yet this did not stop the Chinese government in 1982. The question remains, then, as to why the Chinese government reacted to the history textbooks in 1982 when it had never done so previously despite similar circumstances.

The second question about China's initiation of the Textbook Issue relates to the so-called 'spontaneous', 'automatic response' of the Chinese government and people to the alleged changes in Japanese textbooks. If the Textbook Issue was indeed a case of an 'automatic response triggered by provocative Japanese action' as Whiting would argue,[27] then why had the earliest Chinese press reports on the textbooks not carried some sort of criticism or analysis? Furthermore, why was there a three-week gap between the first report in the *Renmin Ribao* at the end of June and the start of the 'anti-Japan' campaign at the end of July? And why had there been no 'spontaneous' outbursts from any of China's mass organisations as soon as the story broke in the Japanese press? These anomalies suggest that the press campaign was in fact centrally controlled, and had been carefully planned during the three-week gap between the first reports in June and the onset of the campaign at the end of July. Doi Masayuki, for example, attributes the silence in the Chinese media from the end of June to 20 July to preparation time needed by the central leadership to plan a large-scale critical campaign, and comments that the similar tone and content of the articles in the *Renmin Ribao* and other newspapers shows the thoroughness of the preparation.[28] Even proponents of the 'Chinese-protesting-at-historical-revisionism' argument agree that the campaign was controlled by the party leadership. For example, Whiting's study of the campaign in the *Zhongguo Qingnianbao* revealed so many similarities to that in the *Renmin Ribao* that he concluded that 'the simultaneous treatment in all media indicates direction from above'.[29] Furthermore, Whiting points out that had the *Zhongguo Qingnianbao* campaign been running contrary to official policy, it would not have continued for so long nor with such strong content.[30] Doi Masayuki suggests that the start of the campaign was timed to coincide with the arrival of the Esaki Trade Mission in Taiwan on 20 July[31] (see below), and Tanaka Akihiko argues that the coincidence of a number of key anniversaries (VJ day, the Marco Polo Bridge incident) during the course of the campaign could also have played a role in the planning of the issue.[32]

Moreover, the style and content of the press campaign closely resembled some of the previous anti-Japan campaigns which had warned of revivals of Japanese militarism. The textbook changes, and other events of 1982 (such as plans for a monument to Manchukuo), were portrayed in the Chinese press as further evidence of yet another attempt by certain circles in Japan to revive militarism. Thus from initial complaints about textbooks, the campaign in the PRC rapidly became an anti-militarist revival campaign highly reminiscent of the pre-normalisation campaigns. It seems likely, therefore, that the media campaign was designed to serve another purpose not necessarily related to the issue of Japanese history textbook content. The nature of the media campaign and the PRC's 'real' motives are discussed in more detail below .

The third question relates to the timing of the issue. If one accepts that the newly-authorised textbooks had in fact changed very little from previous years', and that 'advance' had almost become the standard description of Japan's invasion of China in history textbooks, and if one also accepts the view that the Chinese press campaign had been carefully planned to start in July and coincide with key events and anniversaries, then *why* did the Chinese government choose that particular time to raise the matter to a diplomatic level, especially on the eve of the celebrations of ten years of normalisation and just prior to Prime Minister Suzuki's visit to China? A number of analysts have suggested that the Chinese government took advantage of the Japanese press reports, knowing full well that Suzuki's visit was imminent. As Chapter 2 illustrated, however, there is no agreement as to China's objectives: suggestions range from attempts to put more pressure on the Japanese government to comply with Chinese requests for low-interest loans to attempts to humiliate Prime Minister Suzuki before his China trip.

From the questions raised above it appears likely that there were other factors involved in the Textbook Issue than merely an attempt by the Chinese government to persuade the Japanese to 'adopt a correct view of history'. The questions of elevating the issue to a diplomatic level for the first time, the content and duration of the *Renmin Ribao* and other media campaign, and finally the timing of the issue indicate that the Chinese government used the Textbook Issue as a 'lever' or a means to an end. This idea then tallies with the 'standard line' in discussions of Sino-Japanese relations, that China uses history as a lever. As we have seen, the 'end' to which China usually aspires is generally taken to be economic or political concessions. As will be explained in the following sections, however, the objectives of the Chinese government in the Textbook Issue were not economically-inspired, nor were they necessarily directly connected with Sino-Japanese relations. Rather, changes in Chinese domestic and foreign policies will be seen to be the key determinants of Chinese decision making on the Textbook Issue. Before considering the various reasons behind China's behaviour in the Textbook Issue, it is useful to look in more detail at the media campaign since its careful co-ordination and planning, and its resemblance to previous anti-Japan media campaigns, are strong indications that the Textbook Issue was not merely concerned with history alone.

Media campaign

The relatively closed nature of China's decision-making processes in the 1980s, particularly in the area of foreign policy, raises problems for anyone attempting to assess the relative influence of the key determinants of the policy-making process. One method of ascertaining the government's position on a particular matter is through an analysis of the media output. In China, the mass media has been used not just as a way of informing the public on current affairs, but also as a means of educating the public about the government's position on domestic and foreign issues. Thus, to a certain extent, 'a controlled press in communist societies reflects the perceptions and decisions of the leadership'.[33] By examining the nature of the anti-Japan press campaign, it is therefore possible to ascertain the aims of the Chinese government in the Textbook Issue.

The *Renmin Ribao* is considered to be the organ of the Communist Party of China, and as such the Party has a powerful say in the journalistic content of the paper. The function of the *Renmin Ribao*, in the words of A. Doak Barnett, is 'to articulate and interpret policies in an authoritative way once China's top leaders have defined them'.[34] Of particular significance in this respect are certain types of article, for example, editorial department articles (*benbao bianjibu*), and regular editorials (*shelun*) which represent the most authoritative policy statements. Unsigned commentator articles (*pinglunyuan*) and observer articles (*guanchajia*) are also authoritative, but without 'the same kind of collective top-level endorsement that editorials' have. Other commentaries and signed articles are less authoritative because they tend to reflect the author's individual view.[35] Whiting also points out that not every article and photograph is controlled by the Party, and any analysis of particular articles must bear this in mind.[36] Nonetheless, 'to a significant degree the images of [*Renmin Ribao*] projects are those officially held by the Chinese body politic', though not necessarily individuals.[37] Yet even when centrally directed, the *Renmin Ribao* may not be reflecting 'true' leadership opinion, but *what the leadership wants domestic and foreign audiences to perceive as leadership opinion*. So, foreign news may be distorted or exaggerated for several reasons, for example to mobilise the masses for greater productivity, or to create an external 'enemy' in order to spur domestic unity.[38] It is important to bear in mind that although the *Renmin Ribao* audience is largely domestic, the paper is also a source for foreign observers and may be used by the Party for 'signalling', that is, manipulation of content for a specific foreign target. Therefore, increased front page and editorial attention to an issue is not purely for the benefit of the domestic audience.[39]

Content analysis of the *Renmin Ribao*, therefore, is a useful way of determining the Party's official line on a particular issue, or at least how the Party wants its official line to be perceived. Close examination of the style and content of the media campaign during the Textbook Issue gives some indication of the Chinese government's intentions. The *Renmin Ribao* played the leading role in the campaign and will be the focus of this section, although the campaigns in other newspapers and journals will also be discussed briefly since their similarity to the *Renmin Ribao* campaign is significant.

Content analysis of the Renmin Ribao

Tanaka Akihiko's content analysis of the *Renmin Ribao* Textbook Issue campaign from 20 July to 15 September revealed that during that period, of the 287 articles about Japan in general, 232 related to the Textbook Issue. By totalling the number of paragraphs given over to the Textbook Issue or related subjects (e.g. Japanese militarism, distortion of history and so on) on each day, Tanaka's study shows in graph form the varying intensity of the campaign, with a pattern of 'waves'. From 20 July, the number of paragraphs rose sharply reaching a peak around 10 August (an average of sixty paragraphs) before dropping down to half that level around 18 August. The intensity of the campaign remained roughly at the same level until 3 September, after which the level dropped very low. Tanaka concludes that the campaign was planned to revolve around two key dates: 15 August, the anniversary of Japan's surrender, and 3 September, the anniversary of China's victory in the anti-Japanese war. On both of these anniversaries the *Renmin Ribao* printed 'important articles', on the former date an editorial entitled 'The Past If Not Forgotten is a Guide to the Future', and on the latter an article entitled 'We Must Not Allow the Basis of Sino-Japanese Friendship to be Destroyed by Militarist Forces'.[40]

My own analysis of the *Renmin Ribao* campaign in terms of the number of articles devoted to the Textbook Issue per day from 20 July to 18 September shows a similar pattern to Tanaka's pattern of 'waves'. The most intense part of the campaign was from 31 July to 15 August; the 'first phase'. The 'second phase' ran from 16 August to 18 September. However, it is the tone and content of the articles rather than their number that is most revealing. This section will describe the content of the *Renmin Ribao* in both phases of the campaign, extending Tanaka's period of study to 18 September in order to include the anniversary of the September 18 Incident (Manchurian Incident). In terms of the types of articles, in the period studied, there were six short commentaries (*duanping*), one editorial (*shelun*), three unsigned commentaries (*pinglunyuan*), fifteen signed articles, two Xinhua correspondent's commentaries (*shuping*), two signed Xinhua correspondent pieces, and one Xinhua Correspondent commentary (*duanping*).

First phase: 20 July–15 August

The first short commentary (*duanping*) appeared on 20 July, and set the tone of the first phase of the campaign. It summarised the changes made in the Japanese textbooks, and stated that historical facts such as Japan's invasion of China should be respected and not distorted. Only by so doing, the article continued, 'can the friendship between Japan, China and South East Asian countries consolidate and develop. If not, people will be bound to suspect whether some people in the Japanese government still cherish the spirit of militarism.' The article concluded by urging respect for history, so that future generations can always remember the lesson and live in friendship.[41] The commentaries that followed showed a similar pattern, that is with references to Japan's invasion of China, Sino-Japanese friendship (either since 1972 or the 'traditional' two thousand year bond), and the handful of Japanese attempting to revive militarism and harm Sino-Japanese friendship. The articles differed only in the relative weight given to each of these recurring themes. By the end of July (for example, 24 and 30 July) references to the 'militarist- revival group' were beginning to outnumber references to friendship. Also, while criticism was first directed at the Japanese Ministry of Education, it gradually widened to include 'certain high level government leaders' (that is, Matsuno Yukiyasu and those rejecting China's demands as interference in internal affairs), and finally, by mid-August, the Japanese government as a whole. China's criticism, one *Renmin Ribao* article pointed out, was not born of a fear of Japanese militarism, but was necessary for the sake of Sino-Japanese friendship in the way that 'bitter medicine is good for the illness'.[42]

By 6 August, after the Japanese Ministry of Education had carried out its preliminary explanations and indicated that it would not be changing the textbooks, the matter became one of principle for the Chinese government: 'acknowledgement (or not) of the history of Japanese militarist invasion of China is an important matter of principle for the development of Sino-Japanese relations'.[43] In addition to the 'authoritative' articles (four *duanping* between 30 July and 15 August), other coverage of the Textbook Issue in the early stage took the form of interviews with Chinese scholars, jurists and writers, reports on the support of Japanese opposition parties, press and public opinion, and the reaction of Southeast Asian countries. Most striking was the increasing amount of accounts, supplemented with photographs, of some of the atrocities committed by the Japanese military in China during the war. By this stage then the campaign was being used to recount (in the run up to the anniversary of the defeat of the Japanese) the 'unfortunate period' of Sino-Japanese relations, with the subject of Japanese textbook content barely being touched upon.

The first stage of the campaign culminated in a number of particularly hard-hitting articles on 14 and 15 August, the latter being the thirty-seventh anniversary of Japan's surrender. An article written by *Renmin Ribao* reporter Chen Powei on the 14th explained the workings of Japan's textbook authorisation system, before focusing on the recent trend in Japanese education towards greater control over textbooks. This was one of the few articles that actually referred in any detail to Japanese textbooks, but the article went on to read that, 'some people in the [Japanese] leadership see textbooks as a tool for reviving and fostering militarist consciousness'. For the reporter, the Textbook Issue called into question Japan's ability to build lasting friendly co-operation in the Asia-Pacific region.[44] A commentary by a Xinhua correspondent on the same day devoted his article to criticism of the view of history expounded by Matsuno. While the article conceded that Matsuno's view of history represented that of a minority of Japanese attempting to revive militarism, it then pointed out that Matsuno's remarks were nevertheless a 'warning sign that within the Japanese authorities there are some who have not woken up to the forces which are promoting the revival of militarism, and their prejudice has developed to a serious stage.'[45]

The editorial of the 15th, 'Past Experience if Not Forgotten is a Guide to the Future', recounted the history of Japanese aggression in China from 1894 to 1945 not to 'settle old accounts' but as a reminder that history should not be forgotten, much less distorted. The article then cited various international documents which confirmed that the international community regarded Japan's actions in China as aggression, and criticised the Ministry of Education for 'reversing the verdict of history' (*fan lishi de zhi'an*). While the article stressed that it was the wish of only a handful of people to revive the dream of the 'Greater East Asia Co-prosperity Sphere', this small group was described nevertheless as very dangerous to Sino-Japanese relations, and as part of a trend that warranted serious attention. The report cited examples such as visits of Japanese cabinet members to the Yasukuni Shrine, the production of films like the 'Great Japanese Empire', plans for Constitutional revision and Japanese attempts to create official ties with 'China's territory', Taiwan, as evidence of this serious trend.[46]

Second phase: 16 August–18 September

After 15 August there was a brief lull in the campaign when the number of articles dropped to around three per day (in contrast to between six and ten per day previously). After 22 August the campaign began to gain momentum again, though never reaching pre-15 August levels. There were fewer 'authoritative' articles in this period, but still frequent reference to the reaction of the Japanese (and regional) press and public opinion. There were also more articles relating to joint friendship activities in the run up to the celebrations marking the tenth anniversary of normalisation.

The commentaries that appeared after the 22nd started to show signs of impatience with the slow response of the Japanese government. While still targeting the 'handful of Japanese officials who cling to the position of distorting history', the commentary of 23 August widened its criticism to include some 'senior officials' who had expressed willingness to settle the matter quickly but had not yet put these words into action. This was seen 'as a trick to gain a respite or false pretences to get by, rather than a real step in the right direction.'[47] The tone of articles in the ensuing days became even more impatient, calling into question the sincerity of the Japanese government and reiterating that the issue was one of principle and required serious acknowledgement and an early solution.[48] There was a distinct lack of reference to Sino-Japanese friendship in these articles, which ended more with ultimatums ('It is time to make a prompt decision')[49] than with warnings as in the previous phase. The response to the Japanese statement of 26 August appeared in the *Renmin Ribao* on the 29th, with a commentary on the 30th. According to these articles, the Chinese government had no choice but to reject the statement given the lack of clear, concrete measures and the distance between those and the Chinese demands. There was further criticism of the Japanese government for not acknowledging that the textbooks prettified the invasion, and for failing to take responsibility and take immediate corrective measures. The reports stated that such behaviour brought into question the Japanese government's sincerity in resolving the problem, and expressed the hope that the mistakes would be corrected for the sake of the development of Sino-Japanese relations and for Japan's 'international image'.[50]

In the meantime, the *Renmin Ribao* carried a few articles and a *duanping* on the plans of former Japanese Prime Minister Kishi Nobosuke to erect a monument to Manchuria which the newspaper stated was another reminder that 'the aggressive soul of Japanese militarism refuses to leave.' The articles directed their criticism at a handful of rightists, and issued a warning to the Japanese government to stop this type of anti-PRC behaviour that was threatening to harm Sino-Japanese friendly relations.[51] At the beginning of September, the Textbook Issue was overshadowed by coverage of the Twelfth Party Congress, and the few articles given over to the Textbook Issue tended to focus on the reaction of Japanese public opinion and the opposition of Sino-Japanese friendship groups to the Ministry of Education. On 3 September, China's 'Victory Over Japan Day', an article entitled 'We Must Not Allow the Basis of Sino-Japanese Friendship to be Destroyed by Militarist Forces' made up in content for what had been missing in quantity in previous days. The article charted the development of rightist tendencies in Japanese government and education, and described these trends as 'the social basis for militarism'. The use of 'advance' in textbooks was described as not simply a matter of choice of wording, but as a serious political problem for Asia since it was reminiscent of the type of inculcation used in education before and during the war. Furthermore, the visits of Cabinet ministers to the Yasukuni Shrine, plans to build a monument to the founding of Manchuria, and the production of a number of films which prettified militarism were linked to the political and economic situation, specifically to the trend towards Japan becoming a political power as well as an economic power. The article reminded readers that without the economic co-operation of Asia, Japan would not have achieved such success, and warned that Japan should not become arrogant and think merely of its own interests. Yet, as with the reports of the first phase of the campaign, the article concluded with an assurance that Sino-Japanese friendship could not be harmed by the actions of a handful of militarists.[52]

An article on 7 September carried excerpts of the speech given to the Twelfth National Party Congress on 1 September, in which Hu Yaobang laid out China's new foreign policy objectives. The speech referred to the 'profound friendship' between China and Japan, but in familiar fashion also warned against current trends:

> Now some forces in Japan are whitewashing the past Japanese aggressions against China and other East Asian countries and are carrying out activities for the revival of Japanese militarism. These dangerous developments cannot but put the people of China, Japan and other countries sharply on the alert. Together with the Japanese people and with far-sighted Japanese public figures in and out of government, we will work to eliminate all hindrances to the relations between our two countries and make the friendship between our two peoples flourish from generation to generation.[53]

Acceptance of the 'supplementary measures' offered by the Japanese government on 6 September was announced in the *Renmin Ribao* on the 10th. The front page article explained the measures that the Japanese government would take to correct the textbooks, but concluded that the Chinese government reserved the right to comment if the measures were not carried out successfully.[54] The commentary in the same issue entitled 'The Japanese Government is Expected to be True in Word and Resolute in Deed' summed up the issue, reverting to the style used at the beginning of the campaign with more reference to friendship than to harmful militarist forces. It concluded on an optimistic note, anticipating 'a successful visit by Prime Minister Suzuki and the further development of friendly co-operation between China and Japan.'[55]

After 10 September there was a sharp fall in the number of articles relating to Sino-Japanese relations in general, and the tone became increasingly friendly from 11 September. There were only seven articles discussing the issue of a revival of militarism and the textbook issue, compared with thirteen reports relating to the forthcoming celebrations of the tenth anniversary or Japanese delegations to China.

An article in the 12 September issue carried excerpts from Japanese newspapers which were calling upon the Japanese government to revise the errors in the textbooks. The *Renmin Ribao*, reminiscent of the earliest article on the matter (30 June), merely quoted from the Japanese press and carried no comment or analysis. To mark the September 18 Incident, the *Renmin Ribao* carried two articles (one an account of the incident itself, the other a containing 'a few old people's' recollections of Japanese militarism) and one photograph. These appeared on the inside pages of the newspaper. There was no accompanying editorial, and no warnings about a revival of Japanese militarism. The campaign was clearly being wound down in time for Prime Minister Suzuki's visit .

The anti-Japan campaign was of course not restricted to the pages of the *Renmin Ribao* but was treated simultaneously, and similarly, in all media, thus strengthening the argument that the campaign was directed from above. Commentaries and editorials appeared in all the major newspapers and local papers, and in monthly and bimonthly journals.[56] Many of the articles in the journals bore a striking resemblance to those in the *Renmin Ribao* described above, becoming progressively more anti-Japanese as the issue developed. As Whiting's study shows, the *Zhongguo Qingnianbao* campaign closely resembled the *Renmin Ribao* campaign, although it did not last as long. It began at the end of July with coverage of the Japanese press reports and the Chinese government protest, and attested to 'the reported anger and the hurt feelings of Chinese and Japanese youth, who were united in friendship.'[57] The reports then became gradually 'more volatile and concentrated' over the following weeks, with accounts of the Nanjing Massacre and other atrocities committed by the Japanese army accompanied by photographs. The newspaper carried reports on the international reaction to the controversy in addition to Japanese public opinion and opposition party response. While seeking to lay the blame for the distortions at the door of 'certain circles' within the LDP and Japanese government, the predominant theme throughout the campaign was the 'total barbarity of Japanese military behaviour' during the war, and warnings to be 'even more alert'.[58]

It must be noted, however, that the anti-Japan campaign was probably not totally controlled by the central leadership. The Party does not have full control over signed articles, for example. Furthermore, anti-Japanese sentiment extended beyond the media and prompted denunciations by friendship groups and academics; public meetings were held to 'expose Japanese militarists' bloody crimes' (Nanjing, 7 August),[59] and history seminars and forums (Henan on 7 August, Harbin on 9 August, Beijing on 10 August, Liaoning on 11 August, Shanghai on 12 August) also discussed the issue.[60] Photographic exhibitions depicting Japan's barbarity during the war were held in Guangdong and Hunan.[61] It is unlikely that the government organised all these activities, some of which must surely have been arranged 'spontaneously' by Chinese citizens.

Comparison with 1970 campaign

The Textbook Issue was the first large-scale anti-Japan campaign since the signing of the Treaty of Peace and Friendship in 1978. According to Doi, the Chinese media had been showing some interest over the previous year in what were perceived to be trends towards rightism in Japan (for example, the debate on constitutional revision and visits of cabinet members to the Yasukuni shrine). However, because these were considered Japan's internal matters, the Chinese press restricted itself to quoting from the Japanese media.[62] Textbook content had not been touched upon, in contrast to the South Korean press which had been criticising changes in Japanese textbooks (which attempted to rationalise Japan's rule in Korea) ever since September 1981.[63] It is unclear how much research has been carried out in China on the subject of Japanese textbook content. The Chinese media's total reliance on Japanese newspaper reports to fuel its campaign seems to suggest that the Chinese certainly had less to draw on than their Korean counterparts who were, as early as 5 August, able to submit to the Japanese government a list of the sections of textbooks they wished to have corrected.[64] The confusion on the part of the Japanese government as to *which* passages the Chinese government wanted to be changed also highlights the ambiguity of Chinese demands regarding specific passages.

Furthermore, the resemblance of the campaign to previous anti-Japan campaigns suggests that the Chinese government could have been 'replaying' a pattern of behaviour with which the Japanese government would be familiar. Before 1972, Whiting notes that Chinese media images of Japan tended to depict Japanese society in an unfavourable light,[65] and, as noted in Chapter 3, frequently warned of a revival of Japanese militarism. Some of the earliest warnings of a revival of Japanese militarism came in 1951 in response to Japan's signing of treaties with the USA and Taiwan which the Chinese government saw as a sign of Japan preparing for a war of invasion. The same criticisms reappeared after Prime Minister Kishi's visits to Taiwan and Southeast Asia and the revision of the US–Japan Security Treaty in the years from 1957–60.[66] But the most important campaign against a revival of Japanese militarism came in 1970, and was touched off by the signing of the Nixon–Satō Communiqué in 1969 in which the statement 'maintaining peace and security in the Taiwan region is an important factor in Japan's security' was taken by the PRC to be an indication of Japan's revived militarism.[67]

Nakajima has likened the 1982 Textbook Issue campaign to the 1970–2 'revival of Japanese militarism' campaign, noting that the 1970 campaign had been 'strategic-tactical' and stopped immediately after Sino-Japanese normalisation, after which time the PRC, ironically, even encouraged Japan to increase its defence expenditure.[68] Okabe's analysis of the 1970–2 anti-militarist revival campaign does indeed reveal some similarities with that of the Textbook Issue in terms of both the content of the *Renmin Ribao* campaign and the possible internal and external reasons for China's actions. Criticism of Japan in the 1970 campaign was based on a number of factors. The Chinese perceived an increase in militarist propaganda in Japan comparable to prewar levels, and believed that Japan possessed the potential to send troops overseas. The media campaigns portrayed Japan as being in a similar position to the prewar days with no resources and a lack of markets. This, it was argued, would lead a rapidly developing Japan to take the military option.[69] An alternative to this argument was that Japan's remarkable economic success would lead inexorably to a more active (and therefore dangerous) foreign policy stance. For example, Japan's 'economic invasion' (of Taiwan) and anti-PRC activities (because of Japan's links with Taiwan) were seen as trends which would lead inevitably to Japan's political and military control of Asia.[70] Okabe argues that while the PRC may have genuinely feared a revival of Japanese militarism in the early 1970s, it seems more likely that the PRC leadership had other objectives in mind when launching the campaign, and used it as 'instrument' to achieve those objectives.

Okabe suggests, for example, that the PRC wanted to apply pressure on the Japanese government by appealing to the Japanese people, who could then influence Japan's leadership to bring about policy changes in Japan that would be favourable to China. The main policy intentions behind the campaign were diplomatic normalisation with Japan, and the prevention of what the PRC perceived to be a new 'Asia policy' developed by the USA and Japan. In addition, Okabe argues that the Chinese believed that criticism of Japan's militarism could help achieve the goals of closer links with North Korea and the USA, and a relaxation of tension between the USSR and PRC.[71] In addition to these external considerations, domestic policies were also seen to lie behind the criticism of Japan's militarism. Okabe describes the campaign as an attempt to 'unite' China.[72] Nakajima makes a similar point, arguing that it was necessary for China to criticise Japanese militarism at that time in order to 'overcome its internal confusion and wobbling after the Cultural Revolution . . . and to show the 'revolutionary nature' of Chinese diplomacy.'[73]

The purpose of this anti-militarist campaign, then, was not necessarily concerned with genuine fears of a revival of militarism, but was very much linked to changes in China's domestic and external situations and the PRC's 'definition of the situation'. The Textbook Issue must also be seen in this light, and while the specific circumstances were different in 1982, consideration must be taken of the internal and external influences on PRC decision making at the time. As the next section will illustrate, in 1982 the PRC faced similar domestic and external situations to those of the early 1970s described above, in particular a power struggle and a change in the PRC's perception of the international situation. It may follow, therefore, that the 1982 campaign was used as a way of fulfilling a number of internal and external aims, just as the 1970–2 campaign had been.

Decision-making on the Textbook Issue

The study of the 1982 *Renmin Ribao* campaign showed that the Textbook Issue was carefully planned and controlled by top leadership. But who actually makes up the top leadership in Chinese foreign policy decision-making, and what factors influence their decisions? In authoritarian regimes, foreign policy decision-making is normally the domain of the top leader. This was certainly the case in China under Mao Zedong, who was responsible for making 'virtually every strategically important decision regarding foreign policy issues.' Mao's 'next in command', Premier Zhou Enlai, was in 'charge of the conduct of foreign affairs' in concert with members of the Politburo and a small group of foreign affairs specialists, and foreign policy was then implemented by the Ministry of Foreign Affairs.[74] Under Deng Xiaoping, the foreign policy-making process changed in 1982 with the Party Secretariat (headed by General Secretary Hu Yaobang) and State Council (headed by Premier Zhao Ziyang) taking over the day-to-day decision-making. Major issues may still have involved the Politburo, and certainly Deng Xiaoping, like Mao before him, remained the 'ultimate source of authority' on all important issues. A. Doak Barnett describes Deng as 'very actively involved in making foreign policy decisions', especially if such decisions involved problems relating to major bilateral relationships, or 'strategic' issues such as the 'independent foreign policy' or 'open door policy'.[75] Thus it seems reasonable to assume that Deng, Hu and Zhao were instrumental in launching the anti-Japan media campaign and in the decision-making in the Textbook Issue.

Yet the question remains as to which factors were most likely to influence the leadership in their decision-making. Robinson states that during the Mao period, Chinese foreign policy was dominated by three domestic factors: primacy of politics (as opposed to economics), ideology, and the 'weight of the past', while three international factors – the foreign policies of the USA and USSR, the structure of the international system, and China's calculation of its power and national interests – played a minor role.[76] Under Deng Xiaoping, politics gave way to economics, revolutionary zeal to traditional Chinese culture, and ideology was downplayed. These domestic factors were important in altering Chinese foreign policy, but equally important were international factors such as China's position in the USA–USSR–PRC 'strategic triangle' (which led to a distancing from the USA and détente with USSR), economic interdependence, and rapid developments in the global military sphere (new high-tech weapons, increases in nuclear armament).[77] Thus there appears to have been a shift from the dominance of domestic factors in Maoist foreign policy towards a more complex interaction between domestic and international factors in Deng's foreign policy. As the following analysis will show, both types of factors interacted to influence the decision-making process in the Textbook Issue. The following section will examine the major international, regional and finally domestic influences in the early 1980s to assess the extent to which they could have affected China's action on the Textbook Issue.

Systemic and regional factors

Chapters 3 and 4 described how the changes in the international system taking place in the early 1980s prompted China to reconsider its 'definition of the situation' and reassess its domestic and foreign policies as a result. Heightened rivalry between the USA and the USSR with its renewed arms race was perhaps the most significant trend. In addition, the USA's pro-Japan and pro-Taiwan posture made the Chinese leadership more uneasy about its relationship with the USA. These factors no doubt contributed to China's shift in policy towards the USSR. In addition, the PRC no longer saw the Soviet Union as the 'threatening Bear at the Gate', but as a 'declining hegemonist power' troubled by economic problems and military overextension.[78] While the international situation was by no means returning to a Cold War-type scenario (not least because the superpowers were declining in power), a shift to the right amongst the countries of the western 'alliance' prompted China to adopt a more independent stance.[79]

These systemic factors mentioned above inevitably had an effect on East Asian international relations, prompting shifts in the foreign policy postures of the major players in the region, and consequently effecting change in bilateral relationships. Common themes running through China's bilateral relations with the USA, USSR and Japan were the Taiwan issue, a shift away from the PRC–USA–Japan 'alliance' of the 1970s, and an increasingly independent stance. While these themes may not appear to be related to the Textbook Issue, it can be seen that the issue was used as a clear signal, to both foreign and Chinese domestic audiences, of a fundamental shift in Chinese foreign policy.

In terms of the Textbook Issue being a purely bilateral problem between China and Japan, we have seen how the Textbook Issue has been viewed by some academics as a way of extracting economic concessions from Japan, with some suggesting that the 1984 yen loan package was Japan's way of placating the Chinese. However, it is difficult to prove that there was a direct link between the issue and the loan agreement. The 1984 loan was the second in a series of long-term loan packages, and was agreed between China and Japan as the first loan package (1979–84) lapsed. The low-interest loans, though beneficial to China, serve Japanese interests as well and must be seen in terms of Japan's commitment to supplying aid to many developing countries. If any link is to be made between the Textbook Issue and Japanese economic concessions, then one should perhaps consider the Chinese request in June 1982 to increase the existing loan amount by ¥91,200 million in order to continue construction of four projects. The negotiations took place during the summer and concluded at the end of September with the Japanese government agreeing to pay ¥65,000 million.[80] Had the Japanese government been so keen to placate the Chinese government on the Textbook Issue, then one might have expected it to agree to the higher amount. As it was, it seems more likely that the government pledged the funding on the basis of its own economic interests. When Japan and China agreed upon the first yen loan package in 1979, Japan agreed to fund six out of eight construction projects. Of these six, four were deemed particularly important to Japan's interests in that they would create 'energy supply routes'. In 1982, the request for funding was for the same four projects, that is, construction of Shijiusuo Harbour, expansion of Qinhuangdao harbour, (both to be used for exporting coal to Japan) and expansion of railways between Yanzhou and Shijiushuo, and Bejing and Qinhuangdao (both used to service the two ports).[81] It can be argued, therefore, that by agreeing to the Chinese requests the Japanese government was following its own economic priorities rather than capitulating to Chinese demands or giving in on account of the guilt complex.

Other analysts have suggested that the issue was a way to 'bring the Japanese government to heel' or to humiliate Prime Minister Suzuki before his impending visit.[82] This may have been due to China's dissatisfaction with the China policy of the Suzuki administration. Akasaka, for example, states that one of China's main sources of dissatisfaction was the lack of development of economic co-operation between the two countries.[83] This argument is echoed by Doi, who comments on the fact that the PRC may have been perturbed by the distinct cooling in Japan's 'China fever' during the previous year both in the political and business worlds, brought about by the plant cancellations and by an increase in pro-Taiwan leanings in the LDP. The disinterested response of the Japanese side to Zhao Ziyang's enthusiastic calls in his talks with Prime Minister Suzuki for co-operation in rebuilding existing factories and joint development of oil and non-ferrous metals is cited by Doi as one reason for the Chinese government's strong dissatisfaction with Japan's coolness. This dissatisfaction was then manifested in the Chinese leadership's's attitude in the Textbook Issue.[84] As with the 'economic' argument above, this explanation does not provide a convincing explanation as to exactly how the Chinese government sought to 'bring the Japanese government to heel', except to imply that, by appealing to the guilt complex, the Chinese government was attempting to pressure the Japanese into improving economic relations.

Perhaps a more convincing explanation relates the Textbook Issue to another issue in Sino-Japanese relations – Taiwan – and some analysts have suggested that the Textbook Issue was used to indicate the Chinese government's displeasure at the trade talks that had taken place between an LDP trade mission and the Taiwanese government.[85] Indeed, Japanese foreign ministry officials felt that the Chinese press reports on the Japanese textbooks had been carefully timed to coincide with the arrival of the Esaki mission in Taibei, and revealed Chinese worries about possible moves towards restoration of Japan–Taiwan relations.[86] The trade delegation, headed by Esaki Masumi, Chairman of the LDP's International Economic Policy Special Research Committee (*Kokusai Keizai Taisaku Tokubetsu Chōsakai*) arrived in Taibei on 20 July as part of its tour of Southeast Asia. The purpose of the negotiations in Taiwan was to discuss ways to rectify the trade imbalance between Taiwan and Japan. The Taiwanese government hoped to reduce its deficit with Japan by coming to some agreement on an increase in exports and a decrease in imports, in addition to greater capital investment from Japan and 'economic and scientific-technical assistance'.[87]

For the Taiwanese government the Esaki Mission was significant politically as well as economically, in that it considered the delegation to be representing the Japanese government and regarded the visit as a sign that relations with the Japanese government would be revived and strengthened.[88] The PRC government was suspicious about the nature of the Esaki Mission, seeing it as a signal that some in the Japanese government were seeking closer links between Japan and Taiwan in order to create 'two Chinas' and 'sabotage friendly relations' between China and Japan.[89] A report by Xinhua at the beginning of July noted that although on his arrival in Taiwan Esaki stopped using the title 'special envoy of the LDP president', the 'delegation still had strongly official characteristics'.[90] The PRC was further angered by the use of the words 'the two countries' in an agreement signed between the delegation and Taiwan. Since the Sino-Japanese Joint Statement stipulates that Japan recognises the PRC government as the sole legitimate government of China, the use of the word 'country' to denote Taiwan was seen by the PRC to reveal Japan's treatment of Taiwan as a 'political entity'.[91] Thus, in this scenario, the Textbook Issue was used by the Chinese government to indicate its opposition to Japan's pro-Taiwan moves, and simultaneously remind the Taiwanese of the dangers of becoming too closely linked with Japan.

Doi points out that China's nervousness about international trends regarding Taiwan was not merely restricted to Japan–Taiwan developments, but could be seen also in China's dealings with the USA over arms sales to Taiwan. On 18 July a *Renmin Ribao* article criticised US politicians (Goldwater and Shultz) who had denied China's sovereignty

144   *China's response*

over Taiwan. President Reagan was also criticised for referring to the
Taiwanese 'government' in a press conference on 28 July. China's criticism of the USA had in fact begun the previous year, having been
triggered by the issue of US arms sales to Taiwan, and had grown much
stronger in 1982. In addition to the pending issue of arms sales, the PRC
was also concerned about Reagan's campaign for restoration of diplomatic relations with Taiwan, pro-Taiwan sentiment expressed by some
of Reagan's senior advisers, the replacement of pro-PRC Secretary of
State Alexander Haig by pro-Taiwan and pro-Japan George Shultz, and
the reluctance of the USA to permit the sale of 'several types of dual-
use and high technologies' to China.[92]

Doi suggests that the PRC's concerns about the developments in the
relationships between Japan and Taiwan, and the USA and Taiwan, and
the deterioration in Sino-US relations were revealed when Liao
Chengzhi (Vice-Chairman of the Standing Committee of the National
People's Congress and one of China's main 'Japan hands') sent a letter
to Taiwanese President Jiang Jingguo calling for peaceful unification.
The letter advised that unification was a domestic issue and warned that
'flattery and cajolery' from foreign quarters (that is, Japan and the USA)
was a disguise for selfish intentions. This letter, Doi argues, attests to
PRC worries about foreign intervention.[93] Okada also makes a link
between Japan's economic relations with Taiwan and the matter of US
arms sales to Taiwan, suggesting that for Beijing, the Japanese government's loans and economic assistance to Taiwan represented part of the
trend of militarist thinking. Okada quotes the *Mainichi Shimbun* which
stated that part of the reason that Taiwan required foreign capital from
Japan was to acquire the ability to manufacture (and buy) weapons
(from the USA). Thus by furnishing loans to Taiwan, Japan was inad-
vertently helping the USA's defence policy on Taiwan.[94]

The picture that begins to emerge is one of China taking a harder line
towards the USA and Japan at the same time. This suggests that the
Chinese were looking at the 'whole picture' which they perceived to be a
'Western incursion' (Japan included) into Taiwan. Seen in this context,
the PRC's criticisms of Japanese textbooks were not merely (if at all) a
protest against the revival of Japanese militarism, but an attack on, and
a warning against, 'Western' imperialism as a whole. The campaign also
enabled China to distance itself from both Japan and the USA prior to
its announcement of a shift in its foreign policy stance towards an 'independent foreign policy of peace'.

The announcement of the 'independent foreign policy of peace'
at the Twelfth Party Congress indicated China's 'comprehensive reassessment of the international strategic environment',[95] and a number of

writers have linked this new foreign policy stance with the Textbook Issue. Nakajima, for example, suggests that the anti-Japan campaign was used as a way of signalling a shift in its foreign policy posture away from the 'West' (i.e. Japan and the USA) in favour of the Soviet Union.[96] As described above, relations between China and the USA had been under strain for some time over the arms sales problem (and over imposition of quotas on Chinese textile exports to the USA),[97] and the Chinese government had shown its dissatisfaction over Japan's links with Taiwan. At the same time there was speculation that the PRC and USSR were willing to discuss the possibility of opening talks on normalisation. Indeed, Moscow had been attempting to improve relations with the PRC since 1981. The issue of PRC–USSR rapprochement had been high on the agenda of talks between Prime Minister Suzuki and the PRC leadership during Suzuki's visit to China. While the Chinese side had assured Suzuki that there would be no 'drastic changes' to China's Soviet policy,[98] by October 1982, vice-ministerial meetings between the PRC and USSR had taken place in Beijing and follow-up talks arranged for March 1983.[99]

The swing away from the West towards the Soviet Union has been seen not as a return to the policy of 'leaning to one side', but merely a 'correction' of the over-friendly relations with the USA in previous years, and a shift towards the middle ground allowing China to take a more independent posture between the two superpowers.[100] Zhao Ziyang had talked in April 1982 of the need for China to follow an independent foreign policy,[101] but the concept was officially articulated by Hu Yaobang in his report to the Twelfth Party Congress. Hu maintained that there was nothing new in China following an independent and autonomous foreign policy, since 'in the 33 years since the founding of the People's Republic, we have shown the world by deeds that China never attaches itself to any big power or group of powers, and never yields to pressure from any big power'.[102] The 'new' posture did however represent a marked change from the previous policy which had identified an enemy – the USSR until 1982 – and pursued a firm united front against it.[103]

While some see the introduction of the new foreign policy line as a response to the changes in international politics, others argue that it was introduced largely in response to domestic problems and internal criticisms – mainly from the PLA – that Deng's foreign policy line leaned too much in favour of the capitalist countries like the USA and Japan.[104] In fact, Deng was facing a number of domestic problems which can also help to explain China's response to the Textbook Issue.

Domestic influences

A number of analyses have accounted for Chinese behaviour in the Textbook Issue as being influenced by the domestic situation, and not as a bilateral problem or a response to other external influences. These explanations state that the Chinese leadership saw in the Textbook Issue an opportunity to achieve one or more domestic objectives. The main arguments tend to focus on two objectives: resolution of the conflict with the PLA over Deng's consolidation of power, and boosting the youth education campaign related to building a 'Socialist Spiritual Civilisation'. Both objectives are closely linked to what must be seen as Deng's overarching goal in the run-up to the Twelfth Party Congress: his legitimisation as leader.

Conflict with the PLA

Chapter 4 described the power struggle between Deng Xiaoping and some elements in the PLA opposed to his policies, which had been ongoing since the late 1970s. While the influence of the PLA 'Old Guard' group had been considerably weakened by 1982, the PLA was still in a position to attempt to block Deng's final consolidation of power before the Twelfth Party Congress. They attempted to do so in three ways. The first was through an attack on the role of ideology, which the 'Old Guard' feared was moving too far away from Maoist principles. The second was the attack on the leadership's handling of its dealings with the USA, Taiwan, Japan and the USSR. The third was through negotiations on PLA personnel changes to be announced at the Twelfth Party Congress. The first and second methods represented attacks on Deng's legitimacy, and Deng's response can be connected to the Textbook Issue. The third was a means of retaining as much influence as possible in the higher echelons of power, and need not concern us.[105]

Tang Tsou explains that at a time when the Chinese government was facing a 'heap of problems' in 1982 (such as economic difficulties, disrupted education system, inadequately trained labour force, decline in Party prestige and problems in its relations with the USA) it was essential to maintain political stability and unity by retaining 'the loyalty of the major political forces in China and maintain a proper balance between the conflicting interests, demands and views'.[106] Putting an emphasis on ideological work was one way in which Deng could suppress dissent, strengthen Party leadership, promote ideological uniformity and control bourgeois liberalist tendencies.[107] The PLA, however, did not agree with the new methods of ideological work that Deng was introducing because it was perceived to be neglecting Marxist-Leninist–Mao Zedong thought. Even though Deng had tried to concede to his critics in the early 1980s, even enlisting them in the fight against bourgeois liberalisation, the PLA nevertheless began to attack Deng. This began in early 1981 with calls from the head of the General Political Department (GPD) to increase ideological study in the army. The pace of the campaign quickened after April 1981 with the 'Unrequited Love' issue. This concerned a film, originally written as a play by military writer Bai Hua, which angered certain members of the PLA and Party for its critique of Maoism and lack of patriotism. There followed a media campaign orchestrated by the director of the GPD, Wei Guoqing, in which an article, 'The Four Basic Principles May Not Be Violated', criticised the film and its message.[108] The 'Unrequited Love' campaign can be seen as a means by which the PLA could achieve two objectives: firstly, to apply pressure on Deng to soften his position on the Party's evaluation of Mao's role in the Cultural Revolution (to be adopted in the form of the Resolution on CPC History in June 1981), and secondly, to indicate the PLA's dissatisfaction with Deng's lack of emphasis on 'spiritual civilisation' (communist beliefs and so on). After the Sixth Plenum in June 1981 Deng fought back, announcing that while bourgeois liberalisation must be opposed, the *method* of opposition and criticism must adhere to the 'three do nots': 'do not slip back into old methods, do not launch a campaign to settle literary issues, do not launch a joint attack'. In other words, Deng acknowledged that the PLA had been right to criticise Bai Hua, but the methods used had been incorrect.[109]

As Deng's campaign for socialist spiritual civilisation progressed, so too did the PLA's opposition to, for example, Deng's instructions to emphasise culture and general knowledge as part of military training (rather than, say, ideology). The Director of the GPD, Wei Guoqing, for example, opposed Deng's views on military training in 1982 and his subsequent dismissal from the post 'indicated the continued presence of dissent in the military'.[110] Wei's dismissal has been linked to the publication of an article in the GPD-controlled army newspaper, the *Jiefangjunbao*. The article, by army propagandist Zhao Ziya, appeared in the 27 August 1982 edition and brought the conflict between Deng and the PLA to a head because the article criticised not just Party policies but the Party leadership itself. The article discussed the issue of socialist spiritual civilisation versus capitalist civilisation (in other words 'red versus expert'), and 'criticized the overemphasis on material progress at the expense of Communist ideology', blaming the 'lax and weak leadership' for failing to check the growing trend of bourgeois liberalism.[111] The article, which conflicted with certain points in the report to be given by Hu Yaobang to the Twelfth Party Congress, was apparently timed to appear after the report had been 'basically finalised' and 'may have represented a last-ditch effort by Deng's opponents to pressure the leadership into altering the report in line with their views'.[112]

The PLA clearly failed to achieve its objective as far as ideology was concerned, because at the end of September the *Jiefangjunbao* published a self-criticism. The self-criticism stated that the article had been wrong to deny the importance of 'culture' in the building of a socialist spiritual civilisation. Moreover, it read, the article had run 'counter to the Party's policy of building up a force of cadres who are revolutionary in spirit, young in age, and with a high level of knowledge and technical skills' and had 'propagated a "leftist viewpoint" under the pretext of opposing bourgeois liberalization'.[113]

Japanese writers have linked the Textbook Issue with this culmination of the conflict over ideology, suggesting that the issue was used as a 'diversionary measure' and manipulated by the top leadership to fend off PLA criticism. Ijiri, for example, suggests that faced with dissent from the PLA in the form of the Zhao article, Deng Xiaoping and Hu Yaobang ensured that the anti-Japan campaign would continue into September to allow the leaders to consolidate their power in the Twelfth Party Congress and 'to avoid an attack from conservatives in the Liberation Army'.[114]

Tanaka links the Textbook Issue with the other conflict between the central leadership and the PLA, that of dissatisfaction with Deng's foreign policy dealings; in particular, US arms sales to Taiwan. The PLA had criticised the leadership for making too many concessions to the United States in connection with the Sino-American negotiations on reducing arms sales to Taiwan. Tanaka argues that the leadership, unwilling to attract further criticism, could not be seen to take a pro-Japan sentiment by ignoring the Textbook Issue or taking a soft line, so it therefore used the anti-Japanese campaign, adopting a hard line to prove that it could take a strong stand against Japan (that is, the USA by proxy) and thus prevent any further criticisms of weakness from the PLA.[115] With Deng Xiaoping 'fighting off internal attacks from party and military rivals who were trying to embarrass him over his US policy and the Taiwan issue before the opening of the Twelfth Party Congress', the Textbook Issue provided an ideal 'diversionary issue'.[116]

Socialist spiritual civilisation

The other main argument relating to China's domestic situation states that the Textbook Issue was a means of bolstering the youth campaign in China which aimed to raise awareness of Chinese history, to show the superiority of a socialist spiritual civilisation, to remove the pernicious influence of bourgeois culture, and to strengthen support for the Party.[117] Chapter 4 described how the slogan 'Build Socialist Spiritual Civilisation' emerged in the late 1970s and early 1980s, with Deng Xiaoping providing the first authoritative explanation of the term in December 1980. From January 1981 the Party was called upon to develop a sense of 'spiritual civilisation' among the Chinese youth. The concept stemmed from leadership worry that young Chinese were not sufficiently aware either of their history, or their Party's and army's history,[118] and were essentially suffering from a 'crisis of faith'.[119]

The 'Build Socialist Spiritual Civilisation' campaign was stepped up in the summer of 1982. For example, a 'patriotic education' campaign urging all Chinese, but particularly the young, to 'Love the Party, Love Socialism, Love the Army, Love your Country' was planned for just before and after 'Army Foundation Day' on 1 August.[120] A speech by the Vice-Chairman of the Military Commission, Nie Rongzhen, urged all Chinese, but especially the young, to 'study the history of the Chinese Revolution and the glorious history and fine traditions of our Party and our Army', and to 'resist the inroads of bourgeois ideas' which have 'affected the idea of ardently loving the Party, the socialist movement and the People's Army'.[121] From the day of China's protest to the Japanese government until 1 August there were activities held in Beijing for 'Love the Army, and Learn from the Army Week'. Furthermore, when the *Renmin Ribao*'s anti-Japan campaign was reaching its first peak around 8 August, the Central Committee of the Communist Youth League instructed all its units to organise 'Learn History, Love Your Country' movements in August, September and October.

The increase in activities can be seen as a build-up to Hu Yaobang's report to the Twelfth Party Congress in which he devoted a long section to treatment of 'socialist spiritual civilisation' and which Schram considers to be the most authoritative statement on the topic.[122] Schram argues that by introducing the subject of spiritual civilisation into the report before any discussion of political developments, Hu was stressing the importance of the role of ideology.[123] In his report, Hu stressed the need for the Chinese people to be guided by communist ideology in building a socialist spiritual civilisation, warning that if ideology is ignored then 'people will fall into a one-sided understanding of socialism and direct their attention exclusively to the building of material civilization or even only to the pursuit of material gains.' He also addressed the problem of the 'crisis of faith', talking of the need to stop the decline in standards of social conduct, such as 'benefiting oneself at others' expense, pursuing private interests at the expense of public interests, loving ease and despising work, [and] putting money first in everything.'[124]

The Textbook Issue can be seen as a timely opportunity to help educate young Chinese in history and ideology in the run up to the Twelfth Party Congress. As Tanaka notes, that there was relatively little mention in the *Renmin Ribao* campaign about the Japanese textbooks themselves, and rather more attention given to accounts of the Sino-Japanese war, indicates that the campaign was not so much about criticism of textbooks as about history education.[125] In addition, according to Tanaka the 'patriotic education' campaign began in earnest with publication of the speech by Nie Rongzhen in the *Renmin Ribao* on 25 July (the day before China's official protest to Japan). Tanaka concludes that the reason the Textbook Issue was carefully planned to begin in July and continue throughout the summer was because it was necessary to synchronise it with the youth education campaign.[126]

Summary

From the arguments given above, it seems certain that the Chinese government was not merely concerned with settling a conflict of interpretations of Sino-Japanese history. As we have seen, the Textbook Issue was probably not even directly connected with Sino-Japanese bilateral relations, but had more to do with the Chinese domestic situation and changes in foreign policy direction. Johnson's observation that it seemed 'doubtful that the Chinese government was truly interested in Japanese school textbooks'[127] is supported by the analyses discussed above, which, even if they do not agree on any one particular reason for China's actions, nonetheless concur that the issue was not solely about textbook versions of Sino-Japanese history.

As with the anti-Japan campaign of the early 1970s, it seems likely that the Chinese government used the Textbook Issue as a means to achieve a number of aims. External aims were related to the development of a new foreign policy prompted by a changed view of the world and internal criticisms. The Textbook Issue was used as a means of communicating to foreign and domestic audiences that the previously pro-Western stance was shifting to a more central position. Domestically, faced with a power struggle with certain elements of the PLA opposed to leadership policies and a general 'crisis of confidence' among Chinese youth, the Deng–Hu–Zhao triumvirate took a tough position on Japan, and used the Textbook Issue as part of the youth education campaign. By doing so, the leadership aimed to boost confidence and restore faith in, and therefore the legitimacy of, the leadership in time for the Twelfth Party Congress.

In his discussion of succession politics in China, Shambaugh notes that foreign policy represents an issue area which acts as a barometer of 'political maneuvring among the elite' providing 'opportunities for succession contestants to prove their worthiness and test their mettle'.[128] One means of securing one's position, Shambaugh argues, is to take 'high-profile positions or actions that appeal to nationalistic sentiment'. This was clearly the case in the Textbook Issue, which was used by the leadership to appeal to nationalistic sentiment by reminding the Chinese people (and the PLA dissenters) of the humiliation and suffering caused by Japanese imperialism and, thereby, consolidate its legitimacy.

Yet this sort of behaviour is not unique to China. The literature on international relations suggests it is a universal pattern of behaviour. For example, studies that seek links between societal structures and international behaviour have found that at certain times, certain types of elite 'engage in external conflict in order to divert attention from internal societal problems'.[129] This is thought to be particularly the case with totalitarian or authoritarian regimes and less developed countries which are more prone to 'engage in foreign conflict to divert attention from domestic problems' than democratic regimes and developed countries, but only when the domestic situation is not so serious as to require total preoccupation with internal difficulties. Studies have produced many examples to support this 'diversion hypothesis', citing the PRC in the 1960s, Pakistan in 1971, Latin American countries at various times, and African states in the mid-1960s.[130] Viewed in this way, the Chinese government clearly found the Textbook Issue to be (a) an opportune, diversionary measure to detract from the power struggle and (b) a means of easing the discontent expressed by a sector of the population. Japanese commentators writing at the time of the Textbook Issue suspected that the textbooks were indeed being used by the Chinese government for its own domestic reasons. Japanese foreign ministry personnel, perhaps more familiar with Chinese *modus operandi* than journalists, also suspected that the issue was unconnected with textbooks. Shambaugh could be explaining the Textbook Issue itself when he writes:

> By taking tough positions, Chinese leaders demonstrate their nationalist credentials and win vitally important domestic political support. Foreign analysts would do well to remember that strident

Chinese posturing is directed more at home than abroad. For Chinese leaders, there might be greater room for cooperation and compromise in the absence of succession politics, but under such conditions compromise is often cast as capitulation. To make concessions would leave leaders open to charges of selling out sovereignty, which is political suicide in the Chinese system. No Chinese politician can afford to appear soft on 'hegemony' or 'imperialism' and expect to stay in power.[131]

7 The Textbook Issue
Japan's response

Chapter 6 considered the possible reasons the Chinese government had for lodging its protest about Japan's new history textbooks by looking at the international and domestic situation prevailing at the time. It found that explanations that relied solely on the 'history' aspect failed to provide an adequate account of the Chinese government's actions. Other explanations were considered ranging from the international systemic to domestic levels, and found that some of these appeared far more plausible explanations. This chapter will now turn to look at the Japanese reaction to China's protests to examine which factors were most likely to have influenced the decision makers in their choices. As in Chapter 6, this chapter will show that rather than relying on the standard 'historical' argument, better explanations can be found through closer examination of some of the external and internal 'background' factors described in Chapter 4.

The standard explanation of Japanese behaviour in a bilateral issue with PRC states that Japan responds on an *ad hoc* basis, and 'docilely complies' with Chinese demands in order to assuage the guilt complex felt by Japanese for wartime events. As the following analysis will show, the Japanese government did not give in to Chinese demands in the Textbook Issue and the government's actions were not necessarily dictated by any feelings of guilt.

The chapter begins by reviewing the external developments which may have influenced the course of events in the Textbook Issue, but the main focus of the chapter will be on the domestic aspects of the issue since the issue was closely bound up with the on-going education debate and resolution of the inter-ministerial conflict. The section on domestic factors will, therefore, trace the decision-making process on the Textbook Issue in order to ascertain whether the Japanese government responded in any particular way because it was dealing with China, or whether it followed standard methods of procedure.

Decision making on the Textbook Issue

Chapter 2 talked of the need to identify those variables 'potentially relevant' to the foreign policy output before being able to explore the interaction between them. This is not as daunting a task as it may appear since the type of issue determines the nature of the decision-making process and the factors most likely to influence the process. Thus, Minor describes how 'different actors and patterns of interaction will obtain, and the character of the decision output will vary, depending on the issue to be decided'.[1] In the Chinese case, the issue was an important bilateral foreign policy matter and necessitated a small number of top leaders who were responsible for all the major decisions. In the Japanese case, the issue was (eventually) considered to be an important political matter, or a 'critical' issue,[2] and the key decision-making body was also fairly small. Following Fukui's and Minor's categorisation, a 'critical' issue falls short of being a crisis issue since there is no threat to national security. However, in all other aspects a critical issue is identical to a crisis since it involves an element of surprise, requires short decision time and threatens decision makers' values or goals (the 'situational milieu'). In addition, decision making in a critical issue is by horizontal, equal status, small *ad hoc* groups (type of organisational behaviour), which produce 'creative' or 'unpredictable' decisions (nature of decision).[3]

The Textbook Issue and the Japanese government's response contained elements consistent with a critical issue. The surprise element was the sudden and unprecedented attack by the PRC media on the Ministry of Education, followed swiftly by diplomatic representations by both the PRC and ROK governments. Indeed, the Japanese press accounted for its government's slow response to the foreign demands precisely because the government had not expected the issue to go to these levels.[4] The factor of short decision time was present with the Chinese and Korean governments demanding immediate action, with mounting pressure in the form of anti-Japanese media campaigns spreading throughout East Asia, and with Prime Minister Suzuki's impending visit to China.[5] The threat to decision makers' values or goals could be seen most clearly in the response of the Ministry of Education and the 'education tribe' (*bunkyōzoku*)[6] who resolutely opposed all pressures to change the textbooks on the grounds that such action would rock the basis of the textbook authorisation system; a system that, as described earlier, the MOE was in fact in the process of trying to strengthen. In more general terms, there were widespread fears in the LDP that firstly, the ongoing Ienaga Textbook Trial[7] would be adversely affected if the textbooks were changed in response to foreign pressure, and secondly, if the Japanese were seen to be giving in to foreign interference in what was essentially a domestic issue, their international credibility would be affected at a time when they were trying to raise their status in world affairs.

The organisational behaviour was also consistent with that shown in other critical issues, that is, decisions were made by a small number of high-level ministry officials and Diet members. The decision-making core on the Textbook Issue was made up of Foreign and Education Ministry Bureau Chiefs, Vice-Ministers and Ministers, the Chief Cabinet Secretary and the Prime Minister; in all, a group of approximately twelve decision makers. This number matches Fukui's in his case study of Japan's normalisation with the PRC where 'the number of actors directly involved in the crucial decisions was not much larger than one dozen'.[8] Needless to say, this group of key decision makers did not operate in a vacuum, and their decisions were affected by a number of factors, not least of which was foreign reaction; the opinions of the LDP, the *bunkyōzoku*, ministries, opposition parties, media and the public also had to be taken into consideration. The next section will consider the relative influence of these groups in the decision-making process.

External and domestic determinants

Chapter 4 suggested that a number of changes in the international system in the 1970s and early 1980s affected Japanese foreign and domestic policies. The shift from a bipolar to a multipolar world system meant that Japan could begin to take a more independent stance and a more active role in international affairs. The form that this more active role should take became the subject of much debate, with some arguing for a more active defence role and others for a more active political role. Pressure was being brought to bear upon Japan, chiefly by the USA, whose criticisms of Japan's 'free ride' could no longer be ignored. With a growing sense of pride in the country's economic achievements, the governments of the late 1970s and 1980s were gearing up to respond more fully to these external changes and pressures.

While these external factors may have had an indirect effect on Japanese decision makers, it was the specific 'stimuli', i.e. the reactions of foreign governments and media to the alleged changes to the textbooks, which had a direct effect on Japanese decision-making during the Textbook Issue. As the analysis of the decision-making process will show, Foreign Ministry diplomats and bureaucrats in the 'front line' were particularly concerned about the Chinese and Korean requests, the growing attention the issue was attracting within the region, and the effect the issue could have on Japan's regional and international relations. The Foreign Ministry and 'foreign affairs tribe' (*gaikōzoku*) were supported by opposition parties and interest groups who were keen to see a quick and satisfactory settlement of the issue

Opposition parties

The opposition parties were all vociferous in their criticism of the government's attitude towards and dealing of the Textbook Issue, and were quick to produce a petition to the government. Members of various parties questioned LDP dietmen in numerous committees and reiterated their point of view throughout the duration of the Textbook Issue.

On the subject of textbook authorisation, the opposition parties held different views: while the Japan Socialist Party and Japan Communist Party sought abolition of the system, the Kōmeitō and Minshatō (Democratic Socialist Party) wanted democratisation of the system and also publication of screening results. The Textbook Issue however produced a rare unification of opposition party views, in as much as all criticised the government's mishandling of the issue and shared the view that the textbooks should have been revised immediately.[9]

Having 'watched closely' the government's attitude on the issue, the opposition parties clarified their respective positions by the end of August. The Japan Socialist Party position was that China's protest was natural;[10] the Kōmeitō stance was that the truth should be told to younger generations, and they demanded on 2 August that the government correct the history textbooks.[11] The Minshatō believed that it was wrong to mistakenly record objective historical facts;[12] a Shinjiyū Kurabu (New Liberal Club) spokesman said that if this new trend was ignored it could lead to beautification of Japan's prewar actions.[13] Over 160 members of the Japan Socialist Party, Shinjiyū Kurabu and United Social Democratic Party signed a joint statement urging correction of the textbooks, and sent it to the Prime Minister on 21 August.

Criticism continued after Chief Cabinet Secretary Miyazawa issued the government statement on 26 August. The Japan Socialist Party accused the government of using delaying tactics to avoid correcting the textbooks. The Kōmeitō believed it was within the power of the Ministry of Education to correct the textbooks, and that those in government who had harmed Sino-Japanese relations through this issue should be held responsible. The Shinjiyū Kurabu expressed disapproval of the government statement, and demanded that Japanese youth be given a correct education on history.[14] The Japan Communist Party also criticised the statement, but the Minshatō and United Social Democratic Party judged that the measures contained in the statement were acceptable.[15] After China and Korea had accepted the statement, the opposition parties still felt that the matter had not been settled domestically, and agreed on a policy of 'watching the development of the situation as to what revision the government [would] carry out'.[16]

However, the extent to which the efforts of the opposition parties actually influenced the government's decision making on the Textbook Issue was probably minimal. The Liberal Democratic Party has a long history of overriding opposition parties' protests, the most notable occasion being the renewal of the security treaty with the USA in 1960 when the LDP forced ratification through the Diet in the absence of the opposition parties. Given that the LDP had recently regained a stable majority (and therefore more power in the committees), the opposition parties had no direct control in the decision-making process, and little power to influence the outcome of the Textbook Issue.

Business interests

In the general literature on foreign policy-making, interest groups, such as business or agricultural groups, are generally considered to have a limited impact because they 'have no authoritative position in the foreign-policy process.'[17] Japan's case has been described as somewhat different from this general rule, with the popular conception of Japan, Inc. suggesting a close, almost conspiratorial relationship between the Japanese government, bureaucracy and big business. Studies have shown, however, that the concept of the business community (*zaikai*) as united in its support of the LDP and uniformly in favour of the LDP's policies is a myth. Rather, the *zaikai* has been described as reactive and divided, and certainly not as influential in all policy matters as previously thought.

It is difficult, therefore, to estimate the amount of pressure the business community was able to bring to bear on the Japanese government to resolve the Textbook Issue. Given the growth in anti-Japanese sentiment throughout Asia as the issue developed, it is likely that business leaders were worried about the adverse effect the issue could have on trade not only with China and Korea, but also with Southeast Asia. Yet the reaction of these groups was not widely publicised in the Japanese media. There is some direct evidence that some business organisations supported China's protests and that China was applying pressure on the

Japanese government via trade delegations. For example, the Director General of the Japan Association for the Promotion of International Trade, Morita Takamaru, said during a visit to China that the Ministry of Education should 'right its wrong according to the facts'.[18] When Okazaki Kaheita, adviser to the Japan–China Economic Association met with State Councillor Gu Mu on 11 August, he was met with harsh criticisms of the way the Japanese government was dealing with the Textbook Issue and the serious problem it posed for Sino-Japanese relations.[19]

On the whole, though, there was surprisingly little coverage in both the Chinese and Japanese press of the reaction of Japanese business organisations to the Textbook Issue, but it would be safe to assume that some pressure would have been applied on the government by companies worried that trade with China would be adversely affected by the government's slow response. As Kim points out, Japan's trade with Asia made up 38 per cent of its entire exports and 57 per cent of its imports.[20] Furthermore, with South Korean shopkeepers beginning to boycott Japanese products in August, business groups would have been keen to prevent the issue from worsening and anti-Japan sentiment spreading further through Asia.

Public opinion and interest groups

According to the Chinese press reports, the Ministry of Education's distortion of history provoked 'strong dissatisfaction' amongst Japanese public opinion.[21] Given that the general public in Japan are in the main more concerned with the 'educational advancement of their children than with the ideological content of the education they receive',[22] the response of the Japanese public to the Textbook Issue is notable.

On 30 July, a group called 'The Textbook Problem Citizens Group' (set up in 1981) handed to Miyazawa Kiichi a petition demanding that the government revise the textbooks.[23] A peace rally held in Tokyo on 15 August by opposition parties, trade unions and mass organisations criticised the government's textbook screening system and plans to revise the Constitution.[24] On 18 August there was a meeting of 500 people in Tokyo supported by the Japan Socialist Party, Kōmeitō, Shinjiyū Kurabu and others, and addressed by representatives of unions, women's organisations and textbook writers, all calling for the government to correct the textbooks.[25] Two days later there was a joint meeting of eight 'mass organisations' including the 'Textbook Problem Citizen's Group', 'Asian Women's Group', 'Women's Association Against Militarism' and 'Japan National Culture Association'. The meeting was attended by approximately 500 people, and was followed by a rally outside the Ministry of Education in protest at the distortion of history in text-books.[26] The *Renmin Ribao* frequently reported that Chinese embassies and organisations were receiving telephone calls and letters from Japanese citizens and friendship organisations expressing their indignation at the MOE's distortion of history and showing their support for the Chinese protest.[27] Readers' letters to the Japanese newspapers criticised the MOE's attitude,[28] and members of the public interviewed at random by the press also expressed their disapproval.[29]

Teaching unions and textbook authors were also harsh in their criticism of the government's stance on the Textbook Issue. For the Japan Teachers' Union, the Textbook Issue provided a perfect opportunity to reiterate its calls for abolition of the textbook system. In a meeting with Education Minister Ogawa just after China's protest, JTU Chairman Makieda took the opportunity to stir the problem up a bit more by quoting Ogawa as saying that China's protest was interference. Ogawa flatly denied having said this, and accused Makieda of lying. Throughout the controversy the JTU, other teaching unions, teachers delegations to China and scholars in general took every opportunity to reiterate their stance on the issue. A delegation of the Education and Welfare Association of Aomori made up of primary and secondary school teachers which visited Yichang in China in mid-August expressed its opposition to the Japanese Ministry of Education, and talked of the need to teach students about Japan's aggression in China.[30] A JTU delegation to Beijing at the beginning of August also expressed its disapproval of the Ministry's distortion of history.[31] Fifty organisations affiliated to the JTU lodged a protest with Prime Minister Suzuki and Education Minister Ogawa on 11 August, urging them to accept responsibility, express regret about the war of aggression, and correct the school textbooks.[32]

Much of the criticism levelled at the government by textbook writers centred on the harshness of the textbook screening system, in particular the suggestions for improvement (*kaizen iken*) and suggestions for correction (*shūsei iken*). According to one textbook writer quoted in the *Tokyo Shimbun*, the MOE's explanation that *shinryaku* had a *kaizen iken* attached was not true because he had been forced by the compulsory *shūsei iken* to remove *shinryaku* in his 1978 textbooks.[33] Another textbook writer was quoted in the journal *Japan and China* as saying that in his eight- or nine-year experience of textbook writing, the MOE had *never* allowed the word *shinryaku*.[34] When China expressed its disapproval of the government view of 26 August, the textbook writers came out in full support and called for immediate correction of the distortions, and university professors and school teachers criticised the government for evading responsibility.[35]

The Japan–China friendship groups were unanimous in their condemnation of the MOE's attempts to re-write history. At the end of July, Utsunomiya Tokuma, Chairman of the Japan–China Friendship Association criticised the Japanese government for pandering to recent rightist tendencies, and urged it to take corrective measures as soon as possible. On 28 July, the China Research Institute issued a protest statement to Education Minister Ogawa asking that the MOE uphold and respect the spirit of the Sino-Japanese Peace and Friendship Treaty, and to change its attitude on textbook authorisation.[36] Six pro-China groups handed a petition to Prime Minister Suzuki on 5 August demanding that the government take the issue seriously and solve it as early as possible.[37]

The effect of public opinion, the Japan Teachers' Union and Sino-Japanese friendship organisations on the Prime Minister's decision making on the Textbook Issue is difficult to assess. The standard explanation of the influence of public opinion on Japanese domestic and foreign policy-making states that public opinion counts for very little and rarely has a direct influence on policy outcome. This is not just restricted to Japan but is a phenomenon common to many countries. Jensen, for example, states that public opinion has little impact on decision makers who have 'considerable latitude in the making of foreign policy'. Jensen cites examples from USA, British and Japanese foreign policy 'events' where the strength of public opinion was not taken into account in the foreign policy decision.[38] However, it seems likely that the combined weight of public opinion, *zaikai* pressure, opposition group activities, and constant media attention influenced the decision makers to some degree, though to a lesser extent than consideration of the mounting anti-Japan movement, and resolution of the inter-ministerial and subgovernmental conflict.

Resolution of domestic conflict

One of the most striking characteristics of the Textbook Issue was the number of conflicts that emerged, and the way in which they were resolved. The conflict between the Ministry of Education and the Ministry of Foreign Affairs was most evident, but there were also disputes within the LDP, within the *bunkyōzoku*, and amongst the foreign affairs-related dietmen. Many of these conflicts were not necessarily connected with the problem of Japanese history textbooks, or even how best to appease the Chinese and Korean governments. Rather the conflicts were an extension of the domestic debate about the education system described in Chapter 4, or else focused on the issue of whether the protests represented interference in domestic matters.

Since the Textbook Issue was treated as a domestic educational matter from the outset, it is useful to turn to the literature on Japanese domestic decision making which reveals similarities between the behaviour of the bureaucracy, the LDP and the Prime Minister during the Textbook Issue and general patterns of behaviour. The most notable examples are Campbell's description of patterns of conflict and conflict resolution in the Japanese government, and Park's description of interagency co-ordination in controversial issues.[39]

Patterns of conflict and conflict resolution

Campbell's research into policy conflict within the Japanese bureaucracy and the LDP is particularly helpful to an understanding of the types of conflict that arose amongst the bureaucracy and government in the Textbook Issue. He describes a number of regular patterns of conflict or 'cleavage' that occur frequently in the Japanese governmental system, and which are evident in particular in most major conflicts. 'Formal organisation' cleavages refer to conflicts that occur between bureaux within ministries or between different ministries during the policy-making process. Conflicts occur for many reasons, incompatible goals, competition for a share of the budget, 'overlapping jurisdictions' etc., and Campbell comments on the frequency and intensity of 'battles between ministerial feudal domains [which] are the staple of Japanese bureaucratic folklore.'[40] 'Interest-representation' cleavages are divisions according to areas of interest represented by ministries and their clientele (or interest) groups. Interest-representation cleavages occur in the LDP also, where individual dietmen may become associated wih particular 'causes' or interests. While this sort of interest-representation tends to be fairly fluid and flexible, changing according to the type of issue, Campbell identifies more 'stable groupings' within the decision-making system in the form of links between the divisions (*bukai*) of the LDP's Policy Affairs Research Council and the ministries to which they correspond. These alliances are further strengthened by the clientele, or interest, groups which develop ties with the ministry and *bukai* to form 'subgovernments'. Subgovernments, therefore, form a strong and (usually) united front in the face of threats to their particular interests, and 'are crucially reinforced by the deep formal organization cleavages between ministries'.[41]

A third type of cleavage which affects conflict resolution, though more often routine policy making than major conflicts, is the 'informal cleavage'. This refers to groupings such as party factions (*habatsu*), 'university cliques' (*gakubatsu*), study groups, or 'vertical cliques' (*sempai–kohai*) which may divide a ministry, or more likely, a party such as the LDP. While informal groups within ministries are unlikely to be so well organised or strongly identified with a particular viewpoint to impact upon policy conflicts, Campbell argues that factions and opinion groups within the LDP can be seen to influence certain types of policy. In particular, foreign policy matters can be affected since 'foreign affairs offers more scope for ideas and opinion than domestic policy'.[42] Campbell cites the pro-Beijing and pro-Taiwan lobbies as an example of the pressure these sorts of opinion groups can bring to bear on policy-making. Factions tend not to be identified with particular policy issues, but can affect the outcome of some major decisions. More often, however, factional cleavages can be used for purposes of influencing the balance of power within the LDP. Campbell notes, for example, that 'when factional cleavages are *already* activated – most often, because the prime ministership is somehow in doubt – that those opposed to the incumbent leadership will search around for likely issues and make them controversial'. [43]

Campbell's 'model' helps to show that the patterns of conflict behaviour that occurred during the Textbook Issue are consistent with 'normal' patterns of conflict not just in Japan but in other governments also. Thus, as Campbell describes, policy conflict within the bureaucracy is dominated by formal-organisational cleavages, which are reinforced by interest representation cleavages. This was clearly the case in the Textbook Issue with the MOE and MFA arguing for their respective positions. The LDP interest-representation cleavages, the *bunkyōzoku* and *gaikōzoku*,[44] in turn reinforced the interests of their respective ministries and interest groups, thereby creating the conflict between subgovernments. In addition, there was a certain amount of conflict *within* the subgovernments brought about by different views on how to handle the problem. Finally, the issue was further compounded by a certain amount of factional cleavage, with some conflict between the mainstream and anti-mainstream factions, although this tended to break down into interest-representation as the issue progressed.

As there are common types of conflict, so too are there common patterns of conflict resolution depending on issue type. Both Park and Campbell describe similar patterns of conflict resolution, and these can be applied to the Textbook Issue. Campbell states, for example, that where the consensus model does not work, then Japanese decision makers employ alternative methods of conflict resolution such as 'contrived consensus' or 'mediation from above'. A 'contrived consensus 'may be reached when a constantly recurring problem requires ministries to set up 'project teams' or when agencies are set up to deal specifically with the problem. With non-recurring policy conflicts, however, a contrived consensus will probably not emerge, and 'mediation from above' (i.e., the prime minister, chief cabinet secretary and party secretary-general) is necessary. The role of the mediator or go-between is to discuss 'the problem exhaustively with both contending groups, so that each side is confident that the mediator has heard and understood its point of view'. When the mediator suggests a possible solution, 'he then has considerable leverage to persuade each side that it is the best he can do given the situation'.[45]

Park's description of the way in which bureaucratic agencies interact during controversial or complex issues provides a more comprehensive view of the different stages of conflict resolution. When co-ordination with another agency is necessary, Park explains, co-ordination starts at the administrative level (*jimuteki*) with bureau directors and even Administrative Vice-Ministers in charge of negotiations. It is a 'rule of high priority' that the ministry initiating the policy or programme also involves the ruling party (i.e., the LDP) at this stage. This is done through the corresponding Policy Area Research Committee division (*bukai*) and special interest dietmen (*zoku*). In an educational issue then, the MOE would be in contact with the Education Affairs Division (*bunkyōbukai*) and the education tribe (*bunkyōzoku*). It is the ministry's responsibility to keep the corresponding division 'informed of all major developments', and moreover to 'seek its understanding at every important stage of coordination and support mobilization with other ministries, the Diet, and interest groups'.[46] Thus, the LDP becomes involved in all issues – major or routine – at the earliest stage of co-ordination. If co-ordination at the administrative level fails, the next step is to deal with the issue at the 'political' level. This can involve meetings between the appropriate ministers, cabinet committees, or it can mean that the Prime Minister takes on the task of co-ordination. At the political level, the minister plays the key role in mobilising support for his ministry. If the minister is a 'powerful dietman with much clout', the ministry may rely on his influence to persuade relevant committees, party 'elders' (secretary general, faction leader, *zoku* leaders etc.) round to the ministry's proposed policy.[47] Yet there is a limit to how far the minister can go to defend or promote his ministry's policies. He is, after all, first and foremost a member of the ruling party, and owes his allegiance to that party. Thus 'when party policy priorities are conveyed to the minister, he is expected to see that they are incorporated into agency policy. He cannot allow agency considerations to overshadow those of the party on important policy issues.[48] If the minister is unable to reach a satisfactory settlement with another ministry or with the corresponding PARC division, the issue invariably will be referred to the 'final policy arbiter'; the Prime Minister and major faction leaders. At this stage, Campbell's 'mediation from above' takes place. However, if these 'high-level mechanisms' fail to produce an intraparty, interfactional consensus, then the prime minister 'assumes final responsibility for decision making and its political consequences'.[49]

The stages of decision making in the Textbook Issue described in Chapter 5 correspond to the stages of Park's 'model' of decision making (see Table 7.1). From the time of China's official protest until 4 August (Stages 1–2), the issue was treated as a domestic educational and therefore an administrative (*jimuteki*) problem for the MOE to handle. With South Korea's entry into the controversy, the issue became an 'important problem' (Stage 3), in other words a problem requiring co-ordination between the MOE and the MFA. By late August, co-ordination between the two ministries had failed to produce a satisfactory settlement, and it became a matter requiring a 'high-level political judgement', in other words, mediation by the Prime Minister, Chief Cabinet Secretary and LDP Secretary General (Stage 4). When mediation failed, it was necessary for the Prime Minister to 'take final responsibility' (Stage 5).

Campbell argues that the key to understanding conflict in domestic policy-making is to analyse the relationship both between and within subgovernments.[50] The two agencies most deeply involved in the Textbook Issue were the MOE and the MFA, and the conflicting opinions of the ministries and the support provided by respective *zoku* dietmen and interest groups represented a 'typical' subgovernmental dispute of the type Campbell discusses. The next section will therefore

Table 7.1 Japanese decision-making process

Stage	Level of decision-making process	Type of conflict	Method of conflict resolution
1. Domestic	Administrative		
2. Diplomatic	Administrative	Inter-ministerial	Co-ordination
3. International	'Important' political	Sub-government	Co-ordination
4. Compromise	High-level political	Inter- and intra-sub-government	Mediation from above
5. Settlement	Prime Minister's responsibility		'Final policy arbiter'

consider the way the conflicts between and within the subgovernments developed as the issue progressed through its various stages, and how they were resolved.

Administrative problem (Stages 1 and 2)

When the Chinese press picked up on results of the textbook screening process at the end of June, the Ministry of Education was sufficiently worried that Head of the Textbook Authorisation Division, Fujimura Kazuo, took the matter up with the Foreign Ministry. The Ministry of Foreign Affairs, however, was unconcerned, dismissing Fujimura's concerns. Indeed, according to Ishiyama, the head of the China desk reassured Fujimura that the Chinese press reports were nothing to worry about, and that China would not make an issue of the textbook screening process; after all, Zhao Ziyang's recent visit to Japan had reconfirmed Sino-Japanese friendship on the eve of the tenth anniversary. When China protested, the MFA was clearly caught off guard. One MFA official stated, 'in the history of international relations, there are no examples of such a thing becoming a diplomatic matter'.[51] The MFA notified the Education Ministry of Xiao Xiangqian's protest on the evening of 26 July. Ishiyama's account of the MOE's initial reaction to China's official protest describes the debate that took place amongst the top MOE personnel who were unclear as to whether the protest was just a warning to the MOE to take care in its next round of textbook authorisation, or whether it was more serious. If it was a serious protest, the MOE had to find out what China's objectives were, and how much the MOE would have to concede to satisfy China's demands. The Education Administrative Vice-Minister, Misumi Tetsuo, therefore made the decision to contact the MFA to ascertain China's intentions, to arrange a meeting with the Chinese Embassy staff to explain the textbook screening process, and to inform the press.[52]

As Chapter 5 showed, from the very outset the Ministry of Education's reaction to China's diplomatic protest was that although it was willing to listen humbly and to explain the situation, it had no intention of changing the textbook authorisation policies.[53] This was also the 'officially sanctioned' means of dealing with the issue. Meetings between the Prime Minister, Chief Cabinet Secretary and Education Minister Ogawa on 27 July confirmed the decision to explain the textbook screening system in response to China's protest, and at a Cabinet meeting on the same day Prime Minister Suzuki announced the decision to make all efforts to 'explain the real truth (*shin'i*)' in order to calm the situation and avoid it becoming a diplomatic problem.[54]

The MOE were confident that the Chinese government could be made to understand. After the first round of explanations on 29 July, when Bureau Chief Suzuki described the mechanism of the textbook authorisation system (emphasising that the government played a minor role) and assured the Chinese side that Japanese education reflected the spirit of the Sino-Japanese Joint Statement, the MOE was therefore surprised by Wang Xiaoyun's cool reaction and his 'personal' statement that the Chinese people could not be satisfied. This was a response which, according to the Asahi, the MOE did not expect.[55] Yet despite the Chinese dissatisfaction with the preliminary explanation, their subsequent retraction of Ogawa's invitation to China and then Korea's official protest, the MOE – at least as far as the media portrayed it – still maintained that the matter could be resolved through explanation of the textbook authorisation system.[56] In fact, Ishiyama notes that there *were* doubts in the MOE that China could be made to understand, and some suspicions that the Textbook Issue was not really about textbooks.[57] At a meeting of education-related 'Old Boys', there was general agreement that the PRC probably had an ulterior motive for its protest, since for many years the controversial *shinryaku* to *shinshutsu* recommendation had been the subject of Japanese press reports but had not attracted Chinese attention.[58] The retraction of Ogawa's invitation to visit China came as a severe blow to the MOE, and was taken as an indication that 'explanation' was not going to work. Nonetheless, the 'Old Boys' were unanimous on the decision not to give in to the external pressures, since any change to the textbook screening process would have huge implications. [59]

In contrast to its initial dismissal of the Chinese news reports, once the issue became a diplomatic matter, the MFA was keen to get it under control as soon as possible. Ironically, however, it was prevented from doing so by the MOE's 'stubborn' attitude, and the beginnings of the conflict between the two ministries emerged with the MFA criticising the Education Ministry for its 'lack of international awareness'.[60] As might be expected, the chief worry for the MFA was how the issue would affect friendly relations with China and Korea, but like the MOE, there were suspicions amongst Foreign Ministry personnel as to whether China's protests were genuinely concerned with textbooks. Some perceived that Chinese caution over the Reagan administration's Taiwan arms sales and the LDP's Esaki Mission to Taiwan lay behind the criticisms. However, despite growing worries about possible escalation of the issue, the MFA was nevertheless powerless to do anything since the textbook authorisation system was a domestic educational matter in which the MFA could not interfere.[61]

'*Important*' *political problem (Stage 3)*

When Korea made its official protest and China reiterated its demand for correction of the textbooks, Prime Minister Suzuki began to apply pressure on the Ministry of Education to 'co-ordinate its view' with the Ministry of Foreign Affairs. Now considering the issue an 'important problem' requiring an 'early solution', Prime Minister Suzuki also called for the government and party to act as 'one body' (*ittai*) in their efforts to solve the problem. The *Asahi Shimbun* saw this as evidence that it would be inevitable to solve the issue on the basis of a 'political judgement' (i.e. high-level decision) since dealing with it at administrative level had not been successful. According to the *Asahi Shimbun*, the decision to reconfirm the principles of the Sino-Japanese Joint Statement was an unprecedented act, which revealed the Prime Minister's strong feeling that the issue must be handled cautiously.[62]

The Ministry of Education continued its 'desperate defence of TAS [textbook authorisation system]'[63] and refused to change the textbooks on the grounds that altering textbooks at the request of foreign governments would destroy the basis of the textbook system. But the MFA, now with the added worry about how the issue would affect trade talks with Korea, declared that it was nonetheless still unable to take action (*myōshu ga nai*) despite growing fears that if not handled correctly it could lead to repercussions in Japan's diplomatic relations with China and Korea.[64] Both the Prime Minister and the MFA stepped up their pressure on the MOE to change the passages in the textbooks after 7 August, but as the conflict with the MFA grew, the MOE became even more adamant that the textbooks could not be changed. The conflict, not just between the two ministries but between the education and foreign affairs subgovernments, became increasingly obvious at this point.

By this stage, the MOE was fully supported, or more likely, directed by the *bunkyōzoku*, which took a particularly hard line on the issue.[65] The *bunkyōzoku* is considered to have considerable influence in education policy making, with the relationship often described as one in which the *zoku* is the 'senior partner' and the MOE the 'junior partner'.[66] In the Textbook Issue, for example, Takayama describes the MOE's attitude as submissive to the *bunkyōzoku*,[67] playing the role of 'hand-maiden'. Throughout the Textbook Issue the educational subgovernment presented a formidable 'united front' in its battle with the Ministry of Foreign Affairs and the Prime Minister. The initial MOE statements gained the full support of the Education Affairs Division and 'the MOE relied on zoku members to prevent the MFA from intervening in its area of responsibility'.[68] For example, on 27 July, a joint meeting of the Education Affairs Division and Education System Research Council confirmed its support for the MOE's view that the textbooks could not be changed in response to a protest from a foreign country.[69] On 4 August, 'education-connected' LDP Diet members in a meeting with MOE officials agreed that the problem 'be settled as an educational problem, to the last'.[70] On 6 August, at a joint meeting of the LDP's Policy Affairs Research Council education bodies, the Educational Affairs Division and the Educational System Research Council (ESRC),[71] former Education Ministers expressed the view that 'an easy-going compromise will not be good for the future of Japan–China and Japan–ROK relations'. Thus they rejected the 'compromise' of changing the textbooks, favouring instead the policy of 'obtaining the understanding' of the Chinese and Korean governments.[72] Thus, the education subgovernment was adamant that the textbook authorisation system be maintained at all costs. If changes were made, especially at the behest of a foreign government, the system would be weakened just when the MOE and the *bunkyōzoku* were trying to strengthen it. Furthermore, any changes to the system would be tantamount to an admission that textbook authorisation methods and results had hitherto been wrong.

Yet despite the education subgovernment's unerring position, signs that the MOE might be willing to compromise began to emerge at the beginning of August. At a Lower House Educational Affairs Committee meeting held on 6 August, for example, the MOE appeared to be willing to take a softer position on the issue. Education Minister Ogawa was reported as saying the MOE 'was ready to accept applications by textbook publishers for corrections of controversial descriptions in those textbooks which anger China and other countries.'[73] Bureau Chief Suzuki also 'hinted' at the 'possibility of the MOE side's agreeing to the correction of errors' according to a report in the *Nihon Keizai Shimbun*. Suzuki said that 'if applications for the correction of errors are presented by the school textbook companies, we will have no choice but to accept them and study them', although he qualified this statement by saying that a re-revision would not be 'in conformity with the purport of examination and authorisation'. The *Nihon Keizai* regarded this statement as indicative of pressure being applied from top party leadership:

> It is viewed that this statement contained the implication that compliance with the request for a re-revision is entrusted to high-level political judgement, going beyond the Education Ministry

officials concerned, and the administrative official concerned will have no choice but to accept such a political judgement.[74]

High-level political problem (Stage 4)

The high-level involvement to which the *Nihon Keizai* referred was probably related to Prime Minister Suzuki's announcement on 7 August that he was determined to settle the Textbook Issue by accepting Chinese and Korean requests for revision of the passages in the textbooks. Furthermore he set a deadline, indicating that he expected the problem to be resolved before his visit to China in September.[75] The LDP, though fairly divided on the issue, appeared willing to show self-restraint in order to avoid an intraparty struggle. However, the Prime Minister's statement indicated that in addition to the key problem of dealing with the conflict between the Ministry of Foreign Affairs and the Ministry of Education, maintaining harmony within the party was also important. The Prime Minister stated, for example, that he had informed Education Minister Ogawa of his intention, and that the key was to try to persuade the MOE and LDP to agree to the proposal.[76]

Publication of the Education Ministry's *kenkai* of 9 August eradicated any impression the MOE had given earlier about softening its stance, reconfirming as it did the standard line that the Ministry was willing to listen and explain, but make no corrections to the textbooks. The subsequent publication of the Foreign Ministry's *kenkai* further underlined the lack of progress that was being made in the Prime Minister's attempts to mediate from above. The decision taken on 13 August to produce a Prime Minister's view (*shushō kenkai*), in other words a unified government statement, which would declare Japan's war responsibility and self-reproach for past history was reached after Hashimoto and Osaki returned from Beijing. The Prime Minister instructed both the MFA and the MOE to work out a policy response on the basis of the reports of the Bureau chiefs, the MOE to continue to work out concrete means for revising the textbooks, and the party to 'coordinate itself'.[77] Chief Cabinet Secretary Miyazawa announced that he hoped a solution could be found before Foreign Minister Sakurauchi's departure for India on 27 August, thereby imposing a time limit on the conflicting parties.

As the issue developed, the MOE became increasingly isolated and it finally appeared willing to concede to Chinese and Korean requests. An initial compromise was reached between the MFA and MOE on 17 August at a meeting between MFA representatives Kiuchi and Hashimoto, and MOE representatives Suzuki and Osaki. It is possible that this concession came about because the MOE had come under pressure from some of the *bunkyōzoku* to agree on some sort of compromise with the MFA. The *Asahi Shimbun* suggested, for example, that the MFA and *gaikōzoku* made the *bunkyōzoku* their chief target in persuading the MOE to make concessions.[78] In this scenario, the *bunkyōzoku* came under pressure from the LDP, the Prime Minister and the Foreign Ministry to try and persuade the MOE to soften its attitude, and the MOE eventually submitted to *bunkyōzoku* pressure. The two key people who appeared to have been entrusted with the task of negotiating a compromise were Mitsuzuka Hiroshi and Mori Yoshirō, which is ironic since these two politicians were keen advocates of moves to strengthen textbook authorisation system and the 'ringleaders' in the 1980–1 'biased textbook campaign'.[79] This does indicate, however, that the education subgovernment was not completely united on the issue, with some *bunkyōzoku* preferring to take a more cautious approach. Indeed, closer examination of some of the discussions being held within the education and foreign affairs subgovernments, but particularly within the LDP, reveal further conflicts which are worth examining in more detail.

In terms of intra-party conflict, Campbell's third type of cleavage, the informal grouping, was described as likely to affect routine policy-making rather than major conflicts. Similarly, Fukui's study of the politics of Sino-Japanese normalisation in 1972 found that ideological and policy-related conflicts had a greater influence on decision making than did factional conflicts.[80] This would appear to be borne out in the Textbook Issue, since one striking characteristic of LDP behaviour appeared to be the lack of factional conflict. Journalist Shimizu Minoru, for example, commented at the time of issue on the lack of intraparty power struggle that would have been expected under the circumstances. Shimizu explains that:

> In the past, when the prime minister of the day and the mainstream group have come up against a difficult problem, the anti-mainstream group has seen it as a good opportunity to undermine the premier's political base and has made it the subject of outspoken arguments strongly critical of the prime minister.[81]

During the Textbook Issue, perhaps with the exception of Nakagawa Ichirō,[82] there was no open criticism of the Prime Minister by non-mainstream faction members. Indeed, according to Shimizu the non-mainstream factions (Fukuda, Komoto and Nakagawa) *co-operated* with the mainstream factions of Suzuki and Tanaka to help settle the problem. Shimizu ascribes this to the complexity of the issue, which required a 'united' approach. Another reason is that the non-mainstream faction contained many *bunkyōzoku* who were in turn members of the Japan–Korea Dietmen's League. Shimizu explains that although there was a strong feeling within the LDP that the Chinese and South Korean protests were 'improper', these feelings were not 'strongly voiced at official party meetings . . . because these dissatisfied dietmen, being pro-Korean, have tried to avoid exacerbating overall relations between Japan and South Korea.'[83] Thus, Korea's entry into the controversy appeared to have a moderating effect on intra-party friction because of a conflict of interest. According to this argument, had the protests come from China alone, it is possible that the LDP would not have been willing to accept the compromises and inter-factional conflict might have played a greater role in the outcome. Shimizu quotes a leader of the LDP mainstream who said that without the South Korean protests, 'the Fukuda faction and other members of the non-mainstream group would probably have strongly opposed the amendment of the textbook accounts and criticised Prime Minister Suzuki and his government for their handling of the issue'.[84]

On closer examination, however, this apparent lack of argument over the Textbook Issue was in fact only superficial, and in reality there *was* a great deal of 'informal argument', criticism of Suzuki's leadership, and factional and ideological conflict.[85] Indeed, since the textbook controversy touched upon a number of sensitive issues – domestic and diplomatic – disagreement between various party groups was inevitable. Thus, while the party appeared to be fairly united on the Textbook Issue, behind closed doors there was a great deal of discussion and conflict.

Schoppa describes the LDP's response as 'a typical "hawk" versus "dove" conflict',[86] with the hawks rejecting the criticisms as interference in internal affairs, and the doves advocating a cautious response. Japanese observers have also tended to apply this broad categorisation to the Textbook Issue. Following this classification then, the issue can be seen in terms of the 'traditional' conflict between on the one hand, the hawk non-mainstream factions (such as Fukuda), which contain many *bunkyōzoku*, many of whom also happen to be Korea-friendly, and on the other hand, the dove mainstream factions (such as Tanaka), which are pro-China, a standpoint supported by many *gaikōzoku*-related dietmen (see Table 7.2).[87]

There are however a number of anomalies in the classification suggested in Table 7.2, and the boundaries between the opposing groups were in fact not as clearcut as the categorisation suggests. Firstly, some LDP members who normally could be considered hawks took a dovish

Table 7.2 Conflict in the Textbook Issue

Doves	Hawks
Tanaka (i.e. mainstream) faction	Fukuda (i.e. non-mainsteam) faction
China-friendly group	Korea-friendly group
Gaikōzoku	*Bunkōzoku*

stand on the issue, and members of the supposedly mainstream dove factions took a hawkish stand. Perhaps the best example of the cross-factional nature of the issue is the so-called *sanninzoku* (Matsuno Yukiyasu, Minowa Noboru, Nakagawa Ichirō),[88] who were the 'spokesmen' for the LDP hawks, yet belonged to the (mainstream) Tanaka faction, or headed their own (Nakagawa). In addition, since none of the *sanninzoku* were education-related dietmen, the reasons for their position appears more to do with the expression of the new sense of nationalism (discussed in Chapter 4) and fears about maintaining national sovereignty than with concern for the preservation of the text-book authorisation system.

The second problem with the classification is that dietmen who held concurrent 'membership' of *bunkyōzoku* and PRC Dietmen's League or *gaikōzoku* and ROK Dietmen's League were faced with the dilemma of which stand to take. Two examples can be cited to illustrate the complexity of the issue for individual dietmen. Mitsuzuka Hiroshi was a member of the Fukuda faction and a *bunkyōzoku* hawk. He was active in the 1980 'Biased Textbook Campaign' and was therefore in favour of stricter textbook authorisation and opposed to revising textbooks in response to foreign requests. He was also a member of the (supra-Party) Pro-Korean Dietmen's League (KDL), and whereas under normal circumstances membership of both the *bunkyōzoku* and the KDL would not be problematic, the Textbook Issue created a conflict of interests. Moreover, Mitsuzuka was sent as a Japanese government representative to Korea, where needless to say the Korean press criticised him as a 'ringleader' of the textbook campaign. Furthermore, the LDP entrusted Mitsuzuka with the job of persuading the Ministry of Education to reach a compromise with the Ministry of Foreign Affairs. Education Minister Ogawa faced a similar dilemma to that of Mitsuzuka. A member of the Suzuki (therefore dove) faction and 'self-professed' China friend, Ogawa nevertheless took a hard-line position in support of the *bunkyōzoku* and the ministry he represented.[89]

Third, the *gaikōzoku* and *bunkyōzoku* were not uniformly for or against revision of the textbooks because there were varying degrees of 'hawkish' and 'dovish' attitudes within the groups. This indicates the presence of intra-subgoverment conflict. The *bunkyōzoku* did not agree unanimously on a hard-line policy, and similarly not all of the *gaikōzoku* agreed upon the adoption a moderate policy. The various meetings of the Education and Foreign Affairs related groups held on 18 and 19 August, respectively, best represent this lack of cohesion. Various opinions were voiced at the joint Education Affairs Division and Education System Research Council meeting. Whereas some dietmen rejected the requests as interference in internal affairs, others advocated a cautious response, or even acceptance of the Chinese and Korean requests for revision.[90] The Foreign Affairs Division and Foreign Affairs Research Council Vice-Chairmen's meeting produced similar discussions, with a range of viewpoints from rejection to acceptance of the demands.[91]

The myriad of conflicting and competing views and interests expressed by the LDP dietmen, albeit behind closed doors, gives some indication of the complexity of the task facing Party and government leaders in their attempt to bring about a solution to the Textbook Issue. Nevertheless, despite all this 'informal argument', it was important to create an impression of party cohesion because the Party executive hoped for an early settlement of the issue.[92] This appearance of unity was achieved through a great deal of 'groundwork' (*nemawashi*) carried out by party executives (*tōkanbu*) who talked to important participants of Education Division and Foreign Affairs Division prior to meetings to request that they avoid any argument on the Textbook Issue.[93] Party General Secretary Nikaido Susumu said at the beginning of August that the party was refraining from discussion of the issue, and requested that the government settle the matter as soon as possible.[94] When China made its official protest, Nikaido (who was known for his pro-PRC leanings) had taken immediate steps to prevent intra-party disputes.[95] In addition, *bunkyōzoku* and party hawks had been asked to refrain from making sensational speeches,[96] though this clearly had little effect on the more outspoken LDP members such as Matsuno Yukiyasu and Minowa Noboru.

While LDP dietmen agreed to disagree, the 'battle' between ministries continued. When the Ministry of Education agreed to bring forward by one year the triannual revision (*kaitei kentei*) of the 'problem' textbooks, the Ministry of Foreign Affairs pushed for further concessions. The MFA's attitude angered the MOE which criticised the MFA for fawning upon foreign countries and promptly rescinded the proposal to bring forward the *kaitei kentei*. Miyazawa, having sided with the MFA, called a halt to the meeting and ordered the MOE and MFA to 're-adjust' their positions by the beginning of the week. Thus, by 17 August, although the MFA, MOE and *bunkyōzoku* had agreed on the need for Japan to express self-reproach in the government view, they had reached a deadlock on the issue of revision of the textbooks. It was at this stage that calls for a 'political judgement' were being made by government leaders who felt that the MOE and MFA would be unable to resolve their differences.[97]

Prime Minister's political judgement (stage 5)

With negotiations at a standstill, the Ministry of Education rapidly 'retreated into its shell'[98] and gave no public response to the Prime Minister's indication on 23 August that the government might correct the textbooks. Education Minister Ogawa voiced his concerns to Prime Minister Suzuki on 24 August, asking that the government make no promises that could not be fulfilled. According to the *Asahi Shimbun*, the MOE was still prepared to stand firm on the issue even though it was becoming more and more isolated. Ogawa had even been willing to discuss resignations of MOE staff, including his own, but the subject was not raised.[99]

With the external pressure of anti-Japanese feelings in Asia, and the domestic pressures of conflict between the MOE and MFA, divisions within the LDP, and opposition from the media, public opinion and big business groups, the Prime Minister and the Chief Cabinet Secretary were forced to abandon their attempts to 'mediate from above' and instead make a decision that would be acceptable to as many sides as possible. This was no easy task since, as an *Asahi Shimbun* commentary pointed out, the Prime Minister would be faced with criticisms of diplomatic failure from the LDP if relations with China and Korea worsened, but would face 'strong repulsion' from the education subgovernment if the textbooks were revised.[100]

Nonetheless, for Suzuki, prompt and satisfactory solution of the Textbook Issue was essential for a number of reasons. Firstly, if it was allowed to drag on it would threaten his impending visit to China to celebrate the tenth anniversary of normalisation. Secondly, if not checked, it threatened to lead to a region-wide anti-Japan movement, ironic given his adherence to the concept of politics of harmony (*wa no seiji*) towards Asia.[101] Thirdly, if not handled well it could ignite nascent intra-party dissatisfaction with Suzuki's leadership (over administrative reform, for example) in addition to ruining his already weakening popularity in the opinion polls, thereby jeopardising his chances for re-election later in the year.

Prime Minister Suzuki was not known for his ability to solve 'complicatedly intertwined' problems.[102] Described as 'tone deaf' in the area of foreign policy,[103] he was considered to be less than decisive in tackling the Textbook Issue.[104] Nonetheless, Suzuki's 'political judgement' finally managed to solve the matter, though not necessarily to the satisfaction of all sides. When the MFA and the MOE failed to make headway in their efforts at co-ordination, Prime Minister Suzuki indicated his willingness to 'take final responsibility' if asked for the 'final say' on the problem.[105] Thus, the government statement announced by Chief Cabinet Secretary Miyazawa on 26 August was the result of a 'high level judgement' by the Prime Minister and corresponds to Park's study of bureaucracy–party co-ordination described above, where the Prime Minister becomes the 'final policy arbiter'. The statement, however, did not gain the approval of the LDP and the ministries.

The measures contained in the statement were regarded by the press as a crushing defeat for the MOE,[106] and Ishiyama notes that this was also the feeling among MOE bureaucrats and LDP education-related politicians.[107] The intensity of external and internal pressure had forced the MOE to make concessions, about which the *bunkyōzoku* was furious. Ishiyama, for example recounts how at a meeting on the afternoon of 26 August, *bunkyōzoku* leaders took the Education Administrative Vice-Minister to task for agreeing to the measures in the government *kenkai*. The Administrative Vice-Minister maintained that he had only been notified of the content of the *kenkai* after it had already been submitted to the Chinese and Korean governments. This indicates that neither the *bunkyōzoku* nor the Ministry had taken part in the negotiations that produced the Japanese government's final statement, and that the *kenkai* was indeed the product of a 'high-level political judgement'.[108] Foreign affairs-related LDP members were no more satisfied with the *kenkai*, criticising it for only going half way to fulfilling the foreign requests, and criticisms were raised by other LDP dietmen who felt that the whole matter had been interference in domestic matters. The 'official' LDP party line, however, was expressed by Secretary General Nikaido who accepted the Prime Minister's decision on behalf of the LDP and agreed to co-operate so that the Textbook Issue could be resolved.[109]

Summary

As we saw in Chapter 5, the Chinese response was based upon considerations of domestic pressures and external changes. In the Japanese case, the interplay of external and internal influences was no less complex, but it appears that domestic factors played a more significant role than did external factors. The initial response to the PRC's protest was certainly dealt with on the basis of domestic considerations, such as the ongoing battle in education to gain control over textbook content, and the 'movement' of the 1980s to instil a greater 'love of country' into the Japanese youth. But even as the issue escalated and external pressures mounted, the fundamental problem remained one of maintaining the education system intact while finding a compromise which would satisfy all sides.

The conflict between the Ministry of Education and Ministry of Foreign Affairs appears to be a typical example of issues involving conflicts between subgovernments, as does the way in which the conflict was resolved. The failure of the two ministries to 'co-ordinate' their policies and reach a settlement quickly made it necessary for the Prime Minister to resolve the problem 'on his own responsibility'. This again is fairly typical of Japanese policy-making, as Campbell argues, but it is not unique to Japanese policy-making, and is a phenomenon described in the literature on foreign policy which states that in any sort of political system 'the executive branch of the government, and, within it, the top decision maker – the president, prime minister, or chancellor – has assumed the primary role in the making of foreign policy.'[110] What is more, when an international problem involves a number of bureaucratic units that cannot overrule each other because of their equal status 'decisions tend to be pushed upward to be resolved at the highest executive levels'.[111]

While Suzuki's solution to the issue did not receive the full approval of the LDP, Education or Foreign Ministries it did manage to placate the Chinese and Korean governments and brought the issue to a close in time for the Prime Minister's China trip. Moreover, as the concluding chapter will illustrate, the issue was resolved with no apparent long-term serious damage to Sino-Japanese friendship, and the Education Ministry was not in fact obliged to make major changes to the textbook screening process as it had feared.

8   Conclusion

Repercussions of the Textbook Issue

The Textbook Issue was resolved just over two weeks before Prime Minister Suzuki's visit to China to celebrate ten years of normalisation. In the run-up to Suzuki's visit, reviews of Sino-Japanese relations and press coverage of forthcoming anniversary celebrations in China contained very little reference to the Textbook Issue. In fact, the tone of the Chinese press had quickly returned to its pre-Textbook Issue state, that is, extolling the virtues of Sino-Japanese friendship and those Japanese who had struggled to help the development of Sino-Japanese friendship. Although references to 'certain elements obstructing Sino-Japanese relations' were still present in editorials and articles reviewing ten years of normalisation, these were considerably weaker than in the previous months.[1] For example, a report by Xinhua reviewing ten years of normalisation remarked upon the huge developments in Sino-Japanese friendship and co-operation since 1972, and predicted that friendship and economic relations would continue to grow in the future. Apart from a brief reference to a 'handful of rightists' putting 'obstacles' in the way of Sino-Japanese relations, the report was clearly very optimistic about the development of relations between China and Japan.[2]

The Japanese media, on the other hand, continued with the theme of textbooks and textbook authorisation, in addition to reports about Suzuki's impending visit to China and the possible repercussions of the Textbook Issue in his talks with Chinese leaders. There was almost daily coverage of one or other aspect of the Textbook Issue, for example, changes to textbook authorisation, plans for Suzuki's visit to China and so on, in the *Asahi Shimbun* from 10 September onwards. Coverage continued until the end of September with reviews and analyses of Suzuki's visit and the tenth anniversary of Sino-Japanese normalisation. Furthermore the September, October and even November issues of

Japanese current affairs journals and magazines contained many articles, analyses and 'post-mortems' of the Textbook Issue. They also dealt with the state of Sino-Japanese relations, the state of Japanese journalism (in light of the 'false' reporting during the Textbook Issue),[3] and the state of the Japanese education and textbook system.[4]

Sino-Japanese relations

As predicted by the *Asahi Shimbun*, the Textbook Issue – or rather the problem of a revival of Japanese militarism – became one of the focal points of discussion during Prime Minister's Suzuki's talks with the Chinese leadership. To a certain extent, the Japanese government had expected this (despite Miyazawa's earlier remark that the subject would not come up for discussion during the Prime Minister's China visit),[5] and Prime Minister Suzuki and the Ministry of Foreign Affairs had allowed for it in their preparations for the trip.

Nonetheless, the Prime Minister was optimistic that his visit would be fruitful. Prior to his departure for Beijing, Prime Minister Suzuki said in an interview with NHK television that in all the two thousand years of Sino-Japanese exchanges 'I can find no time in this history when Sino-Japanese relations were so friendly and stood on such a firm basis of mutual trust as today.' When asked about the Textbook Issue, the Prime Minister said that even though it had already been settled diplomatically, he intended to 'personally explain Japan's position during his talks in China and explain Japan's postwar diplomacy of peace.'[6]

Suzuki had two rounds of talks with Zhao Ziyang, and he also had separate talks with Hu Yaobang and Deng Xiaoping. During talks with Zhao, Prime Minister Suzuki himself raised the subject of the Textbook Issue, reiterating the Japanese government's position that its awareness of the suffering inflicted upon the Chinese people during the war had not changed in the slightest and any errors in the textbooks would be corrected on the government's responsibility. In his meetings with Hu and Deng, both leaders raised the problem of a revival of militarism in Japan and Prime Minister Suzuki gave reassurances that even if Japan became an economic superpower, it had no plans to become a military power.[7]

In his speech at the Great Hall of the People on 28 September, Suzuki made two short references to the Textbook Issue. First, he referred to Japan's Constitution, stressing that the Japanese people rejected the road to military 'superpowerdom' and were firmly committed to the concept of a peaceful Japan, regardless of how violent the international scene might become. Referring to Japan's history textbooks, Suzuki stated that the spirit and principles of the Joint Statement should be reflected in all areas of Sino-Japanese relations, and he reiterated that with the textbook problem, it was the responsibility of the Japanese government to make sincere efforts [to reflect] the spirit of the Joint Statement.[8]

Suzuki's visit was hailed as a success. The 'fallout' of the Textbook Issue did not appear to have caused irreparable damage to Sino-Japanese relations. Numerous celebrations of the tenth anniversary took place in both countries in the form of receptions, exhibitions and exchanges of delegations of politicians and friendship associations. Nor did the issue mar Suzuki's talks with the Chinese leadership. Even though the Textbook Issue and fears about Japanese militarism were fairly high on the agenda of discussion between Suzuki and the Chinese leaders, the issue did not by any means dominate the talks, which encompassed a number of issues such as Sino-Japanese economic relations and the matter of possible Sino-Soviet rapprochement. Furthermore, Zhao, Deng and Hu all acknowledged that the Textbook Issue had already been resolved, and Zhao Ziyang stated that the Chinese government's policy for the development of relations had not changed.

Japanese textbook screening

Opinion is divided as to the short-term and long-term effect of the Textbook Issue on the Japanese textbook screening system and the state of history education. The results of the TARC inquiry into textbook content were published in November, and were very much as the Ministry of Education had predicted in its supplementary explanations to China and Korea. The MOE stated that the TARC inquiry results would include the addition of a paragraph to the criteria for textbook authorisation (*kentei kijun*) which would read something like 'it is essential to consider friendly and close relations with neighbouring countries'.[9] And indeed, the TARC report of 16 November stated that descriptions referring to Asian countries in history textbooks would 'take into consideration international understanding and co-operation' and that the word 'invade' (*shinryaku*) would not be subjected to compulsory changes (*shūsei iken*).[10]

Schoppa suggests that as a result of the internationalisation of the Textbook Issue, textbook screening became less strict in the years after 1982.[11] The '1983 Textbook Report' produced by a publishing union supports this view to a certain extent. Analysis of the 1982–3 batch of textbooks showed that on the subjects of Japan's invasion of China, the

Nanjing Massacre, the Korean Independence Movement and the forced labour of Koreans, textbook screening had fallen into line with TARC's recommendations and fully reflected Chinese and Korean wishes (*ikō*). The report stated that 'in accordance with the purport of the revised criteria for textbook authorisation into which was incorporated 'consideration for neighbouring countries', there were no *kaizen* or *shūsei iken* relating to historical appraisal or facts attached [to these passages]'.[12]

The Textbook Issue is also considered to have had a deeper effect on the textbook system by revealing the excesses and secrecy of the textbook authorisation system and by prompting the Textbook Subcommittee of the Central Education Council to postpone the announcement of the results of the inquiry it had been carrying out since November 1981. The Subcommittee considered that the report it was due to make, which concentrated on selection procedures, would be inappropriate given the foreign protests over textbook content. The Subcommittee therefore decided to postpone its investigations until 11 September. After an explanation by Bureau Chief Suzuki of the details of the Textbook Issue, the Textbook Subcommittee decided to re-open its inquiry, focusing this time on textbook content and authorisation. Whereas the LDP had hoped that the Central Education Council inquiry would help to support its plans to strengthen the textbook authorisation system through the introduction of a textbook law, the Textbook Issue actually forced the Council to look closer at the textbook system. In May 1983, the Textbook Subcommittee submitted its report to the Council, and on the subject of textbook authorisation made three recommendations: to improve the criteria for authorisation in terms of scope, level and treatment of descriptive passages; to extend the authorisation period; and to ensure excellence of textbooks examiners and the TARC.[13]

It would be unwise to assume, however, that the Textbook Issue brought about a 'revolution' in Japan's textbook authorisation system and in the content of history textbooks. In fact, in contrast to those who consider that the Textbook Issue brought about a relaxation in the textbook authorisation system, many Japanese commentators have argued that textbook screening became stricter in the wake of the Textbook Issue, especially with respect to citing of sources and providing evidence for arguments.[14]

In spite of the recommendations of the Central Education Council, the textbook authorisation system remained unchanged until 1990. Even after the system had been 'streamlined' (to a two-stage process) it was criticised for being stricter than before.[15] History textbooks were slow to change, indicating that the Ministry of Education retained as tight a grip as possible on the screening system. Takahashi cites

Professor Satō Kazuo of Aoyama University, who maintained that ' the [1982] government statement was no more than a political statement explaining a policy. . . . It did not represent a legal obligation.'[16] Ienaga's detailed diary of the 'revision authorisation' (*kaitei kentei*) process for his 1983 textbook *Shin Nihonshi* showed that the MOE was still making 'suggestions' regarding descriptions of the Nanjing Massacre, and the use of the word 'invasion'.[17] In addition, Ienaga describes how passages referring to the rape of Chinese women during the Nanjing Massacre were deleted in the authorised version of the textbook, and an entire passage describing the activities of Unit 731 was deleted on the basis of a suggestion for correction (*shūsei iken*).[18]

Morikawa suggests that, despite the international criticism of 1982, with the LDP's continued strength in the 1980s there was no major change of opinion within the conservative camp on education, nor was there sufficient pressure to force a change of opinion. In fact education-related problems appeared more frequently, with a succession of 'slips of the tongue' being made by Education Ministers and Prime Ministers alike on the matter of history education and the war.[19] Thus the Textbook Issue did not deter the education subgovernment from attempting to place greater emphasis of 'national pride' in Japanese education. The recurrence of the Textbook Issue in 1984 and 1986 suggests that the events of 1982 had not produced any long-term changes in textbook authorisation and content, and the MOE still appeared willing to attempt to let through ultra-nationalist textbooks. While some textbooks of the late 1980s (as some had in the 1970s) contained the term 'Japan's invasion of China', textbook authors in the 1990s were still encouraged to use a lower figure than the Chinese estimate of 300,000 in reference to the number of casualties of the Nanjing Massacre; or else ensure that they indicated that 'other authorities use lower figures'.[20]

If change did occur in the officially accepted view, then it only began in earnest after 1989 with the death of Emperor Hirohito and the end of the Showa era. The Introduction referred to the debate on Japan's war responsibility for its actions in Asia, which had been stifled for decades because of the focus on Japan's Pacific War, and the 'victim's history' that produced. In the 1990s, especially with the removal of the LDP from power in 1993–6, there have been greater moves towards acknowledging Japan's role as victimiser in Asia. Dower argues that 'the popular consciousness of victimization and atrocity has changed in contemporary Japan', and that 'this has entailed greater general acknowledgment of Japan's own war crimes *vis-à-vis* fellow Asians'.[21] This 'greater general acknowledgment' is being reflected in textbooks. Newspaper reports in

1994 commented that the 1993 screening of Civics and History textbooks was more 'relaxed' than in previous years, and noted that an increasing number of high-school history texts contained references to the issue of compensation for comfort women. In addition, textbooks were no longer as vague as they had been on the number of casualties of the Fifteen Year War, since they now contained references to the fact that the number of victims 'exceeded 20 million'.[22] Ironically, in 1994, the Education Ministry found itself on the defensive following criticism by the right-wing press that the textbooks *exaggerated* Japan's wartime excesses.[23]

However, the degree to which this 'acknowledgement' of Japan's actions in Asia will extend is of course limited. The Japanese is not the only government guilty of taking a great interest in the content of school history textbooks and creating a 'sanitised' national history, and a brief comparison with the USA is illuminating. In a study of the US views of the decision to drop the atom bomb, Walker indicates that the US government has been the 'primary agent for shaping popular views of historical events in recent times', and it has done so 'in order to build unity, foster patriotism, and ensure loyalty'.[24] American history textbooks, which 'impress the historical consciousness of nearly every high school student in America', have tended to perpetuate the 'official' view that the decision to drop the bomb was made on the basis of a choice between that or an invasion which would have cost many American lives. The textbooks generally fail to include information about some of the other options open to the Truman administration, nor do they contain information about the 'new' academic debates, the revisionist view, etc., and some contain inaccuracies and even 'flagrant' factual mistakes. In sum they 'sustain myths about and questionable explanations for the use of the bomb'.[25] One of the reasons for this sort of the treatment of the use of the bomb is, Walker suggests, due to the 'demands of the powerful state textbook selection committees and the inherent pressure to avoid controversy'.[26] Thus, just as in Japan, American students leave school with a 'general impression' which conforms to the officially-accepted and popular view of their national, and as a corollary, international history, but which leaves them poorly informed. Even though at the time of writing (August 1997), the Supreme Court in Tokyo has ruled that the Education Ministry's screening of certain sections of Ienaga's *Shin Nihonshi* was unconstitutional, it is unlikely that there will be a rapid sea change in Japanese history education.[27] As Gluck points out 'each country weaves . . . a national "mythistory", in which the myths are as important as the history and both are continually reworked.'[28]

Sino-Japanese relations after the Textbook Issue: learning from history?

If, for the Chinese, the Textbook Issue was concerned with encouraging Japan to adopt the 'correct view' of history and making Japan face up to its war responsibility, then the frequency with which similar issues arose in the 1980s showed that their attempts had failed. If, on the other hand, the Textbook Issue was being used for other, unrelated, reasons, as this study suggests, then a pattern of behaviour in Sino-Japanese political relations can be discerned.

This study set out to challenge the 'theory' that Sino-Japanese relations are particularly sensitive to, if not dominated by history and history-related issues, and can only be understood within this historical context. If a provocative issue arises there is a general assumption that the decision-making process in both countries is influenced (by perceptions of individual decision makers, media, public opinion and so on) to such an extent that the foreign policy output is adversely affected.

The study examined the Textbook Issue in terms of the framework presented in Chapter 2, which advocated an approach to the study of relations between China and Japan that combined the findings of two distinct fields of study: international relations and area studies. Without an 'integrated' approach studies of Sino-Japanese relations tends to overemphasise either the general or the specific. In the case of the former, international systemic factors tend to obscure important domestic influences, while in the latter case, the emphasis can too easily be placed on the historical aspect of the relationship. The concept that Chinese and Japanese governments alike are heavily influenced by history and the perceptions of that history held by individual decision makers places too much emphasis on the role of the 'psychological environment' in the foreign policy process, implying that these variables are the key determining factors in Chinese and Japanese foreign policy output. Clearly there is a need to strike a balance between the general and the specific. The organising framework outlined in Chapter 2 allowed such a balance by setting out all the potentially relevant variables, taking into account both international systemic and nation-state 'idiosyncratic' influences. Some of the variables potentially relevant to the Textbook Issue were examined in Chapters 3 and 4, which revealed that a number of changes were taking place in the Chinese and Japanese international and domestic environments that pointed to the possibility that the Textbook Issue had more to do with these external and internal factors than with the issue of history textbooks. The detailed account of the day-to-day events of the Textbook Issue in Chapter 5 reinforced this idea, showing that the nature of the Chinese media campaign and the response of the Japanese government appeared to have little to do with history textbooks.

Chapters 6 and 7 rejected the idea that, in the Textbook Issue, Sino-Japanese relations were dominated or determined by the legacy of past relations between the two countries. Instead, several possible 'scenarios' were considered to help explain the reasons behind Chinese and Japanese decision-making on the Textbook Issue. Variables such as changes in the international system, shifts in domestic policies, and conflicts within the bureaucracy were seen to be of particular relevance to the way the issue was instigated and resolved. For example, in the Chinese case 'systemic changes', and such domestic factors as a power struggle, social disquiet, and *to a certain extent* the 'legacy of history' all combined and interacted to produce the Chinese response to the Textbook Issue. In the Japanese case, as Chapter 7 illustrated, the educational subgovernment was adamant that the textbook system should not be changed in response to the demands of foreign governments; it was a matter of national sovereignty. Even when the issue worsened and the Japanese government realised that bilateral relations with both the PRC and the ROK were at stake, the divisions of opinion within the LDP and the bureaucracy still appeared to be the major influence on the foreign policy-making process. Only when regional anti-Japan sentiment began to threaten Japan's foreign trade and international image, did Prime Minister Suzuki (concerned, perhaps, about his chances for re-election in November), agree to take responsibility for the final decision. The issue for the Japanese government, therefore, was not about history textbook content, but about protecting national interests, or maintaining the education system by making the smallest concession possible. These factors produced a more convincing explanation of Chinese and Japanese decision-making on the Textbook Issue than the 'unique', 'dominant role of history' approach.

Patterns in Sino-Japanese relations

Both Mendl and Lee have commented separately on the way Sino-Japanese relations before normalisation developed in cyclical patterns, each cycle beginning with the two governments on relatively friendly terms, but culminating in a crisis.[29] A similar pattern can be observed in Sino-Japanese relations since diplomatic normalisation, with the relationship alternating between 'friendship fever' and 'friction' in the early post-normalisation years, thereafter settling into a pattern whereby, as Tanaka notes, problems emerge when they are least expected (such as on the eve of the tenth anniversary of normalisation); or after a period of improved, friendly relations (for example, the Yasukuni Shrine issue in 1985).[30] In the 1980s, 'major' diplomatic problems occurred every two or three years, and the pattern of behaviour in each issue was strikingly similar. For example, the 1985 Yasukuni Shrine issue prompted harsh criticism from the Chinese press which was already commemorating the fortieth anniversary of Japan's defeat with a spate of articles about Japanese aggression during the war. Ijiri comments that given that Sino-Japanese relations were already strained due to a serious trade imbalance, it seems likely that the Chinese side used its warnings about Japan's revival of militarism as a 'convenient tool' to pressurise Japan.[31]

Although the Chinese government did not make a formal protest against Nakasone's visit to the Yasukuni Shrine, the issue escalated in September when Chinese students in Beijing held demonstrations protesting not only against Nakasone's action but also against a perceived revival of Japanese militarism, and Japan's 'second occupation' or 'economic invasion' of China; criticisms reminiscent of those of the early 1900s described earlier. The demonstrations were apparently sparked off by China's growing trade deficit with Japan, and the flood of poor quality Japanese products onto the Chinese market in the early 1980s. The slogans warning against a Japanese 'economic invasion', and condemning the 'second occupation' harked back to Japan's history of colonial expansion in China and, according to Whiting, revealed the persistence of 'traditional' Chinese fears of foreign domination.[32]

The 1986 Textbook Issue was exacerbated by Japanese Education Minister Fujio Masayuki who made a number of insensitive comments about the Nanjing Massacre and about Japanese actions in Korea, and was consequently lambasted in the Chinese and Korean press for attempting to defend and 'whitewash' Japan's invasion of China and annexation of Korea. Fujio was subsequently dismissed, and the Japanese government apologised for his improper comments, but the *Renmin Ribao* carried a commentary warning that Fujio's comments represented part of a growing trend towards a resurgence of militarism in Japan.[33]

In 1987, an ongoing dispute between the Chinese, Taiwanese and Japanese governments concerning the ownership of a Kyoto dormitory for Chinese students was brought to a head in February, when a Japanese high court awarded ownership to Taiwan. This was treated as a serious matter by the Chinese government, which regarded the decision as a violation of the Joint Statement and Treaty of Peace and Friendship. Deng Xiaoping himself criticised the decision, and reprisals were taken in the form of the expulsion of a Japanese journalist from

China. Deng's later criticisms of Japan for reviving militarism and for increasing its defence budget above the 1 per cent ceiling prompted an angry response from some Japanese politicians. Vice-Foreign Minister Yanagiya Kensuke implied in a supposedly 'off-record' response to Chinese criticism that Deng was 'living above the clouds' and did not understand Sino-Japanese relations. This remark in turn incensed the Chinese leadership, which was only pacified after Yanagiya apologised and resigned.[34]

In April 1988, Okuno Seisuke, Director General of the National Land Agency, sparked off another row, when, in answer to a question about visits to the Yasukuni Shrine, he remarked that it was time to put the ghosts of the Japanese army occupation to rest and that because China was a communist country, it had little understanding of religion. When the Chinese Foreign Ministry criticised Okuno for ignoring the facts of history and of disregarding diplomatic courtesy, Okuno commented that Japan had not intended to invade China. This resulted in further criticism from the Chinese foreign ministry and media, joined by North and South Korea. In May the Japanese Government issued a statement saying that this and previous Japanese cabinets adhered to the view that in the Sino-Japanese war 'invasion was a fact'. Okuno resigned shortly after.[35]

In February 1989, Prime Minister Takeshita Noboru commented that the question of whether the Second World War was a war of invasion or not was a problem for future generations of historians to evaluate. The *Renmin Ribao* criticised the statement, but Takeshita managed to prevent the problem from developing further during talks with Foreign Minister Qian Qichen, who was in Tokyo for the funeral of Emperor Hirohito. Takeshita admitted that the comment was a 'slip of the tongue' (*shitatarazu*) and that he regretted that it had become an incident which invited criticism from foreign countries. He added that the fact that Japan's past behaviour was 'invasive' could not be denied. The Chinese government took the issue no further, but a speech by Premier Li Peng (Seventh plenum, Twelfth People's Congress) in March indicated the Chinese dissatisfaction with the state of affairs. Recalling the disaster brought upon the Chinese and Asian people during Japan's war of invasion, Li Peng warned that the nature of the war could not be changed, and added the standard maxim of Sino-Japanese relations that 'the past if not forgotten is a guide to the future'.[36]

In the 1990s, these sorts of issues show no signs of abating, yet this sort of patterned behaviour, of 'cycles' and 'routinisation' of issues, is not unique to China and Japan. Campbell, for instance, points out that any relationship develops repetitive patterns which become institutionalised because of the frequency and complexity of their interactions.

Both sides then establish 'some predictable rules that permit but control conflict, especially for those responsible for maintaining and managing the relationship'.[37] In other words, all bilateral relationships form some way of interacting to deal with conflicts and avoid crises. Campbell describes the 'set of games' – the political process – by which Japan and the United States manage to avoid crisis. The cycle of behaviour that has developed in the area of trade between Japan and the USA shares many similarities with Sino-Japanese political relations. For example, Japan's first response to a problem voiced by the USA is to deny that the problem exists. Japan then agrees to negotiate, at which point the USA 'castigates the Japanese behaviour as unfair'. Japan's next response is to 'explain why things must be done that way and anyway it has done all it can' which in turn provokes the Americans to 'threaten dire consequences'. Japan will then concede to such pressure, and a 'new era in US-Japan relations' is proclaimed. The whole cycle is then repeated; not because the negotiations have not been successful, but precisely because they work so well and have become 'ritualised'. 'Ritualisation' is described in the general literature on international relations. Mansbach, for instance, in describing the nature of 'issue cycles' where issues develop through phases of 'genesis', 'crisis', 'ritualisation' and 'resolution', remarks that in the third stage:

> actors may acquire patterned and stable mutual expectations about how they should interact over the issue in the future. They have learned what they can safely do to each other without triggering hostile spirals. Their actions may be downright unfriendly; but those actions are expected by adversaries, are regarded as posturing, and are considered tolerable.[38]

To return to Campbell's description of relations between the USA and Japan, the cycle of 'issues, the sequence of moves, the rhetoric about unfairness, the threats, the sky-is-falling media campaigns, the last-minute deals' helps to prevent sensitive issues from reaching crisis point by 'channelling and managing conflict'.[39] If one replaces the USA's cries of 'unfairness' with China's accusations of 'revival of militarism' in the pattern, what results is an accurate description of the way Sino-Japanese political relations were conducted in the 1980s and early 1990s. China's frequent protestations over Japanese 'provocative' actions, the media campaigns, and Japan's 'last-minute' response to China's protests over, say, the Yasukuni Shrine and other issues of the 1980s clearly suggests that Sino-Japanese relations have become 'ritualised' through their frequent interaction.

Qianshi buwang, houshi zhishi

As this study has shown, it is essential to consider Sino-Japanese relations within the broad context of the international and domestic situations in order to achieve a better understanding of the complexity of the relationship and the numerous influencing factors. Of course, these factors differ in significance according to time and type of issue, and the key determinants in the Textbook Issue may not be the same as those which determined, say, the outcome of the Yasukuni Shrine Issue. Nevertheless, this study points to the desirability and applicability of an organising framework that allows for comparison over time, between different types of issue, and between other bilateral relationships (in order to consider the influence of different political systems, economic development, capabilities). By carrying out this type of research, and combining the findings from international relations and area studies, it may be possible to build a picture of how and why China and Japan are likely to act/react under certain types of circumstance at certain times. This would enable researchers to veer away from the tendency that places too much emphasis on the 'unique' historical and cultural aspects of Sino-Japanese relations. Thus it is hoped that through methodical, systematic analysis of Sino-Japanese past behaviour, researchers will be able to better understand current patterns of behaviour between the two leading powers of the Asia Pacific: *qianshi buwang, houshi zhishi*.

Appendix 1

Names and positions of Japanese
and Chinese politicians and
bureaucrats involved in the
Textbook Issue

Table A1.1 Japanese politicians and bureaucrats involved in the Textbook
Issue

Name	Position	Faction	Zoku
LDP			
Suzuki Zenkō	Prime Minister	Suzuki	
Ogawa Heiji	Education Minister	Suzuki	
Miyazawa Kiichi	Chief Cabinet Sec.	Suzuki	Gaikō
Sakurauchi Yoshio	Foreign Minister	Nakasone	Gaikō
Fujinami Takao		Nakasone	Bunkyō
Sunada Shigetami		Nakasone	Bunkyō
Kaifu Toshiki	Education System Research Council	Komoto	Bunkyō
Nikaido Susumu	LDP Secretary General	Tanaka	Kensetsu
Matsuno Yukiyasu	DG National Land Agency	Tanaka	
Minowa Noboru	Posts and Telecommunications Minister	Tanaka	Unyū
Kosaka Tokusaburō	Transport Minister	Tanaka	
Nakagawa Ichirō	DG Science and Technology Agency	Nakagawa	
Aoki Masahisa		Nakagawa	Gaikō/Bunkyō
Hasegawa Takashi		Nakagawa	Bunkyō
Ishibashi Kazuya	Education Affairs Division, Head	Fukuda	Bunkyō
Mitsuzuka Hiroshi	Subcommittee on Textbook Problem	Fukuda	Bunkyō
Mori Yoshiro	Educational Affairs Division	Fukuda	
Fujio Masayuki		Fukuda	Gaikō
Okuno Seisuke		None	Bunkyō
MOE			
Tamo Takahisa	Parliamentary Vice-Minister		
Misumi Tetsuo	Administrative Vice-Minister		
Suzuki Isao	Elementary and Secondary Education Bureau Chief (ESEB)		
Fujimura Kazuo	ESEB Textbook Authorisation Division Head		
Osaki Hitoshi	Science and International Affairs Bureau Chief		

Name	Position	Faction	Zoku
MFA			
Tsuji Hideo	Parliamentary Vice-Minister		
Sunobe Ryōzō	Administrative Vice-Minister		
Kiuchi Akitane	Asian Affairs Bureau Chief		
Hashimoto Hiroshi	Public Information and Cultural Affairs Bureau Chief		
Watanabe Kōji	Minister Japanese Embassy, Beijing		
Katori Yasue	Japanese Ambassador, Beijing		

Table A1.2 Chinese politicians and bureaucrats involved in the Textbook Issue

Name	Position
Deng Xiaoping	Chairman, Central Advisory Commission and Central Committee Military Commission
Zhao Ziyang	Premier, State Council
Wan Li	Vice-Premier
Gu Mu	State Councillor
Hu Yaobang	Party General Secretary
Wang Xiaoyun	Chinese Ambassador, Tokyo
Wu Xueqian	Vice-Foreign Minister
Xiao Xiangqian	Foreign Ministry, Director First Asian Affairs Bureau
He Dongchang	Education Minister (State Education Commission)
Li Tao	Education Ministry, Director Foreign Affairs Section

Appendix 2
Literature on Sino-Japanese
relations by category

Table A2.1 Literature on Sino-Japanese relations

Subject category	Reference
History/Overview	Chen, 1986 Cheng, 1985 Coox, 1978 Etō, 1972, 1980 Furukawa, 1983, 1988 Hsiao, 1974b Iriye, 1990 Jain, 1981 Jansen, 1975 Kawahara, 1974 Klein, 1989 Leng, 1958 Mueller and Ross, 1975 Newby, 1988, 1990 Radtke, 1990 Scalapino, 1991 Sladkovsky, 1975 Tanino, 1990 Taylor, 1985 Yang, 1986 Yamaguchi, 1976 Zhang, 1986
Economic	Howe, 1990 Ishikawa, 1987 Kim and Nanto, 1985 Maruyama, 1990 Matsumura, 1988 Morino, 1991 Shimakura, 1986
Political/Economic	Arnold, 1985, 1990 Lee, 1976, 1984 Taylor, 1996 Whiting, 1992
Political/Diplomatic	Bedeski, 1983 Fukui, 1977 Hsiao, 1974a Ijiri, 1990 Johnson, 1986 Kim, 1979 Ogura, 1979 Okabe, 1976 Park, 1978a, 1978b Tanaka, 1983a, 1991

Subject category	Reference
Cultural/Attitudes	Chin, 1989
	Etō, 1981
	Iriye, 1980
	Johnson, 1978
	Liang, 1985
	Takeuchi, 1981
	Ogata, 1965
	Sun, 1986
	Whiting, 1978
	Whiting, 1989

Note: This is by no means an exhaustive list of the literature on Sino-Japanese relations written since 1945, but it does include monographs and articles from major journals which may be considered to have made a significant contribution to the literature and are relevant to this study.

Notes

1 Introduction

1 The 'Textbook Issue' described in this study is not to be confused with the 'textbook trial' or 'textbook controversy', which refers to the long-running court cases brought by historian Ienaga Saburō against the state over the constitutionality of textbook authorisation procedures. While the Textbook Issue did have some connection with the textbook trials (see Chapter 7), the two controversies are to be considered as separate issues.

2 *Renmin Ribao*, 15 August 1982, 1.

3 In the October and November issues of Japanese weekly and monthly journals, however, there was a rash of articles analysing the press, the education system, the state of Sino-Japanese relations and so on. Chapter 7 examines these articles.

4 *Japan Echo*, 1982, 9(4), 15.

5 Quoted in Ijiri, 1990, 640.

6 In Japanese this is referred to as, for example, *nitchūkan no kindai ni okeru fukōna danzetsu*; Fujiie, 1986, 206.

7 Ijiri, 1990, 640.

8 Jiang Zemin, 1992, 9–10.

9 See Yang, 1986, 27–8, citing the *Shanhaijing* and also Sansom, 1987, 15, citing the same source.

10 Sansom, 1987, 16.

11 Hane, 1991, 26.

12 Hane, 1991, 25.

13 See Varley, 1973, 40, and Totman, 1981, 32.

14 Yamamura, 1990, 408.

15 The aim of 'tribute' was the restoration of a Chinese world order based on the exchange (of gifts or trade) in return for tribute from foreign countries; Yamamura, 1990, 424.

16 Fairbank, 1968, 2.

17 Spence, 1990, 119, and Hsü, 1990, 130–1.

18 Yamamura, 1990, 435.

19 Toby, 1984, 196.

20 Toby, 1984, xv. Toby notes that Japanese ships from Tsushima and Satsuma carried out trade with Korea and the kingdom of Ryukyu, which served as 'entrepôts' between Japan and China.

21 Toby, 1984, 199. These 'New Regulations' required Chinese merchants to carry 'credentials' issued by the *bakufu*, and their purpose was to limit the number of trading ships entering Nagasaki, the volume of trade and the export of Japanese specie carried through the port.
22 Toby, 1984, 215–28.
23 Toby, 1984, 5.
24 Jansen, 1992, 77.
25 Jansen, 1992, 119.
26 Jansen, 1992, 86.
27 Jansen, 1975, 130.
28 Varley, 1974, 16.
29 Tsunoda, 1958, 12.
30 The *Kojiki* (compiled 712) and *Nihongi* (or *Nihon Shoki*, compiled 720) are the two main written sources of information about the early period of Japanese history.
31 Hane, 1991, 38.
32 Sladkovsky, 1975, 16.
33 Jansen, 1992, 119.
34 Iriye, 1992, 71.
35 Jansen, 1975, 131; see also Chu, 1980, 82.
36 Chu, 1980, 74–82.
37 Iriye, 1992, 15.
38 Hsü, 1990, 340.
39 Iriye, 1992, 28–9.
40 From 13 students in 1896 to 8,000 by 1905; Fujiie, 1988, 208.
41 Nish, 1990, 602, footnote 1.
42 Fairbank and Reischauer, 1973, 405.
43 Jansen, 1975, 132
44 Japan also gained an indemnity of 200 million taels, navigation rights on the Yangzi and Wusong rivers, manufacturing rights in the treaty ports, and the opening of new ports (Shashi, Chongqing, Suzhou and Hangzhou).
45 Jansen, 1975, 131. This is perhaps an over-generalisation, as such feelings were by no means universal; see Iriye, 1992, 31–2.
46 Wray, 1978, 116–8.
47 Duus, 1988a, 7.
48 Jansen, 1975, 162–3.
49 Duus, 1989a, xiii.
50 Duus, 1989a, xxiv.
51 Trade composition was as follows: China exported to Japan textile raw materials, coal, cereals, fertiliser and agricultural products, and imported from Japan textiles, chemicals, metals, machinery and manufactured goods.
52 Japan had acquired rights in Manchuria after its victory in the Russo-Japanese war of 1904–5. The Treaties of Portsmouth and Peking gave Japan the remainder of the Russian lease on the Liaodong peninsula (thereafter renamed the Kwantung Leased Territory), railway rights in south Manchuria and control in Korea, a 'protectorate' between 1905–11 and thereafter a Japanese colony.
53 Duus *et al.* 1989, 8.

54 Itō, 1974, 90.
55 The Twenty-One Demands called for: the transfer of all German rights in China to Japan; extension of leases in South Manchuria and Inner Mongolia; joint administration of the Hanyebing company; employment of Japanese as advisers in politics, business and the military, Japanese ownership of land and permission for railway construction.
56 Jansen, 1975, 214.
57 Terauchi was superficially friendly towards China to appease the Chinese after 1915 but in reality his objective was a 'forward' policy, that is, development of Japan's continental interests. Jansen, 1975, 219.
58 Beasley, 1987, 10.
59 The Manchurian Incident occurred on 18 September 1931, and was the result of a conspiracy of lower-ranking Kwantung army officers to blow up part of the railway near Mukden, lay the blame on KMT troops and seize Mukden.
60 Wray, 1978, 123.
61 Hata, 1988, 302, 314.
62 On 7 July 1937 fighting broke out between Japanese and Chinese troops near the Marco Polo Bridge in Beijing, and failure to settle the incident as a local matter led to an escalation of fighting by the end of July and then to full-scale hostilities.
63 Coox, 1988, 320–1.
64 Dower, 1986, 43.
65 Chinese estimates suggest a figure of 300,000 dead (see Dower, 1986, 326, footnote 26); a Japanese war veterans' association, *Kaikosha*, has produced the lowest estimates of 30–40,000 (Katsumata, 1994, 1, 16); the Far East International Military Tribunal reached an approximate figure of 200,000.
66 Ienaga, 1978, 9.
67 Unit 731 established in Harbin in the early 1930s, under the guise of an 'Epidemic Prevention and Portable Water Supply Unit', carried out research into the uses of the plague, cholera, typhoid, frostbite and gas gangrene as weapons of warfare. Two other installations, Unit 100 near Changchun, and the Tama Detachment in Nanjing also carried out similar research. For full analysis of Unit 731, see Williams and Wallace, 1989.
68 Powell, 1981, 44–52 .
69 See Ienaga, 1978, 167; Dower, 1986, 42.
70 See Dower, 1986, 295–7, and Sekine, 1992, 146.
71 See for example, Ienaga, 1993a; Fujiwara, 1988; Chiba, 1992.
72 Conroy, 1982, 15.
73 Coox, 1978, 296–7.
74 Whiting, 1989, 41.
75 Gluck, 1993, 83.
76 This phrase was used predominantly by the Japanese, and was particularly popular during the war as a central element of the thinking behind the Greater East Asia Co-Prosperity Sphere. It therefore has negative connotations for many Chinese.
77 *Japan Times Weekly*, 12–18 June, 1995, 1.
78 *Nihon Keizai Shimbun*,10 November 1996, 1.
79 Sekine, 1992, 126.

80 Buruma points out that the debates on the war, and especially the Nanking Massacre, of the 1980s took place 'outside Japanese universities' and were conducted by journalists, 'amateur historians' and so on (Buruma, 1994, 119).
81 Gluck, 1993, 66.
82 Dower, 1996, 123.
83 Gluck, 1993, 70–1.
84 Gluck, 1993, 84.

2 The Textbook Issue: methodology and approaches

1 See Appendix 2 for categories of literature on Sino-Japanese relations.
2 See, for example, Leng, 1958; Ogata, 1965.
3 Ogata, 1965, 392.
4 Leng, 1958, 108–9.
5 Whiting, 1989.
6 Whiting, 1989, 41.
7 Ijiri, 1996, 60.
8 Lee, 1976, 1984; Arnold, 1985, 1990.
9 Lee, 1976, 185.
10 Lee, 1976, 134.
11 Lee, 1976, 190.
12 Whiting, 1992; Zhao, 1993.
13 *Tsukiai* refers usually to social 'networking', after-hour social activities which help to improve and develop relations between company employees. Here it refers to activities which aim to improve relations between countries at government and private levels; Zhao, 1993, 167.
14 Zhao, 1993, 167–9.
15 Zhao, 1993, 169.
16 Zhao, 1993, 170. See also Shambaugh, 1996b, 83–8; Nakajima, 1989, 216–29.
17 Ogata, 1965, 392.
18 Johnson, 1986, 409.
19 Arnold, 1990, 140.
20 Ijiri,1990, 638–49.
21 Kojima, 1988, pp. 24–28.
22 Kojima, 1988.
23 See for example Fukui 1977; Bedeski 1983; Hsiao 1974a.
24 Tanaka, 1991; Fukui, 1977; Okabe, 1976; Tanaka 1983a.
25 Tanaka, 1991, 189–207.
26 Fukui, 1977a, 60–102; Ogata, 1977 (in Scalapino).
27 Tanaka, 1991, 3–22.
28 Brecher, 1972, 1.
29 Rosenau, 1994, 532.
30 Neumann and Waever, 1997, 1–37.
31 Light, 1994, 93–108.
32 Zhao, 1996, 19–20.
33 Kim, 1989, 6.
34 Rosenau, 1987, 2–3.
35 Rosenau, 1987, 53.

36 Waltz, 1959.
37 Singer, 1961, 77–92. For a discussion of the level-of-analysis problem, see Hollis and Smith, 1990, ch. 5.
38 Cited in Hollis and Smith, 1990, 100.
39 Kenneth Waltz is the main advocate of this neo-realistic approach.
40 Ng-Quinn, 1983, 215.
41 Ng-Quinn, 1983, 221.
42 Hollis and Smith, 1990, 105.
43 Rosenau, 1987, 2.
44 Light, 1994, 94.
45 Kim, 1989, 4.
46 For detailed analyses of the 'state' of the literature on Chinese foreign policy see Wu, 1980; Shih, 1990; Kim, 1984, 1989.
47 Wu, 1980, 47 and Kim, 1984, 16, citing Fairbank, 1969, 449. Other examples are Mancall, 1963, and Hunt, 1984.
48 Wu, 1980, 49 citing Feuerwerker, 1972, 5 and Schwartz, 1968.
49 For example Hunt,1984, 1–2; Pann, 1988, 7–8; Papp, 1988, 311.
50 Wu, 1980, 53. Examples of this type of approach are Tsou and Halperin, 1965, and Bobrow, 1979.
51 Examples are Lucian Pye and Richard Solomon.
52 See for example Kokubun, 1986, 517; Wang, 1994, 497–502; Chay, 1990; Gaenslen,1986; Hermann *et al.*, 1987.
53 Wu, 1980, 53–7.
54 Wu, 1980, 57.
55 Examples of multi-causal analyses are Robinson, 1977 and Whiting, 1989b.
56 Langdon, 1973, xi–xiv.
57 Reischauer, 1977, 335, 378.
58 Satō, 1977, 367–89.
59 Reischauer, 1977, 408; see also Scalapino, 1977 and Ward, 1978 for further examples of the importance of cultural identity.
60 Scalapino, 1977, 393; Ward, 1978, 202; Reischauer, 1977, 413.
61 See for example Scalapino, 1977 and 1989.
62 Luard, 1992, 335–65 (citing Rosenau, 1979).
63 Rosenau, 1994, 532.
64 Segal, 1990.
65 Robinson and Shambaugh, 1994.
66 Curtis, 1993.
67 Aruga, 1989.
68 Satō, 1989.
69 For example, Satō, 1989; For more information of Japanese research on international relations see Inoguchi, 1989, 250–60, and Inoguchi, 1992, 73.
70 Wang Jisi, 1994.
71 Easton's model of the political system is perhaps the simplest (see Clarke and White, 1989, 29). McGowan and Shapiro's framework (McGowan and Shapiro, 1973, 42), though fairly simplified in comparison with, for example, Brecher's model of Israel's foreign policy process (Brecher, 1972, 3–4), nonetheless illustrates the foreign policy process in the form of a system or input–output model. A more recent effort at such a framework has been devised by Papadakis and Starr in their work on small states (in

Hermann *et al.*, 1987, 417). Their 'environmental model' builds upon Rosenau's seminal 'pre-theory' and Brecher's model of Israeli foreign policy process, but again is essentially an input–output model.

72 McGowan and Shapiro, 1973, 42.
73 McGowan and Shapiro, 1973, 40–46.
74 McGowan and Shapiro, 1973, 45.
75 McGowan and Shapiro, 1973, 43.
76 For example, studies of key leaders such as Kennedy during the Cuban Missile Crisis, Mao Zedong, Stalin and Hitler.
77 Zhao, 1996, 11.
78 Yayama, 1982, 108–15.

3 Postwar Sino-Japanese relations: an overview

1 Zhongguo Waijiaobu, 1987, 48.
2 Pye and Leites, 1982, 1157, state that one characteristic of Chinese political culture is that 'it is proper to cite events of a distant past to justify current sentiment'.
3 Kawahara, 1974, 430; Tanaka, 1991, 45. The Sino-Soviet Treaty of Friendship, Alliance, and Mutual Assistance was signed in 1950 and spoke of joint prevention of the revival of Japanese imperialism.
4 Jain, 1981, 11–12.
5 Tanaka, 1991, 47; Furukawa, 1988, 144.
6 Morino, 1991, 89.
7 Mendl, 1978, 3 talks of the search for reconciliation and proposals of an 'Apology Mission', and 'Friendship Mission' in mid-late 1940s.
8 Jain, 1981, 30.
9 Mendl, 1978, 6–7; Tanaka, 1991, 48; Iriye, 1992, 94–5.
10 Tanaka, 1991, 45.
11 Lee, 1984, 2.
12 Jain, 1981, 39. Tanaka also makes the same point (1991, 44).
13 Johnson, 1986, 408.
14 Tanaka, 1991, 52.
15 Tanaka, 1991, 50; Lee, 1976, 144.
16 Tensions had been rising between the PRC and USSR since 1956, with Khruschev's denunciations of Stalin, and resulted in the Sino-Soviet split in 1960. In 1958, the Quemoy–Matsu crisis (China's attempts to capture the islands of Quemoy and Matsu) caused tension with the US government.
17 Tanaka, 1991, 52; see also Lee, 1976, 38–9.
18 Jain, 1978, 44–8, Tanaka, 1991, 51–4; Lee, 1976, 38–40.
19 Named after the two principle negotiators, Liao Chengzhi and Takasaki Tatsunosuke, and later renamed Memorandum Trade in 1967.
20 Mendl, 1978, 22.
21 Lee, 1984, 7.
22 Tanaka, 1991, 53–4; Lee, 1976, 43–4.
23 Japan's handling of two incidents in particular – the sale of the Kurashiki vinylon plant to the PRC and the Chou Hung ching incident involving a PRC defector – angered the Taiwanese government, and when Japan tried

to appease Taiwan it was then criticised by the PRC for pursuing a two Chinas policy. See Mendl, 1978, 22–3.
24 Jain, 1981, 54–6; Lee, 1976, 86.
25 Jain, 1981, 55.
26 Japan's decision to commit itself to Taiwan's security has been attributed to its 'anxiety to recover Okinawa from the US'. See for example Jain, 1981, 58–9; Tang, 1978, 407.
27 Lee, 1976, 163. The 'four conditions' stated that the PRC would not trade with Japanese companies that: (1) were pro-South Korea and Taiwan; (2) had large investments in South Korea or Taiwan; (3) supplied arms to US war efforts in Asia; (4) were involved in US–Japan joint ventures or were subsidiaries of US companies. Lee, 1976, 162.
28 Tanaka, 1991, 58–9.
29 Tanaka, 1991, 62–6.
30 The standard account of Sino-Japanese normalisation describes how the 'Nixon Shock' prompted a surprised Japan into following the US lead in seeking diplomatic normalisation with China. But in fact, as both Tanaka and Johnson have pointed out, from 1970 on there were signs within Japanese political and business circles indicating that the Japanese government was ready to start discussing negotiations for normalisation. These signs were, for example, opposition party delegations to China, acceptance of Zhou's 'four conditions' by large corporations, and Satō's use of the official name for China 'the People's Republic'. Tanaka also argues that Nixon's announcement did not come as great a shock to the Japanese government as is generally thought, and that the Japanese foreign ministry had been aware of the thaw in Sino-US relations. Johnson, 1986, 411–13; Tanaka, 1991, 66–9.
31 *China Quarterly*, 1972, no. 52, 782–3.
32 *China Quarterly*,1972, no. 52, 782–3.
33 Tsou *et al.*, 1978, 410.
34 Lee, 1976, 192.
35 Lee, 1976, 191.
36 Jain, 1981, 99.
37 Shambaugh, 1994b, 424.
38 See Zhao, 1993, 119 for a list of agreements.
39 Lee, 1984, 17.
40 Hsiao, 1974, 725.
41 Tsou *et al.*, 1978, 424.
42 Hsiao, 1974, 726.
43 Bedeski, 1983, 28.
44 The Senkaku islands are a group of eight islands southwest of Okinawa to which Japan, China and Taiwan all lay claim.
45 Kim, 1979, 305.
46 Jain, 1981, 106,115–7.
47 Kim, 1979, 311–2. For a detailed study of the international implications of the Treaty of Peace and Friendship, see Bedeski, 1983.
48 Lee, 1984, 140.
49 Lee, 1984, 142.
50 Newby, 1988, 7.
51 Jain, 1981, 149.

52 For detailed accounts and analysis of the Baoshan shock see Kokubun, 1986; Lee, 1984, ch. 2; Francks, 1988.
53 Maruyama, 1990, 105–6.
54 Newby, 1988, 8–9.
55 Newby, 1988, 39.
56 Tanaka, 1991, 114.
57 Arnold, 1985, 104.
58 Matsumura, 1988, 22.
59 Arnold, 1985, 105.
60 *China Quarterly*, 1982, no. 90, Chronicle.
61 Gaimushō, 1983, 72.
62 Gaimushō, 1983, 73.
63 Yang, 1993, 427–8.
64 *Far Eastern Economic Review*, 11 June 1982, 14 (Mike Tharp).
65 *Beijing Review*, 14 June 1982, 5–6.
66 Tanaka, 1991, 116.
67 Tanaka, 1991, 117.
68 *Beijing Review*, 14 June 1982, 5–6.
69 Yang, 1993, 430–1.
70 Arnold, 1985, 106.
71 Kennedy, 1989, 531.
72 Calvocoressi, 1996, 68.
73 McWilliams and Piotrowski, 1993, 230.
74 McWilliams and Piotrowski, 1993, 230; Derbyshire, 1987, 108.
75 Kennedy, 1989, 531, citing A. Ulam.
76 McWilliams and Piotrowski, 1993, 231, 441. The imposition of martial law and arrests of Solidarity leaders was 'generally attributed in the West to the Kremlin'.
77 Kennedy, 1989, 532.
78 Calvocoressi, 1996, 49.
79 Signs that China was considering a more friendly approach to the USSR emerged in February 1982 in China's response to Brezhnev's call for an improvement in relations. Tanaka, 1991, 117; Berton, in Hsiung, 1985, 37.
80 Cumings, 1993, 56.
81 Susumu, 1981, 24.

4 Background to the Textbook Issue: domestic issues in the 1970s and 1980s

1 Jensen, 1982, 261.
2 Jensen, 1982, 261.
3 Ezra Vogel's 'Japan as Number One' (1979) was just one of many studies by 'Westerners' extolling the virtues of Japan and the Japanese.
4 (Murakami in) Okimoto in Rohlen, 1988, 203; Richardson, 1997, 76–7.
5 Farnsworth, 1981, 72.
6 The vote, sponsored by the Japan Socialist Party, was brought on the basis of dissatisfaction with Ohira's economic policies, poor handling of corruption issues and his agreement with the USA to increase defence spending. The LDP 'rebels' belonged to the non-mainstream Fukuda, Miki and Nakagawa factions, and their abstention has been attributed to such

factors as resentment of the Ohira–Tanaka 'axis' and dissatisfaction with Ohira in general. See Stockwin, 1981, 21–7.

7 Farnsworth, 1981, 75–6; Stockwin, 1981, 31.

8 Murakami, in Okimoto and Rohlen, 1988, 204.

9 Pyle, 1987, 251.

10 Aoki, 1994, 3 describes four phases of *Nihonbunkaron/Nihonjinron* writing: 1945–54 ('negative distinctiveness'); 1955–63 (Japan and Europe's parallel development); early 1964–76, late 1977–83 (positive distinctiveness); 1984 to date (universality).

11 Farnsworth, 1981, 78.

12 Farnsworth, 1981, 78.

13 Farnsworth, 1981, 78.

14 Nihon Kyōiku Nenkan Koinkai (hereafter NKN), 1982, 222.

15 Pyle, 1982, 242.

16 In particular Shimizu Ikutaro, cited in Pyle, 1982, 257–9.

17 Pyle, 1982, 248–50, 261.

18 Buzan, 1988, 566–7.

19 Farnsworth, 1981, 78 citing 1980 Blue Book.

20 Dahlby, 1981, 36.

21 Dahlby, 1981, 36.

22 Expenditure had been 0.9 per cent; Farnsworth, 1981, 79.

23 The 'defence lobby' included Michio Sakata, Shin Kanemaru and some LDP hawks such as Okuno Seisuke and Nakagawa Ichirō (Dahlby, 1981, 36–7).

24 Pyle, 1982, 233, citing an *Asahi Shimbun* poll, 4 November 1980.

25 Dahlby, 1981, 38.

26 Schoppa, 1991, 30.

27 Schoppa, 1991, 39.

28 Duke, 1972, 348.

29 Yamazumi, 1988, 97.

30 Duke, 1972, 350.

31 NKN, 1983, 308; Ishizaka, 1989, 25.

32 Takahashi, 1988, 96. The latter point is significant because during the 1982 Textbook Issue the option of *seigo teisei* was rejected by the Ministry of Education on the grounds that it was the publishers' responsibility to apply for such revision, and could not be responded to from a foreign request. The MOE also argued that the nature of the 'errors' also meant that *seigo teisei* was inappropriate.

33 Partial revision involves roughly a quarter of the textbook to be revised; 'new authorisation' applies to completely new textbooks, and those re-submitted following a change in the 'Course of Study'.

34 In 1990–1 the process was reduced to two stages; this account describes the 1982 system.

35 The Course of Study is a set of curriculum guidelines for local school authorities. The courses of study are to be considered only as an outline for curriculum development, and schools have some flexibility in implementing the curriculum (Thomas and Postlethwaite, 1983, 71). The Standards for Textbook Authorisation stipulates that textbooks must comply with the Fundamental Law on Education and the objectives of the Course of Study; that subjects such as religion and politics be treated fairly,

with no bias; that there be no factual errors or inaccuracies and that expressions used must be appropriate and standardised (Monbushō, 1986, 7).

36 TARC is an advisory body attached to the Ministry of Education, made up of university lecturers and schoolteachers and divided into subcommittees according to textbook subject matter.

37 In 1982 for social studies textbooks this could mean anything between 200 and 600 recommendations for corrections (*Asahi Shimbun* 26 June 1982, 1).

38 The article appeared in the 25 October 1979 issue.

39 NKN, 1982, 222.

40 NKN, 1982, 222.

41 NKN, 82, 224.

42 At the end of 1980, the *Keizai Kōhō Sentā* (affiliated to *Keidanren*) in cooperation with the *Nihon Bunka Kaigi* published a document (*Keizai Kyōiku* I.II) which pointed out the 'bias' in new middle school 'Civics' (*Kōmin*) textbooks and also in high school textbooks 'Politics and Economics' (*Seiji Keizai*). The document called on the Ministry of Education and textbook publishers to revise passages relating to pollution problems, consumer problems, energy resources, welfare problems, theories of economic systems, and the role of enterprise. NKN, 1982, 222.

The 'University of Tsukuba Group' headed by Professor Morimoto Shinsō also produced a report based on the content analysis of the *Kōmin* textbook which was distributed to the LDP, the *Minshatō* and business circles (NKN, 1982, 222).

43 The MOE submitted an 'opinion for reference' *(sankō iken)* to textbook companies requesting that the errors be revised and under such pressures, the Textbook Association (*Kyōkasho Kyōkai*) decided (December 1980) 'independently' to rewrite the criticised parts of the approved (but not yet distributed) *Kōmin* textbooks, which was unprecedented in educational history (NKN, 1982, 223, 296). This incident was cited by critics during the 1982 Textbook Issue to illustrate the Education Ministry's hypocrisy; in 1982 the Ministry steadfastly maintained that errors could not be revised (by *seigo teisei*) *immediately*; clearly this was not the case.

44 The LDP PARC (Policy Affairs Research Council) Education Division (*Jimintō Seichōkai Bunkyōbukai*) and Education System Research Council (*Bunkyō Seido Chōsakai*) jointly set up committees on the Fundamental Law of Education, the School System, Textbooks, and Teacher Training. NKN, 82, 222.

45 This is strikingly similar to the 1955 campaign when the Democratic Party charged that the Japan Teachers' Union had put 'pressure on publishing companies to include more left-wing content in their textbooks in order to obtain teacher recommendation for purchase' (Duke, 1972, 348).

46 NKN, 1983, 226.

47 NKN, 1983, 222.

48 NKN, 1982, 220.

49 Beer, 1984, 271.

50 Beer, 1984, 271.

51 The report had focused mainly on textbook selection procedures; the revised version looked at textbook content and authorisation. NKN, 1983, 224–6 and *Asahi Shimbun* 12 September 1982, 2.

52 NKN, 1983, 304.

206   *Notes*

53 See Chang, 1981, 6–8; Nethercut, 1983, 30–2.
54 Nethercut, 1983, 32–3.
55 Ginsburg, 1984, 5.
56 Introduced by Hua Guofeng in February 1978, the Four Modernisations had been formulated some time before that by Zhou Enlai. Hua's Ten Year plan for 1976–85 was to see implementation of the Four Modernisations, but it was soon realised that it was overambitious and had to be 'reintroduced' by Zhao and Deng, whose interpretation of the programme was different.
57 Dittmer, 1981, 33–6.
58 Zhao, 1996, 85.
59 The First World referred to the USA and Soviet Union, the Second World to developed countries of Europe, and Japan, the Third World to developing countries (China, Asia, Africa and Latin America).
60 Nethercut, 1983, 34.
61 Joffe, 1987, 149–83.
62 Joffe, 1987, 171.
63 Joffe, 1987, 28.
64 Nethercut, 1983, 34; Teiwes, 1984, 123.
65 Teiwes, 1984, 123; see also Dittmer, 1982, 41.
66 Teiwes, 1984, 124.
67 Joffe, 1987, 28 and Nethercut, 1983, 34–5 both remark on the courtesy and respect each group showed the other.
68 Mass demonstrations in Tiananmen Square in April which began as a homage to Zhou Enlai were interpreted by Mao as a criticism of Mao and the Cultural Revolution, and Deng was accused of playing a key role (Spence, 1990, 648).
69 Nethercut, 1983, 35.
70 Joffe, 1987, 28.
71 The full title of the document is 'Resolution on certain questions in the history of our Party since the founding of the People's Republic of China'.
72 Nethercut, 1983, 35. The GPD criticism was linked to the Bai Hua 'incident'. Writer and PLA member Bai Hua's film 'Unrequited Love' received criticism from the PLA and later from the Party and press (see Chapter 6).
73 Joffe, 1987, 28.
74 Dittmer, 1981, 49.
75 Cited in Dittmer, 1982, 39.
76 Discontent was not confined just to the youth and intellectuals, but was widespread. See Dittmer, 1982, 40.
77 Schram, 1984, 30.
78 The four principles are support of the socialist road, the people's democratic dictatorship, leadership by the Communist Party, and Marxism-Leninism/Mao Zedong Thought; Schram, 1984, 10.
79 Dittmer, 1982, 40.
80 Talk with cadres of central propaganda departments on 17 July 1981, in Deng Xiaoping, 1984, 369.
81 Schram, 1984, 30.
82 Schram, 1984, 31.
83 Nethercut, 1982, 697.
84 Nethercut, 1983, 35.

85 Deng, 1984, 348.
86 Deng, 1984, 350.
87 Tanaka, 1983, 205–9.
88 Deng, 1984, 416: 'To have lofty ideals, moral integrity, knowledge and a strong physique; to stress appearance and bearing, manners, and sense of discipline; and to defy hardships and sacrifice.'
89 Dittmer, 1982, 41–3. The focus of the campaign was a film based on the play 'Unrequited Love' by PLA member and writer Bai Hua. The military criticised the film for its 'implicit critique of Mao and apparent lack of patriotism,' and in so doing was criticising Deng's emphasis on material civilisation; see Chapter 6.
90 Pollack, 1984, 356.
91 Calvocoressi, 1996, 69.
92 See Deng, 1984, 'The Present Situation and the Tasks Before Us', 225.
93 Jian, 1993, 3.
94 That is, couched in terms of the Chinese people never allowing themselves to be humiliated again by big powers. See for example Hu Yaobang's speech to Twelfth Party Congress, *Beijing Review* 13 September 1982, 29–33.
95 Whiting, 1983, 915.
96 Whiting, 1983, 915.
97 Farnsworth, 1981, 78.
98 Pyle, 1987, 254.
99 Otake remarks upon assertive nationalism among some Japanese – especially young businessmen – see Pyle 1987 252, note 11 referring to Otake Hideo's *Nihon no bōei to kokunai seiji*, 1983.

5 The Textbook Issue: outline of events

1 NHK TV news reported on the issue on 25 June, showing passages apparently from the textbooks in question (Watanabe, 1982, 25), and all the major newspapers carried articles similar to the *Asahi Shimbun*. See for example, *Mainichi Shimbun*, *Sankei Shimbun*, *Yomiuri Shimbun* and *Nihon Keizai Shimbun*, 26–7 June 1982.
2 The Japanese word *shinryaku* can mean aggression, invasion, invading etc., depending on the context. In the Textbook Issue, *shinryaku* can be translated as invasion when referring to Japan's invasion of China, and aggression when referring to the conduct of the Japanese army during the war.
3 *Asahi Shimbun* 26 June, 1. (Unless otherwise stipulated, all references to newspaper articles in this and subsequent chapters are for 1982.)
4 The Japanese refer to 'the prewar' and 'the postwar', both of which are nouns in Japanese (*senzen* and *sengo*). 'The prewar' as it is referred to in the *Asahi Shimbun* throughout the Textbook Issue describes the period *before the Pacific War*. The term 'the Pacific War' has been, until recently, the only generally accepted way of referring to Japan's part in the Second World War, even though this clearly ignores the fact that Japan and China had been at war since 1937. See Gluck, 1993, 64–95.
5 *Asahi Shimbun* 26 June, 1.
6 *Asahi Shimbun* 26 June, 1.

208 *Notes*

7 *Asahi Shimbun* 26 June, 1.
8 Note that in the *Asahi Shimbun* there were no examples of descriptions of the Nanjing Massacre or the September 18 Incident about which the Chinese government was to complain; these appeared in the *Mainichi* and *Yomiuri*, and were the source of the *Renmin Ribao* article of 30 June. See *Renmin Ribao*, 30 June, 6.
9 Kyōiku Kōryusha, 1991, 188. Okada, 1982, 83 has the Xinhua report down for the 26th, the same day of the Mainichi report to which it referred. Xinhua bulletins are mainly for foreign audiences, so it was not until the issue got into the *Renmin Ribao* that it became a matter for the domestic audience.
10 *Renmin Ribao* 30 June, 6.
11 Kim, 1983, 283.
12 For example, see *Seiron* 18 September, *Sekai Nippō* 21 September, *Sekai* 5 October and also October–November issues of *Shokun* and *Seiron*.
13 Lee, 1979, 85–95.
14 Yayama, 1983, 305.
15 Lee, 1979, 95.
16 Sugiyama, 1982a, 28–31.
17 Sugiyama, 1982a, 28–31.
18 Yayama, 1983, 305.
19 *Asahi Shimbun* 26 July, 22.
20 Sugiyama, 1982a, 28.
21 *Asahi Shimbun* 28 July, 3, interview with Bureau Chief Suzuki.
22 See *Asahi Shimbun* 19 September, 5. This point raises the issue of self-censorship. Did the writers use these terms because they considered them appropriate to descriptions of Japan's actions in China; or were they acting pre-emptively because they knew that *shinryaku* would be subjected to some sort of recommendation from the MOE during authorisation as it had been since the 1960s? See *Asahi Shimbun* 27 June, 23, and Furukawa, 1988, 453.
23 Sugiyama, 1982a, 28–31.
24 Sugiyama, 1982a, 28–9.
25 Yayama, 1983, 307.
26 Sugiyama, 1982b, 159.
27 *Asahi Shimbun* 29 July, 22.
28 *Asahi Shimbun* 29 July, 1.
29 The example given was a map caption which had been changed from 'The invasion of China' (*Nihon no chūgoku shinryaku*) to 'The encroachment into China' (*Nihon no chūgoku shinnyū*). *Asahi Shimbun* 27 July, 3.
30 Daily Summary of Japanese Press, 5 August, 12.
31 *Asahi Shimbun* 30 July, 4; Daily Summary of Japanese Press, 5 August, 12.
32 *Asahi Shimbun* 30 July, 4.
33 *Asahi Shimbun* 30 July, 4; Daily Summary of Japanese Press, 5 August, 12.
34 Daily Summary of Japanese Press, 5 August, 13.
35 *Asahi Shimbun* 30 July, 4.
36 See *Asahi Shimbun* 14 August, 2, 'Analysis' '*Shinryaku o shinshutsu ni nado to, rekishi kyōkasho no kijutsu o kentei ni yotte kakiaratameta, iwayuru kyōkasho mondai wa . . .*' (The so-called textbook problem in which

changes such as invade to advance have been applied to history text-books . . .).

37 *Asahi Shimbun* 25 August, 3.
38 Watanabe, 1982, 30.
39 *Shokun*, November 1982, 75.
40 The newspaper's right-leaning stance may account for this conclusion. Watanabe, 1982, 30.
41 See, for example, *Shokun* and *Seiron*.
42 *Asahi Shimbun* 19 September, 5.
43 *Asahi Shimbun* 27 July, 3.
44 Sugiyama, 1982b, 159. Note that there *had* been a *kaizen iken* to change 'When Nanjing was occupied' to 'Amid the confusion of the occupation of Nanjing'.
45 Sugiyama, 1982a, 32.
46 *Asahi Shimbun* 19 September, 5.
47 *Asahi Shimbun* 25 August, 3.
48 Beer, 1984, 272.
49 *Japan Echo* IX(4), 15.
50 Tanaka, 1983, 219, note 48, says that on discovery of the error the whole basis of the PRC's campaign was lost, which explains China's sudden acceptance of the Japanese *kenkai*.
51 The inconsistencies in the Japanese press reports, noted above, were further compounded in the Chinese press, where Japanese words with no direct translation into Chinese were given Chinese approximations, or else were translated incorrectly. According to this report, for example, *qinlüe* (Japanese, *shinryaku*) had been replaced not by *jinchu* (*shinshutsu*) as in the *Renmin Ribao* report of 30 June, but by *jinji* (advance), the Japanese equivalent of which (*shingeki*) did *not* appear in the Japanese reports as an example of the changes to the textbooks.
52 The Chinese name for what the Japanese call the 'Manchurian Incident' of 18 September 1931.
53 *Renmin Ribao* 20 July, 7.
54 *Daily Report: China* 26 July, D1–3.
55 *Renmin Ribao* 24 July, 6 (English translation in *Daily Report: China* 26 July, D3–4).
56 *Asahi Shimbun* 24 July, 3. It is not clear exactly what Ogawa said. According to the *Kokusai Kyōiku Jiten*, Ogawa said 'TAS is carried out impartially and fairly, it is an internal problem and there is no reason for it to be criticised by foreign countries' (Kyōiku Kōryusha, 1991, 188). The *Asahi Shimbun* states that Ogawa later denied saying these things to Makieda; in fact he called Makieda a liar! (*Asahi Shimbun* 24 July, 3).
57 *Asahi Shimbun* 24 July, 3.
58 *Asahi Shimbun* 21 July, 3.
59 Summary of World Broadcasts, Far East, 28 July, 7089/A3/10.
60 *Renmin Ribao* 28 July, 4.
61 *Renmin Ribao* 28 July, 4. The *Asahi Shimbun* noted that Xiao also referred to the description of the September 18 Incident as 'the bombing of the South Manchurian railway', but this did not appear in the *Renmin Ribao* version. See *Asahi Shimbun* 27 July, 1. For full translation of *Renmin Ribao* articles see Summary of World Broadcasts, Far East, 29 July, 7090/A3/1.

62 *Asahi Shimbun* 27 July,1.
63 *Asahi Shimbun* 27 July, 3.
64 *Asahi Shimbun* 27 July, 1.
65 *Daily Summary of Japanese Press* 4 August, 13, quoting *Nihon Keizai* 27 July, 1; see also *Asahi Shimbun* 27 July, 3 in which Foreign Ministry heads are quoted as saying that 'it is not an inter-governmental issue'.
66 *Asahi Shimbun* 28 July, 1.
67 *Daily Summary of Japanese Press* 4 August, 13–14.
68 *Asahi Shimbun* 27 July, 3.
69 *Asahi Shimbun* 27 July, 3.
70 Summary of World Broadcasts, Far East, 30 July, 7091/A3/5.
71 *Asahi Shimbun* 27 July, 3.
72 *Asahi Shimbun* 27 July, 3.
73 *Asahi Shimbun* pm, 30 July, 1.
74 *Asahi Shimbun* pm, 29 July, 1.
75 *Asahi Shimbun* pm, 29 July, 1.
76 *Daily Summary of Japanese Press* 4 August, 14, quoting *Nihon Keizai* (pm) 27 July, 1.
77 *Asahi Shimbun* pm, 29 July, 1; *Asahi Shimbun* pm, 30 July, 1.
78 *Asahi Shimbun* 30 July, 4.
79 *Renmin Ribao* 30 July, 6, 'Good Advice Grates on the Ear but Benefits Behaviour'.
80 *Renmin Ribao* 30 July, 6.
81 *Asahi Shimbun* 29 July, 1.
82 Summary of World Broadcasts, Far East, 29 July, 7090/A3/2
83 *Asahi Shimbun* 30 July, 1.
84 *Asahi Shimbun* 30 July, 1.
85 *Asahi Shimbun* 30 July, 1, 22.
86 Summary of World Broadcasts, Far East, 31 July, 7092/A3/4; *Asahi Shimbun* 30 July, 22; *Asahi Shimbun* pm, 30 July, 1.
87 *Asahi Shimbun* pm 30 July, 1.
88 *Daily Report: China* 3 August, D5–6.
89 *Daily Report: China* 4 August, D4.
90 Summary of World Broadcasts, Far East, 2 August, 7093/A3/2.
91 *Daily Report: China* 2 August, D1.
92 *Asahi Shimbun* 3 August, 1.
93 *Daily Report: China* 2 August, D2.
94 *Asahi Shimbun* 2 August, 2.
95 *Daily Report: China* 3 August, D3–4.
96 *Daily Report: China* 3 August, D2–3.
97 *Asahi Shimbun* 4 August, 1.
98 *Daily Summary of Japanese Press* 13 August, 16, quoting *Sankei Shimbun* 6 August, 2.
99 The South Korean government regarded the loan from Japan of $6 billion in credits as a way of helping to maintain South Korea's position as a line of defence against communism, but the Japanese government was opposed to the linkage of economic cooperation and security. See Bridges, 1992, 155; Ahn, 1993, 267.
100 *Asahi Shimbun* 4 August, 3.
101 *Asahi Shimbun* 4 August, 1 and 5 August, 1.

102 *Asahi Shimbun* 5 August, 1.
103 *Asahi Shimbun* 5 August, 1.
104 *Asahi Shimbun* 5 August, 1.
105 *Renmin Ribao* 6 August, 1.
106 *Renmin Ribao* 6 August, 1, and *Asahi Shimbun* pm, 5 August, 1.
107 *Asahi Shimbun* pm, 5 August, 1.
108 See Chapter 4.
109 *Asahi Shimbun* pm, 5 August, 1.
110 *Daily Summary of Japanese Press* 13 August, 15 translation of *Sankei Shimbun* 6 August, 2.
111 *Asahi Shimbun* pm, 5 August, 1 and *Asahi Shimbun* 22 August, 2.
112 *Asahi Shimbun* 6 August, 1.
113 *Daily Summary of Japanese Press* 13 August, 10.
114 *Asahi Shimbun* 6 August, 1.
115 Summary of World Broadcasts, Far East, 7 August, 7098/A3/4.
116 *Asahi Shimbun* 7 August, 1. Hashimoto was probably chosen to go to China because at the time of Sino-Japanese normalisation he had been head of the China Desk, and was known to the Chinese negotiators. See Park, 1978, 372.
117 *Daily Summary of Japanese Press* 17 August, 11.
118 *Daily Summary of Japanese Press* 13 August, 11.
119 *Asahi Shimbun* 10 August, 2, also *Asahi Shimbun* 25 August, 3.
120 *Asahi Shimbun* 10 August, 2.
121 *Asahi Shimbun* 10 August, 2. On the changes made during authorisation to passages about Korea, the *kenkai* stated that although the word 'riot' was used to describe the Korean Independence Movement, 'it does not have a bad connotation'. The Korean government had also protested about passages describing the forcible sending of Koreans to Japan, the enforced changing of Korean names to Japanese names, the ban on the use of the Korean language and the forcible paying of homage at shrines. On these aspects the MOE document stated that 'at one point the Koreans went voluntarily to Japan', and that there was 'insufficient historical material' on the subject of enforced use of the Japanese language and visits to shrines (*Asahi Shimbun* 10 August, 2).
122 *Asahi Shimbun* 10 August, 1.
123 Summary of World Broadcasts, Far East, 11 August, 7101/A3/1.
124 *Asahi Shimbun* 10 August, 1 and *Asahi Shimbun* pm, 10 August, 1.
125 According to the *Asahi Shimbun* report, the Foreign Ministry view should be regarded as the equivalent of the government's view (*Asahi Shimbun* 13 August, 2).
126 *Asahi Shimbun* 13 August, 2.
127 Summary of World Broadcasts, Far East, 14 August, 7104/A3/6.
128 *Asahi Shimbun* 5 August, 3.
129 *Daily Summary of Japanese Press* 13 August, 16.
130 *Daily Summary of Japanese Press* 17 August, 11.
131 *Asahi Shimbun* 10 August, 1.
132 *Asahi Shimbun* 14 August, 2.
133 *Asahi Shimbun* 14 August, 2.
134 On 12 August, the South Korean Foreign Ministry (via the Japanese Embassy in Seoul) urged a prompt response by the Japanese government to

its demand made on 3 August for correction of the 'distortions' of facts regarding Korea in Japanese schoolbooks (Summary of World Broadcasts, Far East, 14 August, 7104/A3/6).

135 That the PRC now seemed willing to acknowledge that the issue was a domestic matter and allow the Japanese government to treat it as such appears to be a slight concession. The *Renmin Ribao* changed its wording accordingly to say that 'we do accept it is an internal matter'; a complete turnaround from before.

136 For example, on the evening of the 13th there was a meeting of Education Ministry heads and the LDP Education Committee heads (*bunkyō bukai kanbu*). On the 14th, both the Foreign and Education Ministries held meetings to discuss the strategy (see *Asahi Shimbun* 15 August, 1).

137 *Renmin Ribao* 15 August, 1. English translation in Summary of World Broadcasts, Far East, 16 August, 7105/A3/1–5.

138 *Daily Report: China* 13 August, D4; 16 August, D3.

139 *Daily Report: China* 13 August, D4–5; 16 August, D3–4; 17 August, D6.

140 Summary of World Broadcasts, Far East, 16 August, 7105/A3/7; *Daily Report: China* 17 August, D9.

141 Summary of World Broadcasts, Far East, 19 August, 7108/A3/3 and *Renmin Ribao* 15 August,.7.

142 *New York Times* 11 August, 8.

143 Summary of World Broadcasts, Far East, 16 August, 7105/A3/7.

144 *Asahi Shimbun* 16 August, 3.

145 ROK newspapers carried 946 articles; there were 353 in Hong Kong, 312 in Singapore and 246 in the PRC; Kyōiku Kōryusha, 1991, 188.

146 Kyōiku Kōryusha, 1991, 188.

147 References to the contents of these press reports of other East and Southeast Asian countries are to be found in the July, August and September issues of Summary of World Broadcasts, *Daily Report*, *Daily Summary of Japanese Press*, *Renmin Ribao*, *Asahi Shimbun* and so on.

148 See for example 'China Using Dispute with Japan to Diplomatic Advantage with Other Countries', *The Times* 6 August, 6. See also 22 July, 7; 30 July, 8; 2 August, 6; 8 August, 14; 9 August, 4; 10 August, 4; 14 August, 8.

149 *New York Times* 25 August, 22. See also 28 July, 6; 11 August, 8; 14 August, 4; 24 August, 4; 25 August, 4.

150 Kyōiku Kōryusha, 1991, 188.

151 *Asahi Shimbun* 5 August, 3. The only other government to lodge a protest was the Vietnamese at the beginning of September, as reported in *Asahi Shimbun* 9 September, 3, and Summary of World Broadcasts, Far East, 7127/A3/6. These reports are based on an article in *Nhan Dan* which stated that, via the Japanese Ambassador in Hanoi, the Vietnamese government demanded a 'serious, clear-cut attitude, and correction of distortions'. The Japanese response is unclear.

152 *Asahi Shimbun* 17 August, 1.

153 Summary of World Broadcasts, Far East, 19 August, 7108/A3/2.

154 *Asahi Shimbun* 22/8.2; Summary of World Broadcasts, Far East, 23 August, 7111/A3/5.

155 *Asahi Shimbun* 22 August, 2.

156 The process of 'revision authorisation' is described in Chapter 4.

157 *Asahi Shimbun* 20 August, 1.
158 *Asahi Shimbun* 20 August, 1.
159 *Renmin Ribao* 21 August, 6; *Asahi Shimbun* 20 August, 2.
160 *Asahi Shimbun* 20 August, 2; 22 August, 2.
161 *Asahi Shimbun* 22 August, 2.
162 *Asahi Shimbun* 21 August, 1.
163 *Asahi Shimbun* 24 August, 1.
164 *Asahi Shimbun* 24 August, 1.
165 *Asahi Shimbun* 24 August, 1; *Daily Report: China* 25 August, D1; Summary of World Broadcasts, Far East, 26 August, 7114/A3/2.
166 *Asahi Shimbun* 24 August, 1.
167 *Asahi Shimbun* 24 August,1. Mitsuzuka and Mori left for Seoul on the evening of 22 August.
168 *Asahi Shimbun* 25 August, 1.
169 *Asahi Shimbun* 26 August, 1; Summary of World Broadcasts, Far East, 26 August, 7114/A3/3, 'Japanese Lawmakers' Visit to Korea'.
170 *Asahi Shimbun* 26 August, 1.
171 For full text in English, see Summary of World Broadcasts, Far East, 27 August, 7115/i , and in Japanese see *Asahi Shimbun* 27 August, 1.
172 *Asahi Shimbun* 27 August, 1; Summary of World Broadcasts, Far East, 27 August, 7115/A3/8.
173 *Asahi Shimbun* 27 August, 1; Summary of World Broadcasts, Far East, 27 August, 7115/A3/8.
174 *Asahi Shimbun* 27 August, 1.
175 *Asahi Shimbun* 27 August, 1.
176 *Asahi Shimbun* 27 August, 1, 3; Summary of World Broadcasts, Far East, 28 August, 7116/A3/8; Takahashi, 1988, 103.
177 *Renmin Ribao* 29 August, 1; *Asahi Shimbun* 29 August, 1.
178 *Renmin Ribao* 30 August, 6, commentary entitled 'The Japanese Government Must Correct Errors Conscientiously'.
179 *Asahi Shimbun* 5 September, 2.
180 Tanaka, 1983, 197; *Asahi Shimbun* 31 August, 2.
181 *Daily Summary of Japanese Press* 11 September, 2.
182 *Asahi Shimbun* 29 August, 1.
183 Tanaka, 1983, 197; *Asahi Shimbun* 3 September, 1.
184 *Asahi Shimbun* 30 August, 1.
185 The Education Ministry announced on 7 September that it was to bring forward the TARC Inquiry (originally scheduled for the end of September) to 14 September. This move was seen as a 'demonstration of Japan's desire for an early solution to the problem, especially in time for Prime Minister Suzuki's visit to China beginning on 26th September' (Summary of World Broadcasts, Far East, 9 September, 7126/A3/2; see also *Asahi Shimbun* 8 September, 3).
186 *Asahi Shimbun* 1 September, 1.
187 *Asahi Shimbun* 2 September, 2.
188 *Asahi Shimbun* 3 September, 1; Tanaka, 1983, 197–8, citing *Nihon Keizai Shimbun* 3 September.
189 See for example *Asahi Shimbun* 10 September, 1, which refers to *zaisetsumei/aratani shimeshita mondai kaiketsu no sotchi*, with one reference to *aratanasotchi* but no detail to explain the new measures.

214   *Notes*

190 Summary of World Broadcasts, Far East, 10 September, 7127/A3/5.
191 *Asahi Shimbun* 10 September, 1; 8 September, 1.
192 *Asahi Shimbun* 9 September, 1; 8 September, 1.
193 *Asahi Shimbun* 10 September, 1.
194 Summary of World Broadcasts, Far East, 10 September, 7127/A3/5.
195 *Renmin Ribao* 10 September, 1; Summary of World Broadcasts, Far East, 10 September, 7127/A3/5.
196 *Asahi Shimbun* 10 September, 1.
197 *Asahi Shimbun* 10 September, 1.
198 *Renmin Ribao* 10 September, 1; Summary of World Broadcasts, Far East, 10 September, 7127/A3/5.
199 Summary of World Broadcasts, Far East, 11 September, 7128/A3/1.

6 The Textbook Issue: China's response

1 Yang, 1986, 208.
2 Yang, 1986, 208 for Chinese version of events; Nakajima, 1982c, 145 for the Japanese version.
3 Nagano, 1982, 164–7.
4 Nagano, 1982, 165. On the matter of war reparations the wording was as follows: 'The government of the People's Republic of China announces that for the sake of Sino-Japanese friendship it renounces the request for war reparations from Japan.' Note that Ohira deleted the word 'right' in 'right to request' with the consent of the Chinese side.
5 Gluck, 1992, 15.
6 For details on historical revisionism in France and Germany see Harriss, 1994, 8–25, 64–73.
7 Buruma, 1994, 114.
8 Furukawa, 1983, 5–6.
9 Furukawa, 1983, 7.
10 Furukawa, 1983, 7; Deng, 1984, 396.
11 Furukawa, 1983, 7; Hu Yaobang, 1982, 30.
12 *Far Eastern Economic Review* 1982, August 20, 38.
13 Whiting, 1989, 65.
14 Whiting, 1989, 28.
15 During Suzuki's explanation to a Diet committee at the end of July, he said that *shinryaku* had been changed to *shinshutsu* in the past.
16 Yoneda, 1973, 34–6; Uchida Tomoyuki, 1980, 34–6.
17 Yoneda, 1973, 36–8.
18 Yoneda, 1973, 2.
19 Beer, 1984, 264.
20 For more details of the Ienaga Textbook Trials see Beer, 1984; Herzog, 1993; Buruma, 1994; Morikawa, 1991; Takahashi, 1988.
21 Fujiwara, 1988, 19–23.
22 Buruma, 1994, 122.
23 Fujiwara, 1988, 23–4.
24 Buruma, 1994, 126; Buruma, 1991, 51.
25 Fujiwara, 1988, 24.
26 Buruma, 1991, 51.
27 Whiting, 1989, 41.

28 Doi, 1982a, 7.
29 Whiting, 1989, 47.
30 Whiting, 1989, 51.
31 Doi, 1982a, 8.
32 See for example, Johnson 1986; Ijiri, 1991; Buruma 1994, 1991; Tanaka, 1983a.
33 Ng-Quinn, 1983, 205, citing Liao and Whiting, 1973, 83.
34 Doak Barnett, 1985, 118.
35 Doak Barnett, 1985, 118–9.
36 Whiting, 1989, 42.
37 Whiting, 1979, 5.
38 Whiting, 1979, 4.
39 Whiting, 1979, 4–5.
40 Tanaka, 1983, 198–202; see also Doi, 1982b, 7.
41 *Renmin Ribao* 20 July, 7.
42 *Renmin Ribao* 30 July, 6.
43 *Renmin Ribao* 6 August, 1.
44 *Renmin Ribao* 14 August, 6, 'Riben xiugai jiaokeshu de qianqianhouhou'.
45 *Renmin Ribao* 14 August, 6, 'Dangdai zui huangmiu de lishiguan'.
46 *Renmin Ribao* 15 August, 1, 'Qianshibuwang,houshizhishi'.
47 *Renmin Ribao* 23 August, 6, 'Jin biaoshi jiuzheng cuowu de "yiyuan" shi bugou de', translated in *Daily Report* 23 August, D2.
48 *Renmin Ribao* 26 August, 6.
49 *Renmin Ribao* 23 August, 6; *Renmin Ribao* 26 August, 6.
50 *Renmin Ribao* 29 August, 1, 'Wu Xueqian fuwaizhang jiu jiaokeshu wenti juejian riben zhuhuadashi'; *Renmin Ribao* 30 August, 6, 'Riben zhengfu yingdang qieshi jiuzheng cuowu'.
51 See *Renmin Ribao* 23 August, 6; 27 August, 6.
52 *Renmin Ribao* 3 September, 6, 'Zhongri youhao jichu burong junguozhuyi shilipohuai'.
53 *Renmin Ribao* 7 September, 4; *Beijing Review* 37, 13 September, 30, for translation of Hu Yaobang's speech.
54 *Renmin Ribao* 10 September, 1, 'Riben jiuzheng cuowu de cuoshe bi guoqu qianjinle yibu'.
55 *Renmin Ribao* 10 September, 4 'Xiwang Riben zhengfu yanbixin,xing-buguo'.
56 See August issues of *Hongqi*, *Zhongguo Qingnian Bao*, *Banyuetan*, *Shijie Zhishi* and *Daily Report: China*.
57 Whiting, 1989a, 47.
58 Whiting, 1989a, 47–9.
59 *Daily Report* 9 August, D2.
60 *Daily Report* 10 August, D3; 12 August, D2; 13 August, D1, D4; 16 August, D3–4.
61 *Daily Report* 17 August, D9.
62 Doi, 1982, 7.
63 Jinnō, 1982, 122; also Kobori, 1982a, 52, who says that Korean historians have been studying Japanese history textbooks for many years, and since 1975 the subject has become of great interest to Korean academics; journalists brought the subject into the mainstream in Autumn 1981.

64 *Asahi Shimbun* 5 August pm, 2. The ROK National History Compilation Committee pointed out twenty-four cases of distortion in history and social science textbooks, fifteen of which related to modern history such as the independence movement and Japan's aggression in Korea (translated in *Daily Summary of Japanese Press* 13 August, 10).
65 Whiting, 1989, 80.
66 Kawahara, 1974, 430.
67 Kawahara, 1974, 431.
68 Hsiao, 1974, makes the same point: 'China does not object to Japan's military build-up and its continued alliance with the United States . . . Premier Chou 'understood' the basis for Tanaka's greatly expanded fourth five-year defence programme' (p.118).
69 Okabe, 1976, 144.
70 Okabe, 1976, 142.
71 Okabe, 1976, 131.
72 Okabe, 1976, 133.
73 Nakajima, 1982c, 136–9, and for an English version of a similar argument see *Daily Summary of Japanese Press* 27 August,12, citing *Sankei Shimbun* 20 August, 11.
74 Zhao, 1992, 161.
75 Barnett, 1985, 9–13.
76 Robinson, 1994, 555.
77 Robinson, 1994, 567–87.
78 Lieberthal, 1983, 28.
79 Calvocoressi, 1996, 52–3 points to a general move to the right in the USA and Western Europe with the emergence of Reagan, Thatcher, Kohl, etc. although he acknowledges that the Europeans were not always behind Reagan on USSR policies.
80 Summary of World Broadcasts, Far East, 28 September, 7142/A3/5.
81 For a discussion of Japan's ODA to China see Zhao, 1996, 148–82.
82 Johnson, 1986, 420–4.
83 Akasaka, 1982, 163.
84 Doi, 1982, 10.
85 Okada, 1982, 84; Doi, 1982, 9.
86 Doi, 1982, 8.
87 *Daily Report* 27 July, V2–3.
88 Okada, 1982, 84–5.
89 See *Renmin Ribao* 23 July, 7; Summary of World Broadcasts, Far East, 7 August, 7098/A3/2, quoting NCNA report, 5 August.
90 *Daily Report* 6 August, W1–2.
91 *Daily Report* 6 August, W1–2.
92 Shambaugh, 1994, 203–4.
93 Doi, 1982, 10.
94 Okada, 1982, 89.
95 Shambaugh, 1994, 204. Note that this 'new' independent foreign policy had actually been advocated in the early 1960s; see Robinson, 1994, 574.
96 Nakajima, 1982d, 12. Others, however, have seen it as tilt more towards the West (Robinson, 1994, 574).
97 Wang, 1989, 311.
98 Summary of World Broadcasts, Far East, 30 September, 7144/A3/2.

99 For an account of Sino-Soviet rapprochement, and China's rationale, see Berton, in Hsiung, 1985, 24–55

100 Tanaka, 1983, 203–5; Jūjō, 1982, 21.

101 Wang, 1989, 310.

102 Hu Yaobang, 1982, 29.

103 Tanaka, 1983, 204.

104 Tanaka, 1983, 204; Jūjō 1982, 20.

105 See Joffe, 1987, 175 and Nethercut, 1983 for a discussion of the struggle over personnel changes.

106 Tsou, 1984, 42.

107 Tsou, 1984, 42.

108 Dittmer, 1982, 42.

109 Dittmer, 1982, 43; see also Deng, 1984, 369.

110 Wang, 1989, 199.

111 Joffe, 1987, 173–4.

112 Joffe, 1987, 175.

113 Tsou, 1984, 46.

114 Ijiri, 1990, 646.

115 Tanaka, 1983, 210. Tanaka also suggests that taking a hard-line on Japan would have the added benefit of showing the Party's commitment to its new independent and autonomous foreign policy line to be announced by Hu Yaobang at the Twelfth Party Congress (pp. 204–5).

116 Johnson, 1986, 424.

117 Tanaka, 1983, 202–3.

118 Tanaka, 1983, 205–9.

119 Schram, 1984, 33.

120 The campaign was not merely aimed at Chinese youth, and caused controversy among some in the military who felt that there was no need for a cultural emphasis in military training; see Wang, 1989, 199.

121 Summary of World Broadcasts, Far East, 31 July, 7029/BII/4.

122 Schram, 1984, 33.

123 Schram, 1984, 33.

124 Hu, 1982, 26.

125 Tanaka, 1983, 207.

126 Tanaka, 1983, 208–9.

127 Johnson, 1986, 424.

128 Shambaugh, 1996, 189.

129 Jensen, 1982, 61. 'External conflict' can be protests and threats and not simply warfare; 'domestic conflict' can be general discontent, demonstrations, riots, coups etc.

130 Jensen, 1982, 62–4, citing Wilkenfeld, 1973.

131 Shambaugh, 1996, 190.

7 The Textbook Issue: Japan's response

1 Minor, 1985, 1229.

2 In the context of Japanese decision making, Minor categorises issues into routine, political, crisis and critical. Routine issues are characterised by a long deliberation and formulation time, involve many decision makers, and show elements of the 'bureaucratic politics' model where the outcome is

the result of the 'pulling and hauling among various players'. Political issues are characterised by 'politically sensitive and controversial decisions that have been anticipated in advance'. There is sufficient decision time to allow for a build-up of media and public opinion, but there is less involvement of the bureaucracy, and more factional conflict and extragovernmental pressure than in a routine issue. A crisis issue demands a rapid response in the face of a threat to a nation's security (Minor, 1985, 1233–40).

3 Minor, 1985, 1235.
4 *Asahi Shimbun* 28 July, 1.
5 Minor, 1985, points out that time here is not absolute time but 'refers to the ratio of the time available for decision to the time that is needed to take the preferred action' (p. 1237).
6 The 'education tribe' (*bunkyōzoku*) refers to LDP Diet members who hold or have held the key education posts of the Education Minister, MOE Parliamentary Vice Minister, LDP Education System Research Council Chairmanship, LDP Education Affairs Division Chairmanship, Lower House Education Committee Chairmanship and Directorship (*riji*). The influence of the *bunkyōzoku* on MOE matters grew throughout the 1970s so that by the 1980s the MOE was described as 'lady-in-waiting' to the *bunkyōzoku* (Takayama, 1982, 73).
7 In 1982, Ienaga's second lawsuit, originally brought in 1967, was awaiting ruling from the High Court. Beer, 1984, 264–69; Herzog, 1993, 216.
8 Fukui, 1977, 99.
9 *Daily Summary of Japanese Press* 18 September, 5, quoting *Mainichi Shimbun* 10 September, 2.
10 One somewhat paranoid line of thought within the LDP was that the issue had in fact been contrived by the Japan Socialist Party and the PRC as a way of discrediting the government.
11 *Daily Report* 4 August, D4.
12 *Daily Report* 13 August, D2.
13 *Renmin Ribao* 28 July, 6, citing *Yomiuri* 27 July.
14 *Daily Report* 31 August, D2–3.
15 *Daily Summary of Japanese Press* 8 September, 6, quoting *Yomiuri* 27 August.
16 *Daily Summary of Japanese Press* 18 September, 5, quoting *Mainichi* 10 September.
17 Jensen, 1982, 137.
18 *Daily Report* 9 August, D3.
19 *Asahi Shimbun* 12 August, 1.
20 Kim, 1983, 293.
21 *Renmin Ribao* 23 July, 7.
22 Beer, 1984, 259. 'School children, left to themselves, may be more influenced by the kaleidoscope of mass media images and values than by ideological differences expressed in textbooks; and the general public tends to look on without much interest or concern, unless violence occurs which is very rare. Thus the well-publicized polarization over textbooks involved only specialized elite groups and did not threaten the fabric of society.'
23 *Renmin Ribao* 31 July, 6.
24 *Daily Report* 17 August, D7.

25 *Renmin Ribao* 20 August, 6.
26 *Renmin Ribao* 22 August, 6.
27 *Renmin Ribao* 28 July, 6; 3 August, 6; 18 August, 6; 22 August, 6; 28 August, 6.
28 *Renmin Ribao* 31 July, 6 quoting from *Mainichi* and *Asahi Shimbun* 30 July.
29 *Daily Report* 26 August, D3 quoting *Tokyo Shimbun*.
30 *Daily Report* 18 August, D4.
31 *Renmin Ribao* 10 August, 4.
32 *Daily Report* 13 August, D2.
33 *Renmin Ribao* 31 July, 1.
34 *Renmin Ribao* 26 July, 6; see also *Daily Report* 26 August, D2–3.
35 *Daily Report* 30 August, D4.
36 *Daily Report* 3 August, D5.
37 *Daily Report* 13 August, D3. The groups were: Dietmen's League for Japan–China Friendship, Japan–China Friendship Association, Japan Association for the Promotion of International Trade, Japan–China Cultural Exchange Association, Japan–China Association on Economy and Trade, and the Japan–China Society.
38 Jensen, 1982, 141–4.
39 Park, 1986; Campbell, 1984.
40 Campbell, 1984, 299.
41 Campbell, 1984, 301.
42 Campbell, 1984, 305.
43 Campbell, 1984, 306.
44 Officially there is no foreign affairs tribe or *gaikōzoku*, presumably because this is not a vote-catching area; there are however a group of politicians who are associated with foreign affairs, and the term *gaikōzoku* is used in reference to them.
45 Campbell, 1984, 317.
46 Park, 1986, 115–6.
47 Park, 1986, 117–9.
48 Park, 1986, 144.
49 Park, 1986, 102.
50 Campbell, 1984, 301.
51 Kanagawa, 1982, 98; also Ishiyama, 1986, 124.
52 Ishiyama, 1986, 121.
53 *Asahi Shimbun* 27 July, 1.
54 *Asahi Shimbun* 28 July, 2.
55 *Asahi Shimbun* 30 July, 22.
56 *Asahi Shimbun* pm, 30 July, 1; 3 August, 1; 5 August, 1.
57 Ishiyama, 1986, 127–8.
58 Ishiyama, 1986, 127.
59 Ishiyama, 1986, 128.
60 Ishiyama, 1986, 125.
61 *Asahi Shimbun* 27 July, 3.
62 *Asahi Shimbun* 5 August, 1.
63 Ishiyama, 1986, 127.
64 *Asahi Shimbun* 5 August, 3.
65 Habara, 1982, 65–71.

66 See for example, Park, 1986; Schoppa, 1991; Habara, 1982; Takayama, 1982.
67 Takayama, 1982, 73.
68 Schoppa, 1991, 117.
69 *Daily Summary of Japanese Press* 4 August, 13, translation of *Nihon Keizai* pm, 27 July, 1.
70 *Daily Summary of Japanese Press* 13 August, 8, translation of *Mainichi* 5 August, 2. The LDP members were Kaifu, Ishibashi, Mori, Nishioka and Mitsuzuka.
71 The Educational Affairs Division and the ESRC are the two education-related committees of the LDP's Policy Affairs Research Council (PARC), and with the MOE they form part the educational subgovernment.
72 *Daily Summary of Japanese Press* 13 August, 11.
73 Summary of World Broadcasts, Far East, 9 August, 7099/A3/8. Note that this contradicts a report in the *Nihon Keizai* that Ogawa stated at the same meeting that re-revision was not being considered (*Daily Summary of Japanese Press* 13 August, 12); see also Suzuki Isao's comments of 9 August.
74 *Daily Summary of Japanese Press* 13 August, 12; however, see Suzuki Isao's comments of 9 August.
75 *Asahi Shimbun* 8 August, 2.
76 *Asahi Shimbun* 8 August, 1.
77 *Asahi Shimbun* 14 August, 1.
78 *Asahi Shimbun* 27 August, 4.
79 *Asahi Shimbun* 22 August, 3.
80 Fukui, 1977, 101.
81 Shimizu, 1982, 4.
82 His motives may have been twofold: to criticise the Prime Minister, and/or because of nationalist sentiment and anti-JTU stance.
83 Shimizu, 1982, 4.
84 Shimizu, 1982, 4.
85 Shimizu, 1982, 4.
86 Schoppa, 1991, 61.
87 Shimizu, 1982, 4; Akasaka, 1982, 164.
88 The term 'sanninzoku' was coined by the Chinese press (*Asahi Jānaru* 10 September, 10).
89 *Asahi Shimbun* 5 August, 3.
90 Of the seventeen members whose opinions were recorded, nine rejected the requests, four recommended caution and four suggested revision (*Daily Summary of Japanese Press*, 26 August, 9–10).
91 Five rejections, three recommending caution, one acceptance of the requests (*Daily Report* 20 August, D1, and *Daily Summary of Japanese Press*, 26 August, 9–10).
92 *Asahi Jānaru* 27 August, 6.
93 *Asahi Jānaru* 27 August, 6.
94 *Asahi Shimbun* pm, 5 August, 1.
95 *Asahi Shimbun* 27 August, 2.
96 *Asahi Shimbun* 5 August, 3.
97 *Asahi Shimbun* 22 August, 2.
98 Kanagawa, 1982, 96.

99 *Asahi Shimbun* 27 August, 4.
100 *Asahi Shimbun* 8 August, 2
101 *Far Eastern Economic Review* 9 January, 1981, 26–7.
102 *Asahi Shimbun* 27 August, 4.
103 Akasaka, 1982, 164.
104 *Asahi Shimbun* 27 August, 4.
105 *Daily Report* 25 August, D1.
106 *Asahi Shimbun* 27 August, 4.
107 Ishiyama, 1986, 129.
108 Ishiyama, 1986, 140–1.
109 *Daily Summary of Japanese Press* 8 September, 6, translation of *Nihon Keizai Shimbun* 27 August, 2.
110 Jensen, 1982, 116.
111 Jensen, 1982, 117.

8 Conclusion

1 See *Renmin Ribao* 29 September, 2; *Shijie Zhishi* 18, 8–9. Other articles, such as a *Renmin Ribao* article by Zhang Bei, 28 September, 6, contained no reference to the Textbook Issue at all.
2 Summary of World Broadcasts, Far East, 27 September, 7141/A3/4.
3 This is discussed in Chapter 5.
4 See for example *Chūō Kōron, Sekai, Keizai Ōrai, Shokun*, etc.
5 *Asahi Shimbun* 10 September, 1.
6 Summary of World Broadcasts, Far East, 27 September, 7141/A3/5–6.
7 *Asahi Shimbun* 28 September, 1; 29 September, 1; Summary of World Broadcasts, Far East, 29 September, 7143/A3/1–2; 30 September, 7144/A3/1–9
8 Gaimushō, 1983, 414–5.
9 *Asahi Shimbun* 10 September, 1. When the TARC inquiry opened on 14 September, some of the committee members expressed their dissatisfaction over the way the government had already promised to correct (*zesei*) the passages because, not only was this promise made in anticipation of the report, but also because 'correction of errors' implied that hitherto errors had been made. The members were urged not to feel restricted by the views expressed in the government statement *Asahi Shimbun* 15 September, 1.
10 NKN, 1984, 257.
11 Schoppa, 1991, 62.
12 NKN, 1984, 252.
13 *Asahi Shimbun* 12 September, 2; NKN, 1984, 254–5.
14 Kyōiku Kōryusha, 1991, 189.
15 Kyōiku Kōryūsha, 1991, 187.
16 Takahashi, 1988, 113.
17 Ienaga, 1993b, 165.
18 Ienaga, 1993b, 211–23. These changes and deletions became the subject of Ienaga's third suit against the Ministry of Education.
19 Morikawa, 1990, 105.
20 Smith, 1994, 26.
21 Dower, in Hogan, 1996, 141.

22 *Asahi Shimbun*, 1 July 1994, 1, 33, 34. This figure tallies with the number given in Chinese middle-school history textbooks; see Sekine, 1992, 146.
23 *Far Eastern Economic Review*, 25 July 1994, 26.
24 J. Samuel Walker citing J. Bodnar in Hogan, 1996, 188–9.
25 J.Samuel Walker in Hogan, 1996, 188–199.
26 J.Samuel Walker in Hogan, 1996, 193.
27 This was the final ruling on Ienaga's third suit, orginally brought in 1984, in which Ienaga claimed compensation for deletion and rejection of some descriptive passages (notably Unit 731 and the Nanjing Massacre) during the screening of his textbooks in 1980 and 1983. See *Asahi Shimbun*, 30 August, 1997, 1.
28 Gluck, 1992, 1.
29 Mendl, 1978, 17; Lee, 1986, 185–6.
30 Tanaka, 1991, 108.
31 Ijiri, 1990, 649; see also *Far Eastern Economic Review* 25 April 1991, 54.
32 Whiting, 1989, 76–9.
33 Tanaka, 1991, 150–2; Newby, 1988, 53; Whiting, 1989, 62–5.
34 Tanaka, 1991, 155–62; Whiting, 1989, 152–62; Newby, 1988, 59–60.
35 Tanaka, 1991, 168–9; Whiting, 1989, 200.
36 Tanaka, 1991, 169.
37 Campbell, 1993, 54.
38 Mansbach, 1994, 110–12.
39 Campbell, 1993, 51.

Bibliography

Ahn Byung-joon (1993) 'Japanese policy toward Korea', in Gerald Curtis (ed.), *Japan's Foreign Policy: After the Cold War. Coping with Change*, New York: M.E. Sharpe, 263–73.

Akasaka Tarō (1982) 'Kyōkasho ni mo "Kakuei" ari' (Kakuei's Influence can be Seen Even in Textbooks), *Bungeishunjū*, October, 162–6.

Amako Satoshi (1991) 'In Search of New Linkages: Chinese Diplomacy and Domestic policy in the Post-Cold War Era', JETRO *China Newsletter*, 94, 2–17.

Anderson, Ronald S. (1959) *Japan: Three Epochs of Modern Education*, Washington, DC: Government Printing Office.

Aoki Akira (1982) 'Kyōkasho "gohō" o hikiokoita shimbun no taishitsu" (The Character of the Press that Gave Rise to the Textbook Issue), *Seiron*, 10, 30–43.

Aoki Tamotsu (1994) 'Anthropology and Japan: Attempts at Writing Culture', *Japan Foundation Newsletter*, October, 1–6.

Arnold, Walter (1985) 'Japan and China', in Robert S. Ozaki and Walter Arnold (eds), *Japan's Foreign Relations*, Boulder, CO: Westview Press, 102–16.

—— (1990) 'Political and Economic Influences in Japan's Relations with China since 1978', in K. Newland (ed.), *International Relations of Japan*, Basingstoke and London: Macmillan, 121–46.

Aruga Tadashi *et al.* (1989) *Kōza Kokusai Seiji: Nihon no Gaikō* (Introduction to International Politics: Japan's Foreign Policy), Tokyo: Tokyo Daigaku Shuppankai.

Asahi Jānaru (1982) ' "Hato" "taka" tomoni omokurushii chinmoku', (Hawks and Doves are Suddenly Silent), *Asahi Jānaru*, 27 August, 6–7.

Asai Motofumi (1989) *Nihon Gaikō* (Japan's Diplomacy), Tokyo: Iwanami Shōten.

Baerwald, Hans (1986) *Party Politics in Japan*, Sydney: Allen & Unwin.

Barnett, A. Doak (1985) *The Making of Foreign Policy in China*, London: I.B. Tauris.

Beasley, W.G. (1987) *Japanese Imperialism 1894-1945*, Oxford: Clarendon Press.

—— (1990) *The Rise of Modern Japan*, London: George Weidenfeld & Nicolson.

Beauchamp, Edward R. and Dubinger, Richard (1989) *Education in Japan: A Source Book*, New York and London: Garland.

Bedeski, Robert E. (1983) *The Fragile Entente: The 1978 Japan–China Peace Treaty in a Global Context*, Boulder, CO: Westview Press.

—— (1990) 'Japan: Diplomacy of a Developmental State', *Journal of Asian and African Studies*, XXV: 60–87.

Beer, Lawrence Ward (1984) *Freedom of Expression in Japan: A Study in Comparative Law, Politics and Society*, Tokyo: Kodansha International.

Belloni, Frank P. and Beller, Dennis C. (eds) (1978) *Faction Politics: Political Parties and Factionalism in Comparative Perspective*, Santa Barbara, CA: ABC-Clio.

Benewick, Robert and Wingrove, Paul (eds) (1988) *Reforming the Revolution: China in Transition*, Basingstoke: Macmillan.

Blaker, Michael (1977) 'Probe, Push and Panic: Japanese Tactical Style in International Negotiations', in Robert A. Scalapino (ed.), *The Foreign Policy of Modern Japan*, Berkeley, CA: University of California Press, 55–101.

Boardman, Robert (1980) 'Chinese Foreign Policy: Options for the 1980s', *The Year Book of World Affairs*, 135–52.

Bobrow, Davis (1979) *Understanding Foreign Policy Decisions: The Chinese Case*, New York: The Free Press.

Bobrow, Davis B. and Chan, Steve (1984) 'On a Slow Boat to Where? Analysing Chinese Foreign Policy', in Samuel S. Kim (ed.) *China and the World*, Boulder, CO: Westview Press, 32–56.

Boulding, Kenneth (1969) 'National Images and International Systems', in J. Rosenau (ed.), *International Politics and Foreign Policy*, New York: The Free Press, 422–31.

Boyle, John (1982) 'China and Japan: The Images and Realities of Asian Brotherhood', in David J. Lu (ed.), *Perspectives on Japan's External Relations*, Lewisburg, PA: Bucknell University, Centre for Japanese Studies, 1–75.

Brecher, Michael (1972) *The Foreign Policy System of Israel: Setting, Images, Process*, London: Oxford University Press.

—— (1974) *Decisions in Israel's Foreign Policy*, London: Oxford University Press.

Breuilly, John (1982) *Nationalism and the State*, Manchester: Manchester University Press.

Bridges, Brian (1992) 'Japan and Korea: Closer Neighbours?' *Asian Affairs* 79: 153–60.

Buruma, Ian (1991) 'War and Remembrance', *Far Eastern Economic Review*, 5 September: 51–2.

—— (1994) *The Wages of Guilt*, London: Jonathan Cape.

Buzan, Barry (1988) 'Japan's Future: Old History Versus New Roles', *International Affairs*, Spring: 557–73.

Calvocoressi, Peter (1996) *World Politics since 1945*, 7th edn, London and New York: Longman.

Camilleri, Joseph (1980) *Chinese Foreign Policy: The Maoist Era and its Aftermath*, Oxford: Martin Robertson.

Campbell, John Creighton (1984) 'Policy Conflict and its Resolution within the Governmental System', in Ellis S. Krauss, Thomas P. Rohlen and Patricia G. Steinhoff (eds), *Conflict in Japan*, Honolulu: University of Hawaii Press, 294–334.

—— (1993) 'Japan and the United States: Games that Work', in Gerald D. Curtis (ed.), *Japan's Foreign Policy: After the Cold War: Coping with Change*, New York: M.E. Sharpe, 43–61.

Chan, Steve and Sylvan, Donald A. (eds) (1984) *Foreign Policy Decision Making: Perception, Cognition and Artificial Intelligence*, New York: Praeger.

Chang, Parris H. (1981) 'Chinese Politics: Deng's Turbulent Quest', *Problems of Communism* XXX: 1–21.

Chay, Jongsuk (ed.) (1990) *Culture and International Relations*, Westport, CT: Praeger.

Chen Qimao (1986) 'Mianxiang ershi yi shiji de Zhong Ri guanxi' (Towards Sino-Japanese Relations in the Twenty-First Century), *Riben Wenti* 4: 1–38.

Cheng, Joseph Y.S. (1985) 'China's Japan policy in the 1980s', *International Affairs* 61: 91–107.

Cheung Tai Ming and Smith, Charles (1990) 'Rocks of Contention', *Far Eastern Economic Review*, 1 November: 19–20.

Cheung Tai Ming and Rosario, Louise de (1991) 'Seal of Approval', *Far Eastern Economic Review*, 22 August: 10.

Chiba Hitoshi (1992) *Nitchū Sensō* (The Sino-Japanese War), Tokyo: Futtowāku.

Chin Shunshin (1989) *Nihonjin to Chūgokujin* (The Japanese and the Chinese), Tokyo: Shodensha.

Chou, David S. (ed.) (1989) *Peking's Foreign Policy in the 1980s*, Taipei: National Chengchi University, Institute of International Relations.

Choucri, Nazli, North, Robert C. and Susumu Yamakage (1992) *The Challenge of Japan Before World War II and After*, London: Routledge.

Chu, Samuel C. (1980) 'China's Attitudes Toward Japan At The Time Of The Sino-Japanese War', in Iriye Akira, *The Chinese and the Japanese*, Princeton, NJ: Princeton University Press, 74–95.

Clarke, Michael and White, Brian (eds) (1989) *Understanding Foreign Policy: The Foreign Policy Systems Approach*, Aldershot: Edward Elgar.

Conroy, Hilary (1982) 'Comparing America's War in Vietnam and Japan's War in China', in David J. Lu (ed.), *Perspectives on Japan's External Relations*, Lewisburg, PA: Bucknell University, Centre for Japanese Studies, 15–24.

Coox, Alvin D. (1978) 'Recourse to Arms: The Sino-Japanese Conflict, 1937–1945', in Alvin D. Coox and Hilary Conroy (eds), *China and Japan: Search for Balance since World War I*, Santa Barbara, CA: ABC-Clio, 295–321.

—— (1988) 'The Pacific War', in Peter Duus (ed.), *The Cambridge History of Japan*, Volume 6, *The Twentieth Century*, Cambridge: Cambridge University Press, 315–82.

Coox, Alvin D. and Conroy, Hilary (eds) (1978) *China and Japan: Search for Balance since World War I*, Santa Barbara, CA: ABC-Clio.

Coplin, William D. (1974) *Introduction to International Politics. A Theoretical Overview*, Chicago: Rand McNally College.

Couloumbis, Theodore A. and Wolfe, James H. (1990) *Introduction to International Relations: Power and Justice*, 4th edn, Englewood Cliffs, NJ: Prentice-Hall International.

Crowley, James B. (1970a) 'A New Deal For Japan and Asia: One Road to Pearl Harbour', in James B. Crowley (ed.), *Modern East Asia*, New York: Harcourt, Brace & World, 235–64.

—— (ed.). (1970b) *Modern East Asia: Essays in Interpretation*, New York: Harcourt, Brace & World.

Cumings, Bruce (1993) 'Japan in the World System', in Andrew Gordon (ed.), *Postwar Japan as History*, Berkeley, CA: University of California Press, 34–63.

Curtis, Gerald D. (ed.) (1993) *Japan's Foreign Policy: After the Cold War. Coping With Change*, New York: M.E. Sharpe.

Dahlby, Tracy (1981) 'Defence Without Militarism', *Far Eastern Economic Review*, 29 May: 33–8.

Davies, Derek (1981) 'Suzuki: A Saint or a Samurai', *Far Eastern Economic Review*, 9 January: 33–43.

Delfs, Robert (1991) 'Sense or Sensibility', *Far Eastern Economic Review*, 25 April: 52–5.

De Rivera, Joseph H. 1968. *The Psychological Dimension of Foreign Policy*, Columbus, OH: Charles E. Merrill.

Deng Xiaoping (1984) *Selected Works of Deng Xiaoping, 1975–1982*, Beijing: Foreign Languages Press.

Derbyshire, Ian (1987) *Politics in China: From Mao to Deng*, Edinburgh: Chambers.

Deutsch, Karl W. and Merritt, Richard L. (1965) 'Effects of Events on National and International Images', in H.C. Kelman (ed.), *International Behaviour*, New York: Holt, Rinehart & Winston, 132–44.

Ding, Arthur S. (1991) 'Peking's Foreign Policy in the Changing World', *Issues and Studies* 27(8): 17–30.

Dittmer, Lowell (1981) 'China in 1980: Modernization and its Discontents', *Asian Survey* XXI(1): 31–50.

—— (1982) 'China in 1981: Reform, Readjustment, Rectification', *Asian Survey* XXII(1): 33–46.

Doi Masayuki (1982) 'Kyōkasho hihan no uragawa ni aru mono' (The Truth Behind Textbook Criticisms), *Asahi Jānaru* 24(34): 6–10.

Dou Hui (ed.) (1989) *Zhonghua renmin gongheguo duiwai guanxi gaishu* (An Outline of the Foreign Relations of the PRC), Shanghai: Shanghai Waiyu Jiaoyu Chubanshe.

Dougherty, James E. and Pfaltzgraff, Robert L., Jr (1990) *Contending Theories of International Relations*, 3rd edn, New York: HarperCollins.

Dower, John W. (1986) *War Without Mercy. Race and Power in the Pacific War*, New York: Pantheon Books.

—— (1996) 'The Bombed: Hiroshimas and Nagasakis in Japanese Memory', in Michael J. Hogan (ed.) *Hiroshima in History and Memory*, Cambridge: Cambridge University Press, 116–42.

Drifte, Reinhard (1990) *Japan's Foreign Policy*, Chatham House Paper, London: Routledge.

—— (1996) *Japan's Foreign Policy in the 1990s: From Economic Superpower to What Power?*, Basingstoke: Macmillan.

Drysdale, Peter and Hironobu Kitaoji (eds) (1981) *Japan & Australia: Two Societies and Their Interaction*, Canberra: Australian National University Press.

Duke, Benjamin C. (1972) 'The Textbook Controversy', *Japan Quarterly* 19: 337–52.

Dunbabin, J.P.D. (1994) *The Post Imperial Age: The Great Powers and the Wider World*, London: Longman.

Duus, Peter (1988a) 'Introduction', in Peter Duus (ed.), *The Cambridge History of Japan*, Volume 6, *The Twentieth Century*, Cambridge: Cambridge University Press, 1–30.

—— (1988b) *The Cambridge History of Japan*, Volume 6, *The Twentieth Century*, Cambridge: Cambridge University Press.

—— (1989a) 'Introduction', in Peter Duus, Ramon Myers and Mark Peattie (eds), *The Japanese Informal Empire in China, 1895–1937*, Princeton, NJ: Princeton University Press, xi–xxix.

—— (1989b) 'Zaikabo: Japanese Cotton Mills in China, 1895–1937', in Peter Duus, Ramon Myers and Mark Peattie (eds), *The Japanese Informal Empire in China, 1895–1937*, Princeton, NJ: Princeton University Press, 65–100.

Duus, Peter, Myers, Ramon H. and Peattie, Mark R. (eds) (1989) *The Japanese Informal Empire in China, 1895–1937*, Princeton, NJ: Princeton University Press.

Dyer, Hugh C. and Mangasarian, Leon (eds) (1989) *The Study of International Relations: The State of the Art*, Basingstoke and London: Macmillan.

Eastman, Lloyd E. (1980) 'Facets of an Ambivalent Relationship: Smuggling, Puppets, and Atrocities During the War, 1931–1945', in Iriye Akira, *The Chinese and the Japanese*, Princeton, NJ: Princeton University Press, 275–303.

Eisanstadt, S.N. and Ben-Ari, Eyal (eds) (1990) *Japanese Models of Conflict Resolution*, London and New York: Kegan Paul International.

Endicott, John E. and Heaton, William R. (1978) *The Politics of East Asia*, Boulder, CO: Westview Press.

Etō Shinkichi (1972) 'Postwar Japanese-Chinese Relations', *Survey* 18: 55–65.

—— (1976) 'Foreign Policy Formation in Japan', in Japan Centre for International Exchange, *The Silent Power: Japan's Identity and World Role*, Tokyo: Simul Press, 119–39.

—— (1980) 'Recent Developments in Sino-Japanese Relations', *Asian Survey*, XX(7): 726–43.

Fairbank, John K. (ed.) (1968) *The Chinese World Order*, Cambridge, MA: Harvard University Press.

—— (1969) 'China's Foreign Policy in Historical Perspective', in *Foreign Affairs* 47: 449–63.

Fairbank John K. and Reischauer, Edwin O. (1973) *China: Tradition and Transformation*, Sydney: Allen & Unwin.

Farnsworth, Lee W. (1981) 'Japan in 1980: The Conservative Resurgence', *Asian Survey* XXI(1): 70–83.

—— (1982) 'Japan in 1981: Meeting the Challenges', *Asian Survey*, XXII(1): 56–68.

Feuerwerker, Albert (1972) 'Chinese History and the Foreign Relations of Contemporary China', *Annals of the American Academy of Political and Social Science* 402: 1–11.

Francks, Penelope G. (1988) 'Learning from Japan: Plant Imports and Technology Transfer in the Chinese Iron and Steel Industry', *Journal of the Japanese and International Economies* 2: 42–62.

Frankel, Joseph (1988) *International Relations in a Changing World*, 4th edn, Oxford: Oxford University Press.

Fujiie Reinosuke (1988) *Nitchū kōryū nisennen* (2000 Years of Sino-Japanese Exhange) revised edn, Tokyo: Tōkai Daigaku Shuppankai.

Fujiwara Akira (1988) *Nankin Daigyakusatsu* (The Nanjing Massacre), Tokyo: Iwanami Shōten.

Fukui Haruhiro (1970) *Party in Power: The Japanese Liberal-Democrats and Policy Making*, Berkeley, CA: University of California Press.

—— (1977a) 'Tanaka Goes to Peking: A Case Study in Foreign Policymaking', in T.J. Pempel (ed.), *Policymaking in Contemporary Japan*, Ithaca, NY: Cornell University Press, 60–102.

—— (1977b) 'Policy-Making in the Japanese Foreign Ministry', in Robert A. Scalapino (ed.), *The Foreign Policy of Modern Japan*, Berkeley, CA: University of California Press, 3–35.

—— (1977c) 'Foreign-Policy Making by Improvisation: The Japanese Experience', *International Journal* XXXII: 791–812.

—— (1981) 'Bureaucratic Power in Japan', in Peter Drysdale and Hironobu Kitaoji (eds), *Japan & Australia: Two Societies and Their Interaction*, Canberra: Australian National University Press, 275–303.

Furukawa Mantarō (1983) *Nitchū Sengo Kankeishi Nōto* (Notes on the History of Postwar Sino-Japanese Relations), Tokyo: Sanseido.

—— (1988) *Nitchū Sengo Kankeishi* (A History of Postwar Sino-Japanese Relations), Tokyo: Hara Shobō.

Gaenslen, Fritz (1986) 'Culture and Decision-Making in China, Japan, Russia and USA', *World Politics* 39: 78–103.

Gaimushō (1983) *Waga gaikō no kinkyō* (The Recent Situation in Japan's Diplomacy), Tokyo: Gaimushō.

Gaimushō gaikō shiryokan (1992) *Nihon Gaikōshi Jiten* (A Dictionary of the History of Japanese Foreign Policy), Tokyo: Yamakawa Shuppansha.

Garver, John W. (1993) *Foreign Relations of the People's Republic of China*, Englewood Cliffs, NJ: Prentice-Hall.

Ginsburg, Norton, and Lalor, Bernard A. (eds) (1984) *China: The 80s Era*, Boulder, CO: Westview Press.

Gladue, E. Ted, Jr (1982) *China's Perceptions of Global Politics*, Washington, DC: University Press of America.

Gluck, Carol (1992) 'The Idea of Showa', in Carol Gluck and Stephen R. Grambard (eds), *Showa: The Japan of Hirohito*, New York and London: W.W. Norton, 1–26.

—— (1993) 'The Past in the Present', in Andrew Gordon (ed.), *Postwar Japan as History*, Berkeley, CA: University of California Press, 64–95.

Gluck, Carol and Grambard, Stephen R. (eds) (1992) *Showa: The Japan of Hirohito*, New York and London: W.W. Norton.

Goldstein, Avery (1994) 'Trends in the Study of Political Elites and Institutions in the PRC', *China Quarterly* 139: 714–30.

Goodman, David S. (ed.) (1984) *Groups and Politics in the People's Republic of China*, Cardiff: University College Cardiff Press.

Gordon, Andrew (ed.) (1993) *Postwar Japan as History*, Berkeley, CA: University of California Press.

Groom, A.J.R. and Light, Margot (eds) (1994) *Contemporary International Relations: A Guide to Theory*, London: Pinter.

Haas, Michael (1973) 'The Asian Way to Peace', *Pacific Community* 4: 498–514.

Habara Kiyomasu (1982) 'Jiminto bunkyōzoku no jitsuryoku' (The Power of the LDP's Education Tribe), *Sekai* 444: 65–71.

Hall, Robert King (1949) *Education for a New Japan*, New Haven, CN: Yale University Press.

Han Nianlong (ed.) (1990) *Diplomacy of Contemporary China*, Hong Kong: New Horizon Press.

Hane Mikiso (1991) *Premodern Japan. A Historical Survey*, Boulder, CO: Westview Press.

Harada Saburō (1982) 'Sengo monbu gyōsei', (The Postwar Education Administration), *Sekai* 444: 55–64.

Harding, Harry (ed.) (1984) *China's Foreign Relations in the 1980s*, New Haven, CN and London: Yale University Press.

Harriss, Geoffrey (1994) *The Dark Side of Europe: The Extreme Right Today*, Edinburgh: Edinburgh University Press.

Harvey, Robert (1994) *The Undefeated: The Rise, Fall and Rise of Greater Japan*, London and Basingstoke: Macmillan.

Hasegawa Keitaro (1986) *Sayōnara Ajia* (Farewell to Asia), Tokyo: Nesco Books.

Hata Ikuhiko (1988) 'Continental Expansion', in Peter Duus (ed.), *The Cambridge History of Japan*, Volume 6, Cambridge: Cambridge University Press, 271–314

Hearn Dorfman, Cynthia (1987) *Japanese Education Today*, Washington, DC: US Department of Education.

Hellmann, Donald C. (ed.) (1976) *China and Japan: A New Balance of Power: Critical Choices for Americans*, Volume XII, Lexington, MA: Lexington Books.

Hermann, Charles F., Kegley, Charles W., Jr, and Rosenau, James N. (eds) (1987) *New Directions in the Study of Foreign Policy*, Sydney: Allen & Unwin.

Herzog, Peter J. (1993) *Japan's Pseudo-Democracy*, Folkestone: Japan Library.

Hill, Christopher and Light, Margot (1985) 'Foreign Policy Analysis', in Margot Light and Arthur J.R. Groom (eds), *International Relations: A Handbook of Current Theory*, London: Pinter, 156–73.

Hirasawa Kazushige (1975) 'Japan's Emerging Foreign Policy', *Foreign Affairs* 54: 155–72 .

Ho, Samuel P.S. and Huenemann, Ralph, W. (1984) *China's Open Door Policy*, Vancouver: University of British Columbia Press.

Hobsbawm, E.J. (1990) *Nations and Nationalism since 1780*, Cambridge: Cambridge University Press.

Hocking, Brian and Smith, Michael (1990) *World Politics: An Introduction to International Relations*, London and New York: Harvester Wheatsheaf.

Hogan, Michael J. (ed.) (1996) *Hiroshima in History and Memory*, Cambridge: Cambridge University Press.

Hollis, Martin and Smith, Steve (1990) *Explaining and Understanding International Relations*, Oxford: Oxford University Press.

Holsti, K.J. (1988) *International Politics: A Framework for Analysis*, 5th edn, Englewood Cliffs, NJ: Prentice-Hall International.

Hosojima Izumi (1982) 'Kyōkasho kentei chōsakan ni atau' (Facing a Textbook Examiner), *Chūō Kōron*, October: 98–107.

Hosoya Chihiro (1973) 'Characteristics of the Foreign Policy Decision-Making System in Japan', *World Politics* 26: 353–69.

—— (1993) *Nihon Gaikō* (Japan's Foreign Policy), Tokyo: NHK Books.

Howe, Christopher (1990) 'China, Japan and Economic Interdependence in the Asia Pacific Region', *China Quarterly* 124: 662–93.

—— (ed.) (1996) *China and Japan: History, Trends and Prospects*, Oxford: Clarendon Press.

Hsiao, Gene T. (1974a) 'The Sino-Japanese Rapprochement', *China Quarterly* 57: 101–23.

—— (1974b) 'Prospects for a New Sino-Japanese Relationship', *China Quarterly* 60: 720–49.

Hsiung, James C. (ed.) (1985) *Beyond China's Independent Foreign Policy: Challenge for the U.S. and its Asian Allies*, Philadelphia: Praeger.

Hsü, Immanuel C.Y. (1990) *The Rise of Modern China* 4th edn, Oxford: Oxford University Press.

Hu Yaobang (1982) 'Create a New Situation in All Fields of Socialist Modernization', *Beijing Review* 37, September 13: 11–40.

Hunt, Michael (1984) 'Chinese Foreign Relations in Historical Perspective', in Harry Harding (ed.) *China's Foreign Relations in the 1980s*, New Haven, CN and London: Yale University Press, 1–42.

Hunter, Janet E. (1984) *Concise Dictionary of Modern Japanese History*, Berkeley, CA: University of California Press.

—— (1989) *The Emergence of Modern Japan: An Introductory History since 1853*, London and New York: Longman.

Ienaga Saburō (1978) *The Pacific War, 1931–1945*, New York: Pantheon.

—— (1993a) *Sensō Sekinin* (War Responsibility), Tokyo: Iwanami Shōten.

—— (1993b) *Misshitsu Kentei no Kiroku* (Records of Secret Authorisation), Tokyo: Meichokan Gyōkai.

Ijiri Hidenori (1990) 'Sino-Japanese Controversy since the 1972 Diplomatic Normalization', *China Quarterly* 124: 639–61.

Imai Shun *et al.* (eds) (1988) *Chūgoku Gendaishi* (Contemporary History of China), Tokyo: Yamakawa Shuppansha.

Inoguchi Takashi (1986) 'Japan's Images and Options: Not a Challenger But a Supporter', *Journal of Japanese Studies* 12(1): 95–119.

—— (1989) 'The Study of International Relations in Japan', in Hugh C. Dyer and Leon Mangasarian (eds), *The Study of International Relations: The State of the Art*, Basingstoke and London: Macmillan, 250–64.

—— (1991) *Japan's International Relations*, London: Pinter.

—— (1992) 'International Relations', in *Introductory Bibliography for Japanese Studies* III, Part 1, *Social Sciences 1988–1989*, Tokyo: Japan Foundation, 63–84.

Inoguchi Takashi and Daniel I. Okimoto (eds) (1988) *The Political Economy of Japan*, Volume 2, *The Changing International Context*, Stanford, CA: Stanford University Press.

Iriye Akira (1970) 'Imperialism in East Asia', in James B. Crowley (ed.), *Modern East Asia*, New York: Harcourt, Brace & World, 122–50.

—— (1980) *The Chinese and the Japanese: Essays in Political and Cultural Interactions*, Princeton, NJ: Princeton University Press.

—— (1987) *The Origins of the Second World War in Asia and the Pacific*, New York: Longman.

—— (1990) 'Chinese-Japanese Relations, 1945–90', *China Quarterly* 124: 624–38.

—— (1992) *China and Japan in the Global Setting*, Cambridge, MA: Harvard University Press.

Ishihara Shintarō (1991) *The Japan that Can Say No: Why Japan Will be First Among Equals*, New York: Simon and Schuster.

Ishida Takeshi (1983) *Japanese Political Culture. Change and Continuity*, New Brunswick, NJ and London: Transaction Books.

Ishii Akira and Seiichiro Takagi (1984) *Chūgoku no seiji to kokusai kankei* (China's Politics and International Relations), Tokyo: Tokyo Daigaku Shuppankai.

Ishikawa Shigeru (1987) 'Sino-Japanese Economic Co-operation', *China Quarterly* 109: 1–21.

Ishiyama Morio (1986) *Monbu kanryō no gyakushū* (The Education Bureaucracy's Counteroffensive), Tokyo: Kodansha.

Ishizaka Kazuo (1989) *School Education in Japan*, Tokyo: International Society for Educational Information, Reference Series 5.

Itō Kazihiko (ed.) (1990) *Gendai Chūgoku 6, Gendai Chūgoku Kenkyu Annai* (Contemporary China Volume 6, Research on Contemporary China), Tokyo: Iwanami Shōten.

Itō Teruo (1974) *Chūgokujin no nihonjinkan hyakunenshi* (Chinese Views of the Japanese – a One Hundred Year History), Tokyo: Jiyū Kokuminsha.

Jain, R.K. (1981) *China and Japan 1949–1980*, 2nd edn, Atlantic Highlands, NJ: Humanities Press.

Jansen, Marius B. (1975) *Japan and China: From War to Peace 1894–1972*, Chicago: Rand McNally.

—— (1992) *China in the Tokugawa World*, Cambridge, MA: Harvard University Press.

Japan Center for International Exchange (ed.) (1976) *The Silent Power: Japan's Identity and World Role*, Tokyo: Simul Press.

Japan Echo (1982) 'Who's in Charge of Social Studies?' IX(1): 81–100.

Jenner, W.J.F. (1992) *The Tyranny of History. The Roots of China's Crisis*, London: Allen Lane Penguin Press.

Jensen, Lloyd (1982) *Explaining Foreign Policy*, Englewood Cliffs, NJ: Prentice-Hall.

Jervis, Robert (1969) 'Hypotheses on Misperception', in James Rosenau (ed.), *International Politics and Foreign Policy*, New York: The Free Press, 239–54.

—— (1976) *Perceptions and Misperceptions in International Politics*, Princeton, NJ: Princeton University Press.

—— (1989) *The Logic of Images in International Relations*, New York: Columbia University Press, Morningside Edition.

Jian Sanqiang (1993) *Foreign Policy Restructuring and Adaptive Behaviour*, University Microfilms International.

Jiang Zemin (1992) *International Situation and Sino-Japanese Relations*, Consulate General of PRC (Manchester) Press Bulletin (92) 004.

Jinjiin Kanrikyoku (1982) *Gyōsei kikan sōshikizu* (General Administrative Structure Charts), Tokyo: Jinjiin Kanrikyoku.

Jinnō Takayoshi (1982) 'Seifu dake denaku, nihonjin no ishiki sono mono ga towarete iru' (It is not just the Government, but the Japanese People's Consciousness Itself that is Called into Question), *Asahi Jānaru* 24(34): 122–5.

Joffe, Ellis (1987) *The Chinese Army After Mao*, London; Weidenfeld & Nicolson.

Johnson, Chalmers (1978) 'How China and Japan See Each Other', in Alvin D. Coox and Hilary Conroy (eds) (1978) *China and Japan*, Santa Barbara, CA: ABC-Clio, 5–16.

—— (1986) 'The Patterns of Japanese Relations with China, 1952–1982', *Pacific Affairs* 59: 402–28.

Joji Watanuki (1977) *Politics in Postwar Japanese Society*, Tokyo: University of Tokyo Press.

Jūjō Koji (1982) 'Aratana dankai ni haitta nitchū kankei' (A New Stage in Sino-Japanese Relations) *Sekai Shūbō* 63(42): 19–23.

Kakizawa Koji (1993) 'A New Stage in Sino-Japanese Ties', *Japan Echo*, XX special issue: 45–51.

Kanagawa Michio (1982) 'Kōritsu shita monbushō no ronri to shinri', (The Logic and Mentality of the Isolated MOE), *Keizai Ōrai*, October, 96–105.

Katsumata Michio (1994) 'Time Cools Clash of Passions over Pilgrimages to War Shrine', *Nikkei Weekly*, 15 August: 1, 16.

Kau, Michael Ying-mao and Marsh, Susan H. (eds) (1993) *China in the Era of Deng Xiaoping: A Decade of Reform*, New York: M.E Sharpe.

Kawahara Hiroshi and Fujii Shozo (eds) (1974) *Nitchū kankeishi no kisō chishiki* (Basic Knowledge about the History of Sino-Japanese Relations), Tokyo: Yūhikaku.

Kelman, Herbert C. (ed.) (1965) *International Behaviour: A Social-Psychological Analysis*, New York: Holt, Rinehart & Winston.

Kennedy, Paul (1989) *The Rise and Fall of the Great Powers: Economic Change and Military Conflict from 1500–2000*, London: Fontana.

Kesavan, K.V. (1990) 'Japan and the Tiananmen Square Incident', *Asian Survey*, XXX(7): 669–81.

Kim, Hong N. (1979) 'The Fukuda Government and the Politics of the Sino-Japanese Peace Treaty', *Asian Survey* XIX(3): 297–313.

Kim, Hong N. and Nanto, Richard K. (1985) 'Emerging Patterns of Sino-Japanese Economic Co-operation', *Journal of Northeast Asian Studies*, 4(3): 29–47.

Kim, Paul S. (1983) 'Japan's Bureaucratic Decision-Making On The Textbook', *Public Administration* 283–94.

Kim, Samuel S. (ed.) (1984) *China and the World: Chinese Foreign Policy in the Post-Mao Era*, Boulder, CO: Westview Press.

—— (1989) *China and the World* 2nd edn, Boulder, CO: Westview Press.

—— (1990) 'Chinese Foreign Policy After Tiananmen', *Current History* 9: 245–8, 280–2.

Kim, Young C. (1972) *Japan in World Politics*, Washington, DC: Institute for Asian Studies.

Klein, Donald W. (1989) 'Present and Future Peking–Tokyo Relations, 1986–(1990)', in David S. Chou, *Peking's Foreign Policy in the 1980s*, Taipei: Institute of International Relations, 287–306.

Knorr, Klaus and Rosenau, James N. (eds) (1969) *Contending Approaches to International Politics*, Princeton, NJ: Princeton University Press.

Knorr, Klaus and Verba, Sidney (eds) (1961) *The International System: Theoretical Essays*, Princeton, NJ: Princeton University Press.

Kobori Keiichirō (1982a) 'Kyōkasho mondai:watashi no teigen' (My Suggestions about the Textbook Issue), *Shokun*, October, 46–62.

—— (1982b) 'The Pitfalls of Easy Compromise', *Japan Echo*, IX(4): 43–51.

Kodama Tetsuhide (1982) 'Monbusho to no kōbō' (The Attack on Monbusho), *Asahi Jānaru* 24(34): 125–8.

Kojima Tomoyuki (1988) 'Japan's China Policy: The Diplomacy of Appeasement', *Japan Echo* XV(4): 24–8.

Kokubun Ryosei (1986) 'The Politics of Foreign Economic Policy-making in China: The Case of Plant Cancellations with Japan', *China Quarterly* 105: 19–44.

—— (1986) 'The Current State of Contemporary Chinese Studies in Japan', *China Quarterly* 107: 505–18.

Krauss, Ellis S., Rohlen, Thomas P. and Steinhoff, Patricia G. (eds) (1984) *Conflict in Japan*, Honolulu, HI: University of Hawaii Press.

Kuwabara Takeo (1983) *Japan and Western Civilization: Essays on Comparative Culture*, Tokyo: University of Tokyo Press.

Kyogoku Jun-ichi (1987) *The Political Dynamic of Japan*, trans. Ike Nobutaka, Tokyo: University of Tokyo Press.

Kyōiku Kōryusha (1991) *Kokusai Kyōiku Jiten* (International Dictionary of Education), Tokyo: Aruku.

Lampton, David (1987) 'Chinese Politics: The Bargaining Treadmill', *Issues and Studies* 23(3): 33–58.

Langdon, Frank (1973) *Japan's Foreign Policy*, Vancouver: University of British Columbia Press.

Lee Chae-Jin (1976) *Japan Faces China*, Baltimore: Johns Hopkins University Press.

—— (1984) *China and Japan: New Economic Diplomacy*, Stanford, CA: Stanford University, Hoover Institution Press.

Lee Deng-ker (1990) 'Communist China's Foreign Policy since June 4, 1989', *Issues and Studies* 26: 83–99.

Lee Jung Bock (1979) *The Political Character of the Japanese Press*, Ann Arbor, MI: University Microfilms International.

Lee O-young (1982) 'Rekishi no hokori to hokori' (The Wheat and Chaff of History), *Chūō Kōron*, October: 116–26.

Leng Shao Chuan (1958) *Japan and Communist China*, Kyoto: Doshisha University.

Liao Kuangsheng (ed.) (1981) *Modernization and Diplomacy of China*, Hong Kong: Public Affairs Research Centre, Chinese University of Hong Kong.

—— (1984) *Antiforeignism and Modernization in China 1860-1980: The Linkage Between Domestic Politics and Foreign Policy*, Hong Kong: Chinese University Press.

Liao Kuangsheng and Whiting, Allen S. (1973) 'Chinese Press Perceptions of Threat: The United States and India, 1962', *China Quarterly* 53: 80–97.

Lieberthal, Kenneth (1977) 'The Foreign Policy Debate in Peking', *China Quarterly* 71: 528–44.

—— (1983) 'China in 1982: A Middling Course for the Middle Kingdom', *Asian Survey* XXIII(1): 26–37.

—— (1984) 'Domestic Politics and Foreign Policy', in Harry Harding (ed.), *China's Foreign Relations in the 1980s*, New Haven and London: Yale University Press, 43–70.

Lieberthal, Kenneth G. and Lampton, David M. (eds) (1992) *Bureaucracy, Politics, and Decision Making in Post-Mao China*, Berkeley, CA: University of California Press.

Light, Margot and Groom, Arthur J.R. (eds) (1985) *International Relations: A Handbook of Current Theory*, London: Pinter.

Little, Richard and Smith, Steve (eds) (1988) *Belief Systems and International Relations*, Oxford: Basil Blackwell.

Lu, David J. (1992) *Perspectives on Japan's External Relations*, Lewisburg, PA: Bucknell University, Centre for Japanese Studies.

Luard, Evan (1992) *Basic Texts in International Relations*, Basingstoke and London: Macmillan.

Macridis, Roy C. (ed.) (1989) *Foreign Policy in World Politics*, 7th edn, Englewood Cliffs, NJ: Prentice-Hall.

Mancall, Mark (1963) 'The Persistence of Tradition in Chinese Foreign Policy', *Annals of the American Academy of Political and Social Sciences* 329: 14–26.

Mansbach, Richard W. (1994) *The Global Puzzle: Issues and Actors in World Politics*, Boston: Houghton Mifflin Co.

Martin, Jurek (1990) 'Japanese Foreign Policy in the 1990s', *Asian Affairs* 77: 268–76.

Maruyama Masao (1963) *Thought and Behaviour in Modern Japanese Politics*, London: Oxford University Press.

Maruyama Nobuo (1990) 'Nitchū keizai kankei' (Sino-Japanese Economic Relations), in Okabe Tatsumi (ed.), *Gendai Chūgoku. Chūgoku o meguru kokusai kankyo* (Contemporary China: China in the International Environment), Tokyo: Iwanami Shōten, 78–114.

Matsumura Seizo (1988) 'Japan–China Trade in Retrospect: the 15th Anniversary of Normalizing Relations', JETRO *China Newsletter*, 72: 19–23.

May, Ernest R. (1973) *Lessons of the Past*, New York: Oxford University Press.

McCormack, Gavan and Yoshio Sugimoto (eds) (1988) *The Japanese Trajectory: Modernization and Beyond*, Cambridge: Cambridge University Press.

McGowan, Patrick J. and Shapiro, Howard B. Shapiro (1973) *The Comparative Study of Foreign Policy*, Beverley Hills, CA: Sage.

McNelly, Theodore (1984) *Politics and Government in Japan* 3rd edn, Lanham: University Press of America Inc.

McWilliams, Wayne C. and Piotrowski, Harry (1993) *The World Since 1945: A History of International Relations*, Boulder, CO: Lynne Rienner.

Mendl, Wolf (1978) *Issues in Japan's China Policy*, London and Basingstoke: Macmillan.

—— (1990) 'Unravelling Japan's Foreign Policy', *Japan Digest* 1(2): 45–8.

Merle, Marcel (1987) *The Sociology of International Relations*, Leamington Spa: Berg.

Minor, Michael (1985) 'Decision Models and Japanese Foreign Policy Decision Making', *Asian Survey* XXV(12): 1229–41.

Miura Shumon (1982) 'Don't Leave History to the Historians', *Japan Echo* IX(4): 29–35.

Monbushō Shotōchūtō Kyōikukyoku (1986) *Kyōkasho seido no gaiyō* (An Outline of the Textbook System), Tokyo: Monbushō.

Moody, Peter R., Jr (1994) 'Trends in the Study of Chinese Political Culture', *China Quarterly* 139: 731–40.

Morgan, Patrick M. (1982) *Theories and Approaches to International Politics*, 3rd edn, New Brunswick, NJ and London: Transaction Books.

Morgenthau, Hans J. (1973) *Politics Among Nations: The Struggle for Power and Peace*, 5th edn, Alfred A. Knopf.

Morikawa Kinju (1990) *Kyōkasho to saiban*, Tokyo: Iwanami Shōten.

Morino, Tomozo (1991) 'China–Japan Trade and Investment Relations', in Frank J. Macciarola and Robert B. Oxnam (eds), *The China Challenge, Proceedings of the Academy of Political Science* 38(2): 87–94.

Morley, James William (ed.) (1983) *The China Quagmire: Japan's Expansion on the Asian Continent 1931–1941*, New York: Columbia University Press.

Morris, Ivan S. (1960) *Nationalism and the Right Wing in Japan: A Study of Postwar Trends*, London: Oxford University Press.

Mueller, Peter G. and Ross, Douglas A. (1975) *China and Japan : Emerging Global Powers*, New York: Praeger.

Myers, Ramon H. and Peattie, Mark R. (1984) *The Japanese Colonial Empire, 1895–1945*, Princeton, NJ: Princeton University Press.

Nagano Nobutoshi (1982) 'Kyōdō seimei to sensō sekinin no shori' (Dealing with the Joint Statement and War Responsibility), *Chūō Kōron*, October: 151–67.

—— (1991) *Nihon Gaikō no Subete* (All About Japanese Diplomacy), Tokyo: Gyōsei Mondai Kenkyūjo.

Nakajima Mineo (1982a) 'Chūgoku hodo de kangaeta koto' (My Thoughts on China), *Seiron*, October.

——. (1982b) *Chūgoku: Rekishi, Shakai, Kokusai Kankei* (China: History, Society and International Relations), Tokyo: Chūō Kōronsha.

—— (1982c) 'Ikasarenai nitchū kōsho no kyōshun' (The Lessons of Sino-Japanese Negotiations that can not be Revived), *Chūō Kōron*, October, 136–50.

—— (1982d) 'Problem of Textbooks and Internal Circumstances of China', *Daily Summary of Japanese Press*, 25 August: 12.

—— (1989) *Chūgoku no higeki*, Tokyo: Kodansha.

Nathan, Andrew J. (1973) 'A Factionalism Model of CCP Politics' *China Quarterly* 53: 34–66.

Nethercut, Richard D. (1982) 'Deng and the Gun: Party–Military Relations in the People's Republic of China', *Asian Survey* XXII(8): 691–704.

—— (1983) 'Leadership in China: Rivalry, Reform and Renewal', *Problems of Communism*, March–April: 30–46.

Neumann, Iver B. and Waever, Ole (eds) (1997) *The Future of International Relations*, London and New York: Routledge.

Newby, Laura (1988) *Sino-Japanese Relations*, London and New York: Routledge.

—— (1990) 'Sino-Japanese Relations', in Gerald Segal (ed.), *Chinese Politics and Foreign Policy Reform*, London: Kegan Paul for the Royal Institute of International Affairs, 195–213.

Newland, Kathleen (ed.) (1990) *The International Relations of Japan*, Basingstoke and London: Macmillan.

Ng-Quinn, Michael (1983) 'The Analytic Study of Chinese Foreign Policy', *International Studies Quarterly* 27: 203–24.

—— (1984) 'International Systemic Constraints on Chinese Foreign Policy', in Samuel S. Kim (ed.), *China and the World*, Boulder, CO: Westview Press, 82–109.

Nihon Bōekishinkōkai (JETRO) (1990) *Chūgoku dētā fairu* (China data file), Tokyo: JETRO.

Nihon Kyōiku Nenkan Koinkai (1982–4, 1993) *Nihon Kyōiku Nenkan* (Japan Education Yearbook), Tokyo: Gyosei.

Nihonshi Kenkyūshitsu Tōdai Kyōyō Gakubu (ed.) (1988) *Nihonshi gaisetsu* (An Outline History of Japan), Tokyo: Tokyo Daigaku Shuppankai.

Nish, Ian (1977) *Japanese Foreign Policy 1869–1942: Kasumigaseki to Miyakezaka*, London: Routledge & Kegan Paul.

—— (1990) 'An Overview of Relations between China and Japan, 1895–1945', *China Quarterly* 124: 601–23.

North, Robert C. (1978) *The Foreign Relations of China* 3rd edn, North Scituate: Duxbury Press.

Ogata Sadako (1965) 'Japanese Attitude Toward China', *Asian Survey* V: 389–98.

– (1977) 'The Business Community and Japanese Foreign Policy: Normalization of Relations with the People's Republic of China', in Robert A. Scalapino (ed.), *The Foreign Policy of Modern Japan*, Berkeley, CA: University of California Press.

Ogura Kazuo (1979) 'How the Inscrutables Negotiate with the Inscrutables', *China Quarterly* 79: 529–52.

Okabe Tatsumi (1976) *Chūgoku no tainichi seisaku* (China's Japan Policy), Tokyo: Tokyo Daikagu Shuppankai.

—— (ed.) (1983) *Chūgoku gaikō: seisaku kettei no kōzō* (China's Foreign Policy: The Structure of Policy-Making), Tokyo: Nihon Kokusai Mondai Kenkyūjo.

—— (ed.) (1990) *Gendai Chūgoku: Chūgoku o meguru kokusai kankyo* (Contemporary China: China in the International Environment), Tokyo: Iwanami Shōten.

Okada Hidehiro (1982) 'Kyōkasho kentei wa Chūgoku no naisei mondai da' (Textbook Authorisation is a Chinese Domestic Matter), *Chūō Kōron*, October: 82–97.

Okazaki Kaheita (1982) 'In Defense of Truth in Education', *Japan Echo* IX(4): 36–9.

Okimoto, Daniel I. and Rohlen, Thomas P. (eds) (1988) *Inside the Japanese System*, Stanford, CA: Stanford University Press.

Oksenberg, Michel (1987) 'China's Confident Nationalism' *Foreign Affairs* 65(3): 501–24.

Oksenberg, Michel and Goldstein, S. (1974) 'The Chinese Political Spectrum', *Problems of Communism* 23(2).

Ōkurashō. (1982) *Shokuinroku* (Directory of Government Officials), Tokyo: Ōkurasho Insatsukyoku.

O'Leary, Greg (1980) *The Shaping of Chinese Foreign Policy*, London: Croom Helm.

O'Neill, P.G. (1989) *Japanese Names: A Comprehensive Index by Characters and Readings*, New York: Weatherhill, Inc.

Osamu Miyoshi (1972) 'How the Japanese Press Yielded to Peking', *Survey* 18: 103–25.

Owada Hisashi and Kosaka Masataka (1992) 'The Post-Cold-War Diplomatic Agenda', *Japan Echo* XIX(1): 8–15.

Pann, Lynn (1988) *The New Chinese Revolution*, London: Sphere Books.

Pap, Daniel S. (1988) *Contemporary International Relations*, 2nd edn, London and New York: Macmillan.

Papadakis, Maria and Starr, Harvey (1987) 'Opportunity, Willingness and Small States: The Relationship between Environment and Foreign Policy', in Charles F. Hermann, Charles W. Kegley, Jr, and James N. Rosenau (eds) *New Directions in the Study of Foreign Policy*, Sydney: Allen & Unwin, 409–32.

Park, Yung H. (1978a) 'The Roots of Détente', in Alvin D. Coox and Hilary Conroy (eds) *China and Japan*, Santa Barbara, CA: ABC-Clio, 355–84.

—— (1978b) 'The Tanaka Government and the Mechanisms of the China decision', in Alvin D. Coox and Hilary Conroy (eds) *China and Japan*, Santa Barbara, CA: ABC-Clio, 387–97.

—— (1986) *Bureaucrats and Ministers in Contemporary Japanese Government*, Berkeley, CA: University of California, Institute of East Asian Studies.

Passin, Herbert (1963) *China's Cultural Diplomacy*, New York: Praeger.

—— (1965) *Society and Education in Japan*, New York: Teachers College, Columbia University.

Peattie, Mark R. (1984) 'Introduction', in Ramon H. Myers and Mark Peattie (eds) *The Japanese Colonial Empire*, Princeton, NJ: Princeton University Press, 3–52.

—— (1989) 'Japanese Treaty Port Settlements in China, 1895–1937', in Peter Duus, Ramon H. Myers and Mark Peattie (eds) *The Japanese Informal Empire*, Princeton, NJ: Princeton University Press, 166–209.

Pempel, T.J. (ed.) (1977) *Policymaking in Contemporary Japan*, Ithaca, NY: Cornell University Press.

Pollack, Jonathan D. (1984) 'China in the Evolving International System', in Norton Ginsburg and Bernard A. Lalor (eds) *China: The 80s Era*, Boulder, CO: Westview Press, 353–74.

Powell, John W. (1981) 'Japan's Biological Weapons, 1930–1945: A Hidden Chapter in History', *Bulletin of the Atomic Scientists* 37(8): 44–53.

Pye, Lucian W. (1968) *The Spirit of Chinese Politics: A Psychocultural Study of the Authority Crisis in Political Development*, Cambridge, MA: MIT Press.

—— (1981) *The Dynamics of Chinese Politics*, Cambridge, MA: Oelgeschlager, Gunn & Hain.

—— (1985) *Asian Power and Politics. The Cultural Dimensions of Authority*, Cambridge, MA and London: Belknap Press.

—— (1990) 'China: Erratic State, Frustrated Society', *Foreign Affairs*, Autumn: 56–74.

—— (1992) *Chinese Negotiating Style: Commercial Approaches and Cultural Principles*, New York: Quorum Books.

Pye, Lucian W. and Leites, Nathan (1982) 'Nuances in Chinese Political Culture', *Asian Survey* XXII(12): 1147–65.

Pyle, Kenneth B. (1982) 'The Future of Japanese Nationality: An Essay in Contemporary History', *Journal of Japanese Studies* 8(2): 223–63.

—— (1987) 'In Pursuit of a Grand Design: Nakasone Betwixt the Past and the Future', *Journal of Japanese Studies* 13(2): 243–70.

Qian Xueming (1987) '1986 nian riben waijiao de xinfazhan' (New Developments in Japan's Foreign Policy in 1986), *Riben Wenti*, 3, 1–5.

Radtke, Kurt Werner (1990) *China's Relations with Japan, 1945–(1983)*, Manchester: Manchester University Press.

Reischauer, Edwin O. (1977) *The Japanese*, Cambridge, MA: Harvard University Press.

Reynolds, P.A. (1994) *An Introduction to International Relations*, 3rd edn, London and New York: Longman

Richardson, Bradley M. (1974) *The Political Culture of Japan*, University of California Press.

—— (1997) *Japanese Democracy: Power, Coordination, and Performance*, New Haven, CN and London: Yale University Press.

Richardson, Bradley M. and Flanagan, Scott C. (eds) (1984) *Politics in Japan*, Boston: Little, Brown & Co.

Riskin, Carl (1987) *China's Political Economy: The Quest For Development Since 1949*, Oxford: Oxford University Press.

Robinson, Thomas W. (1977) 'Political and Strategic Aspects of Chinese Foreign Policy', in Donald C. Hellmann, *China and Japan*, Lexington, MA: Lexington Books, 197–268.

—— (1994) 'Chinese Foreign Policy from the 1940s to the 1990s', in Thomas W. Robinson and David Shambaugh (eds), *Chinese Foreign Policy: Theory and Practice*, Oxford: Clarendon Press, 555–602.

Robinson, Thomas W. and Shambaugh, David (eds) (1994) *Chinese Foreign Policy: Theory and Practice*, Oxford: Clarendon Press.

Rosenau, James N. (1969) *International Politics and Foreign Policy; A Reader in Research and Theory*, New York: The Free Press.

—— (ed.) (1974) *Comparing Foreign Policies*, New York: Sage Publications.

—— (ed.) (1976) *In Search of Global Patterns*, New York: Free Press.

—— (1979) *The Scientific Study of Foreign Policy*, revised edn, New York: Nichols Publishing Co.

—— (1987) 'Introduction', in Charles F. Hermann, Charles W. Kegley, Jr, and James N. Rosenau (eds), *New Directions in the Study of Foreign Policy*, Sydney: Allen & Unwin, 1–10.

—— (1994) 'China in a Bifurcated World: Competing Theoretical Perspectives', in Thomas W. Robinson and David Shambaugh (eds), *Chinese Foreign Policy: Theory and Practice*, Oxford: Clarendon Press, 524–55.

Russett, Bruce and Starr, Harvey (1981) *World Politics: The Menu for Choice*, San Francisco: W.H. Freeman.

Sansom, G.B. (1987) *Japan: A Short Cultural History*, London: The Cresset Library.

Satō Hideo (1989) *Taigai seisaku* (Foreign Policy), Tokyo: Tokyo Daigaku Shuppansha.

Satō Seijiro and Matsuzaki Tetsuhisa (1986) *Jimintō Seiken* (The Political Power of the LDP), Tokyo: Chūō Kōron.

Satō Seizaburo (1977) 'The Foundations of Modern Japanese Policy', in Robert A. Scalapino, *The Foreign Policy of Japan*, Berkeley, CA: University of California Press. 367–389.

Sayle, Murray (1981) 'Blockade and Bushido: The Spurs to Destruction', *Far Eastern Economic Review*, 27 November: 16–18.

—— (1982) 'A Textbook Case of Aggression', *Far Eastern Economic Review*, 20 August: 36–8.

Scalapino, Robert A. (ed.) (1977) *The Foreign Policy of Modern Japan*, Berkeley, CA: University of California Press.

—— (1989) 'The Foreign Policy of Japan', in Roy C. Macridis (ed), *Foreign Policy in World Politics*, 7th edn, Englewood Cliffs, NJ: Prentice-Hall, 299–336.

—— (1991) 'China's Relations with Its Neighbours', *Proceedings of the Academy of Political Science* 38(2): 63–74.

Schoppa, Leonard James (1991) *Education Reform in Japan: A Case of Immobilist Politics*, London and New York: Routledge.

Schram, Stuart R. (1984) *Ideology and Policy in China Since the Third Plenum, 1978–84*, London: Contemporary China Institute, SOAS, University of London.

Schwartz, Benjamin I. (1968) 'The Chinese Perception of the World Order', in John K. Fairbank (ed.), *The Chinese World Order*, Cambridge, MA: Harvard University Press, 267–88.

Segal, Gerald (1981) 'The PLA and Chinese Foreign Policy Decision-Making'. *International Affairs* 57(3): 449–66.

—— (ed.) (1990a) *Chinese Politics and Foreign Policy Reform*, London and New York: Kegan Paul International.

—— (1990b) 'The Challenges to Foreign Policy', *Asian Affairs* 77(3): 295–311.

Sekine Ken (1992) *Chūgoku no kyōkasho no naka no nihon to nihonjin* (Japan and the Japanese in Chinese Textbooks), Tokyo: Ikkōsha.

Shambaugh, David (1994a) 'Sino-American Relations', in Thomas W. Robinson and David Shambaugh (eds), *Chinese Foreign Policy*, Oxford: Clarendon Press.

—— (1994b) 'Pacific Security in the Pacific Century', *Current History*, December: 423–9.

—— (1996a) 'China and Japan towards the Twenty-First Century: Rivals for Pre-eminence or Complex Interdependence?' in Christopher Howe *China and Japan: History, Trends and Prospects*, Oxford: Clarendon Press.

—— (1996b) 'Containment or Engagement of China? Calculating Beijing's Responses', *International Security* 21(2): 180–209.

Shen Shouyuan and Huang Zhongqing (1990) 'The People's Republic of China: An Independent Foreign Policy of Peace', *Journal of Asian and African Studies* XXV(1–2): 71–87.

Shimakura Tamio (1986) 'China's Five-Year Plans and Japan's Exports to China – Fluctuations and Cycles', *China Newsletter* 65: 7–12.

Shimizu Minoru (1982) 'Textbook Ramifications in LDP', *Japan Times Weekly*, 11 September: 4.

Shih Chih-yu (1990) *The Spirit of Chinese Foreign Policy: A Psychocultural View*, Basingstoke: Macmillan.

Singer, J. David (1961) 'The Level-of-Analysis Problem in International Relations', in Klaus Knorr and Sydney Verba (eds), *The International System: Theoretical Essays*, Princeton, NJ: Princeton University Press.

Sladkovsky, M.I. (1975) *China and Japan*, Gulf Breeze, FL: Academic International Press.

Smith, Charles (1994) 'The Textbook Truth', *Far Eastern Economic Review*, 25 August: 25–6.

Snyder, R.C., Bruck, H.W. and Sapin, B.M. (eds) (1962) *Foreign Policy Decision-Making: An Approach to the Study of International Politics*, New York: The Free Press.

Solomon, Richard (1971) *Mao's Revolution and the Chinese Political Culture*, Berkeley, CA: University of California Press.

Spence, Jonathan D. (1990) *The Search for Modern China*, New York: W.W. Norton.

Stockwin, J.A.A. (1981) 'Japan's Political Crisis of 1980', *Australian Outlook* 35(1): 19–32.

Stockwin, J.A.A., Rix, Alan, George, Aurelia, Horne, James, Itō Daiichi and Collick Martin (1988) *Dynamic and Immobilist Politics in Japan*, Basingstoke and London: Macmillan.

Sugiyama Takao (1982a) 'Rekishiteki ōgoho kara kyōkasho sōdō wa hajimatta' (The Textbook Controversy Began from Historic False Reporting), *Shūkan Bunshun* 35: 28–32.

—— (1982b) 'Naze monbushō wa kono "ōgoho" o hochi shita no ka' (Why Did the Education Ministry let the False Reporting Go?), *Shūkan Bunshun* 37: 158–61.

Sullivan, Michael P. (1976) *International Relations: Theories and Evidence*, Englewood Cliffs, NJ: Prentice-Hall.

Susumu Awanohara (1981) 'Shadow of the Warrior', *Far Eastern Economic Review*, 9 January: 23–4.

Sutter, Robert (1986) *Chinese Foreign Policy*, New York: Praeger.

Suzuki Hirō (1982) 'Liberalizing Textbook Screening', *Japan Echo* IX(4): 21–8.

Sylvan, Donald A and Chan Steve (1984) *Foreign Policy Decision Making: Perception, Cognition, and Artificial Intelligence*, New York: Praeger.

Takahashi Shirō (1988) *Kyōkasho Kentei* (Textbook Authorisation), Tokyo: Chūō Kōronsha, Chūko Shinsho 867.

Takayama Yoji (1982) 'Monbusho Kenkyū' (A Study of the Education Ministry), *Sekai* 444: 72–86.

Takeuchi Minoru (1981) 'Japan-China Frienship: Myth and Reality', *Japan Quarterly* 28.

Tanaka Akihiko (1983a) ' "Kyōkasho mondai" o meguru chūgoku no seisaku kettei' (China's Decision Making on the 'Textbook Problem'), in Okabe Tatsumi (ed.), *Chūgoku Gaikō* (China's Diplomacy), Tokyo: Nihon Kokusai Mondai Kenkyūjo, 193–221.

—— (1983b) 'Internal–External Linkage in Chinese International Conflict Behaviour: A Model', *Journal of North East Asian Studies* 2(2): 39–57.

—— (1991) *Nitchū Kankei 1945–1990* (Sino-Japanese Relations, 1945–1990), Tokyo: Tokyo Daigaku Shuppansha.

Tanino Sakutaro (1990) 'The Recent Situation in China and Sino-Japanese Relations', *Japan Review of International Affairs* 4(1): 20–41.

Taylor, Robert (1985) *The Sino-Japanese Axis*, London: Athlone Press.

—— (1996) *Greater China and Japan: Prospects for an Economic Partnership in East Asia*, London and New York: Routledge.

Teiwes, Frederick C. (1984) *Leadership, Legitimacy, and Conflict in China*, London and Basingstoke: Macmillan.

Thayer, Nathaniel (1969) *How the Conservatives Rule Japan*, Princeton, NJ: Princeton University Press.

—— (1988) 'Race and Politics in Japan', *Pacific Review* 1(1): 79–87.

Thomas, R. Murray and Postlethwaite, T. Neville (eds) (1983) *Schooling in East Asia: Forces of Change*, Oxford: Pergamon Press.

Toby, Ronald P. (1984) *State and Diplomacy in Early Japan*, Princeton, NJ: Princeton University Press.

Tōhō Gakkai (1992) *An Introductory Bibliography for Japanese Studies*, Vol. VIII, Part 1, *Social Sciences 1988–1989*, Tokyo: The Japan Foundation.

Totman, Conrad (1981) *Japan Before Perry*, Berkeley, CA: University of California Press.

Townsend, James (1980) *Politics in China*, 2nd edn, Boston: Little, Brown.

Tretiak, Daniel (1981) 'Who Makes Chinese Foreign Policy Today (Late 1980)', *Australian Journal of Chinese Affairs* 5: 137–57.

Tsou Tang (1984) 'Political Change and Reform: The Middle Course', in Norton Ginsburg and Bernard A. Lalor (eds), *China: The 80s Era*, Boulder, CO: Westview Press, 27–69.

Tsou Tang and Halperin, Morton H. (1965) 'Mao Tse-tung's Revolutionary Strategy and Peking's International Behaviour', *American Political Science Review* 54: 80–99.

Tsou Tang, Najita Tetsuo and Otake Hideo (1978) 'Sino-Japanese Relations in the 1970s', in Alvin D. Coox and Hilary Conroy (eds), *China and Japan*, Santa Barbara, CA: ABC-Clio, 401–31.

Tsukase Susume (ed.) (1990) *Bibliography of Studies on the History of Modern Sino-Japanese Relations in Japan*, Tokyo: Ryusuke Shosha.

Tsunoda, R., de Bary, W.T., Keene, D. (1958) *Sources of Japanese Tradition*, New York: Columbia University Press.

Uchida Tomoyuki (1980) 'Nitchū ryō kuni no kyōkasho ni arawareta jūgonen sensū' (Descriptions of the Fifteen Year War in the Textbooks of Both China and Japan), *Chūgoku kenkyū geppō*, 393: 34–40.

Uno Shigeaki (1983) *Chūgoku no Kokusai Kankei* (China's International Relations), Tokyo: Hiyo Shobo.

Usui Katsumi (1989) *Nitchu sensō* (The Sino-Japanese War), Tokyo: Chūō Kōronsha.

Valencia, Mark J. (1992) 'Insular Possessions', *Far Eastern Economic Review*, 28 May: 23.

Varley, H. Paul. (1973) *Japanese Culture: A Short History*, Tokyo: Charles E. Tuttle.

Vogel, Ezra F. (1975) *Modern Japanese Organisation and Decision-Making*, Berkeley, CA: University of California Press.

—— (1979) *Japan as Number One*, Cambridge, MA: Harvard University Press.

Walker, J. Samuel (1996) 'History, Collective Memory, and the Decision to Use the Bomb', in Michael J. Hogan (ed.), *Hiroshima in History and Memory*, Cambridge: Cambridge University Press, 187–99.

Walsh, J. Richard (1989) *Continuity and Commitment: China's Adaptive Foreign Policy*, Lanham, MD: University Press of America.

Waltz, Kenneth N. (1959) *Man, the State and War*, New York: Columbia University Press.

Wang, James (1989) *Contemporary Chinese Politics. An Introduction*, 3rd edn, Englewood Cliffs, NJ: Prentice-Hall.

Wang Jisi (1994) 'International Relations Theory and the Study of Chinese Foreign Policy: A Chinese Perspective', in Thomas W. Robinson and David Shambaugh (eds) *Chinese Foreign Policy: Theory and Practice*, Oxford: Clarendon Press, 481–505.

Wang Xiangrong (1986) *Gudai Zhong Ri guanxi shihua* (A History of Ancient Sino-Japanese Relations), Beijing: Shishi Chubanshe.

Ward, Robert E. (1978). *Japan's Political System*, 2nd edn, Englewood Cliffs, NJ: Prentice-Hall.

Watanabe Akio *et al.* (1989) *Kōza Kokusai Seiji 4: Nihon no Gaikō* (Introduction to International Relations, Vol. 4, Japan's Diplomacy), Tokyo: Tokyo Daigaku Shuppansha.

Watanabe Shoichi (1982) 'Banken kyo ni hoeta kyōkasho mondai' (The Textbook Issue – Guard Dogs Barking at the Shadows), *Shokun*, October: 22–44.

Whiting, Allen S. (1979) *Chinese Domestic Politics and Foreign Policy in the 1970s*, Ann Arbor, MI: Centre for Chinese Studies, University of Michigan.

—— (1983) 'Assertive Nationalism in Chinese Foreign Policy', *Asian Survey*, XXIII(8): 913–33.

—— (1989a) *China Eyes Japan*, Berkeley, CA: University of California Press.

—— (1989b) 'The Foreign Policy of China', in Roy C. Macridis (ed.) *Foreign Policy in World Politics*, 7th edn, Englewood Cliffs, NJ: Prentice-Hall, 251–83.

—— (1992) 'China and Japan: Politics versus Economics', *The Annals of the American Academy of Political and Social Science*, 519: 39–52.

Williams, Peter and Wallace, David (1989) *Unit 731: Japan's Secret Bacteriological Warfare in World War II*, New York: The Free Press.

Wolferen, Karel van (1989) *The Enigma of Japanese Power*, London: Macmillan.

Woronoff, Jon (1988) *Politics, The Japanese Way*, Basingstoke and London: Macmillan.

Wray, Harry (1978) 'China in Japanese Textbooks', in Alvin D. Coox and Hilary Conroy (eds) *China and Japan*, Santa Barbara, CA: ABC-Clio, 115–31.

Wray, Harry and Conroy, Hilary (eds) (1983) *Japan Examined: Perspectives on Modern Japanese History*, Honolulu, HI: University of Hawaii Press.

Wu, Friedrich W. (1980) 'Explanatory Approaches to Chinese Foreign Policy: A Critique of the Western Literature', *Studies in Comparative Communism* XIII(1): 41–60.

Yahuda, Michael (1983) *China's Foreign Policy After Mao: Towards the End of Isolationism*, London and Basingstoke: Macmillan.

Yamaguchi Ichirō (1976) *Chūgoku to Nihon* (China and Japan), Tokyo: Ushio Shuppansha.

Yamamura, Kozo (ed.) (1990) *Cambridge History of Japan*, vol 3. *Medieval Japan*, Cambridge: Cambridge University Press.

Yamane Yukio, Fujii Shozo *et al.* (1992) *Kindai nihon nitchū kankeishi kenkyū nyūmon* (An Introduction to Japanese Research on the Modern History of Sino-Japanese Relations), Tokyo: Kenbun Shuppan.

Yamazumi Masami (1981) 'Textbook Revision: The Swing to the Right', *Japan Quarterly* 28: 472–78.

Yang Kaojin (1986) *Zhong Ri guanxi shigang* (An Outline of Sino-Japanese Relations), Shanghai: Shanghai Waiyu Jiaoyu Chubanshe.

Yang Zhengguang (ed.) (1993) *Dangdai Zhong Ri guanxi sishinian* (40 Years of Contemporary Sino-Japanese Relations), Beijing: Shishi Chubanshe.

Yano Tōru (1982) 'Towarete iru no wa nihon no kokka imēji' (Japan's National Image is Called into Question), *Chūō Kōron*, October: 108–15.

Yao Linghai and Lin Jichuang (eds) (1987) *Guoji seiji yu Zhongguo waijiao* (International Politics and Chinese Diplomacy), Dongbei Caijing Dakue Chubanshe.

Yayama Tarō (1983) 'The Newspapers Conduct a Mad Rhapsody over the Textbook Issue', trans. by Tom Roehl and Junko Roehl, *Journal of Japanese Studies*, 9(2): 301–16.

Yoneda Nobuji (1973) 'Kyōkasho ni okeru chūgokuzō' (Images of China in Textbooks), *Chūgoku Kenkyū*, 302: 1–43.

Zhang Sheng Zhen (1986) *Zhong Ri guanxi shi, juan yi* (History of Sino-Japanese Relations, Vol. 1), Jilin: Jilin Wenshi Chubanshe.

Zhao Quansheng (1992) 'Domestic Factors of Chinese Foreign Policy: From Vertical to Horizontal Authoritarianism', *The Annals of the American Academmy of Political and Social Science* 519: 158–76.

—— (1993) *Japanese Policymaking: The Politics behind Politics, Informal Mechanisms and the Making of China Policy*, Westport, CT: Praeger.

—— (1996) *Interpreting Chinese Foreign Policy: The Micro-Macro Linkage Approach*, Oxford: Oxford University Press.

Zhongguo Renmin Daxue Shubao Ziliao Zhongxin (1982) *Fuyin baokan ziliao D6, Zhonguo Waijiao*, Beijing: Zhongguo Renmin Daxue

Zhongguo Renmin Gongheguo Waijiaobu (1987) *Zhongguo waijiao gailan* (Overview of China's Diplomacy), Beijing: Shijie Zhishi Chubanshe.

—— (1991) *Zhongguo waijiao gailan*, Beijing: Shijie Zhishi Chubanshe.

Journals and newspapers

Asian Affairs.
Asian Survey.
Asahi Jānaru.
Asahi Shimbun.
Beijing Review.
Bungei Shunjū.
China Quarterly.
Chūō Kōron.
Daily Summary of Japanese Press.
Far Eastern Economic Review.
Foreign Affairs.
International Affairs.
International Journal.
Japan Echo.
Japan Quarterly.
Japan Review of International Affairs.

Japan Times Weekly.
Journal of Japanese Studies.
Journal of the Japanese and International Economies.
Keizai Ōrai.
Kōmei.
Nikkei Weekly.
Pacific Affairs.
Problems of Communism.
Renmin Ribao.
Riben Wenti.
Sekai.
Seiron.
Shokun.
Shūkan Bunshun.
Summary of World Broadcasts.
World Politics.
Yearbook of World Affairs.

Index